THE DIALOGUE OF
THE SERAPHIC VIRGIN
CATHERINE OF SIENA

THE DIALOGUE OF
THE SERAPHIC VIRGIN
CATHERINE OF SIENA

DICTATED BY HER, WHILE IN A STATE OF
ECSTASY, TO HER SECRETARIES, AND
COMPLETED IN THE YEAR OF
OUR LORD 1370

TOGETHER WITH

AN ACCOUNT OF HER DEATH BY AN EYE-WITNESS

TRANSLATED FROM THE ORIGINAL ITALIAN, AND PRECEDED
BY AN INTRODUCTION ON THE LIFE AND
TIMES OF THE SAINT, BY

ALGAR THOROLD

A NEW AND ABRIDGED EDITION

TAN BOOKS AND PUBLISHERS, INC.
Rockford, Illinois 61105

Nihil obstat.

JOSEPH WILHELM, S.T.D.,
Censor deputatus.

Imprimi potest.

GULIELMUS,
Episcopus Arindelensis,
Vicarius Generalis.

Westmonasterii,
die 13 Dec., 1906.

Originally published in 1907 by Kegan Paul,
Trench, Trubner & Co., Ltd., London.

ISBN: 0–89555–037–7

PRINTED AND BOUND IN THE UNITED STATES OF AMERICA

TAN BOOKS AND PUBLISHERS, INC.
P.O. Box 424
Rockford, Illinois 61105

1974

CONTENTS

THE DIALOGUE OF
ST. CATHERINE OF SIENA

INTRODUCTION

It would be hard to say whether the Age of the Saints, *le moyen âge énorme et délicat*, has suffered more at the hands of friends or foes. It is at least certain that the medieval period affects those who approach it in the manner of a powerful personality who may awaken love or hatred, but cannot be passed over with indifference. When the contempt of the eighteenth century for the subject, the result of that century's lack of historic imagination, was thawed by the somewhat rhetorical enthusiasm of Chateaubriand and of the Romanticists beyond the Rhine, hostility gave place to an indiscriminating admiration. The shadows fell out of the picture; the medieval time became a golden age when heaven and earth visibly mingled, when Christian society reached the zenith of perfection which constituted it a model for all succeeding ages. Then came the German professors with all the paraphernalia of scientific history, and, looking through their in-

A

struments, we, who are not Germans, have come
to take a more critical and, perhaps, a juster view
of the matter.   The Germans, too, have had
disciples of other nations, and though conclusions
on special points may differ, in every country
now at a certain level of education, the same
views prevail as to the principles on which histo-
rical investigation should be conducted.   And
yet, while no one with a reputation to lose would
venture on any personal heresy as to the standards
of legitimate evidence, the same facts still seem
to lead different minds to differing appreciations.
For history, written solely *ad narrandum*, is not
history ; the historian's task is not over when he
has disinterred facts and established dates : it is
then that the most delicate part of his work
begins.   History, to be worthy of the name,
must produce the illusion of living men and
women, and, in order to do this successfully,
must be based, not only upon insight into human
nature in general, but also upon personal appre-
ciation of the particular men and women engaged
in the episodes with which it deals.   With facts
as such, there can indeed be no tampering ; but
for the determination of their significance, of
their value, as illustrative of a course of policy
or of the character of those who were responsible
for their occurrence, we have to depend in great
measure on the personality of the historian.   It
is evident that a man who lacks the sympathetic
power to enter into the character that he attempts
to delineate, will hardly be able to make that

character live for us.   For in Art as well as Life,
sympathy is power.

Now, while this is true of all history whatever,
it is perhaps truer of the history of the middle
ages than of that of any more recent period, nor
is the reason of this far to seek.   The middle
ages were a period fruitful in great individuals
who moulded society, to an extent that perhaps
no succeeding period has been.   In modern times
the formula, an abstraction such as " Capital " or
the " Rights of Man " has largely taken the place
of the individual as a plastic force.   The one
great Tyrant of the nineteenth century found his
opportunity in the anarchy which followed the
French Revolution.   The spoil was then necessarily to the strong.   But even Napoleon was
conquered at last rather by a conspiracy of the
slowly developing anonymous forces of his time
than by the superior skill or strength of an individual rival.   The lion could hardly have been
caught in such meshes in the trecento.   Then,
the fate of populations was bound up with the
animosities of princes, and, in order to understand the state of Europe at any particular
moment of that period, it is necessary to understand the state of soul of the individuals who
happened, at the time, to be the political stake-
holders.

It must not be thought, however, that the
personality of the prince was the only power in
the medieval state, for the prince himself was
held to be ultimately amenable to an idea, which

so infinitely transcended earthly distinctions as to level them all in relation to itself. Religion was in those days a mental and social force which we, in spite of the petulant acerbity of modern theological controversies, have difficulty in realising. Prince and serf would one day appear as suppliants before the Judgment-seat of Christ, and the theory of medieval Christianity was considerably in favour of the serf. The Father of Christendom, at once Priest and King, anointed and consecrated as the social exponent of the Divine Justice, could not, in his own person, escape its rigours, but must, one day, render an account of his stewardship. Nor did the medieval mind, distinguishing between the office and the individual, by any means shrink from contemplating the fate of the faithless steward. In a "Last Judgment" by Angelico at Florence, the ministers of justice seem to have a special joy in hurrying off to the pit popes and cardinals and other ecclesiastics.

For it is an insufficient criticism that has led some to suppose that the medieval Church weighed on the conscience of Christendom solely, or even primarily, as an arbitrary fact : that the priesthood, aided by the ignorance of the people, succeeded in establishing a monstrous claim to control the destinies of the soul by quasi-magical agencies and the powers of excommunication. Nothing can be further from the truth. Probably at no period has the Christian conscience realised more profoundly that the whole external fabric of Catholicism, its sacraments, its priest-hood, its discipline, was but the phenomenal expression, necessary and sacred in its place, of the Idea of Christianity, that the vitality of that Idea was the life by which the Church lived, and that by that Idea all Christians, priests as well as laymen, rulers as well as subjects, would at the last be judged. When Savonarola replied to the Papal Legate, who, in his confusion, committed the blunder of adding to the formula of excom-munication from the Church Militant, a sentence of exclusion from the Church Triumphant, "You cannot do it," he was in the tradition of medieval orthodoxy. Moreover, even though the strict logic of her theory might have required it, the hierarchical Church was not considered as the sole manifestation of the Divine Will to Christen-dom. The unanimity with which the Christian idea was accepted in those times made the saint a well-known type of human character just as nowadays we have the millionaire or the philan-thropist. Now the saint, although under the same ecclesiastical dispensation as other Christians, was conceived to have his own special relations with God, which amounted almost to a personal revelation. In particular he was held to be exempt from many of the limitations of fallen humanity. His prayers were of certain efficacy; the customary uniformities of experience were thought to be constantly transcended by the power that dwelt within him; he was often accepted by the people as the bearer to Christendom of a Divine message over and above the revelation of which the hierarchy was the legitimate guardian. Not infrequently indeed that message was one of warning or correction to the hierarchy. Sabatier points out truly that the medieval saints occupied much the same relation to the ecclesiastical system as the Prophets of Israel had done, under the older dispensation, to the Jewish Priesthood. They came out of their hermitages or cloisters, and with lips touched by coal from the altar denounced iniquity wherever they found it, even in the highest places. It is needless to say that they were not revolutionaries —had they been so indeed the state of Europe might have been very different to-day; for them, as for other Christians, the organisation of the Church was Divine; it was by the sacred responsibilities of his office that they judged the unworthy pastor.

An apt illustration of this attitude occurs in the life of the Blessed Colomba of Rieti. Colomba, who was a simple peasant, was called to the unusual vocation of preaching. The local representatives of the Holy Office, alarmed at the novelty, imprisoned her and took the opportunity of a visit of Alexander VI. to the neighbouring town of Perugia to bring her before his Holiness for examination. When the saint was brought into the Pope's presence, she reverently kissed the hem of his garment, and, being overcome with devotion at the sight of the Vicar of Christ, fell into an ecstasy, during which she invoked the

Divine judgment on the sins of Rodrigo Borgia.
It was useless to attempt to stop her; she was
beyond the control of inquisitor or guards; the
Pope had to hear her out. He did so; proclaimed
her complete orthodoxy, and set her free with
every mark of reverence. In this highly characteristic episode scholastic logic appears, for
once, to have been justified, at perilous odds, of
her children. . . .

* *

Midway between sky and earth hangs a City
Beautiful: Siena, *Vetus Civitas Virginis*. The
town seems to have descended as a bride from
airy regions, and lightly settled on the summits
of three hills which it crowns with domes and
clustering towers. As seen from the vineyards
which clothe the slopes of the hills or with its
crenellated wall and slender-necked Campanile
silhouetted against the evening sky from the
neighbouring heights of Belcaro, the city is
familiar to students of the early Italian painters.
It forms the fantastic and solemn background of
many a masterpiece of the *trecentisti*, and seems
the only possible home, if home they can have on
earth, of the glorified persons who occupy the
foreground. It would create no surprise to come,
while walking round the ancient walls, suddenly,
at a turn in the road, on one of the sacred groups
so familiarly recurrent to the memory in such
an environment: often indeed one experiences a
curious illusion when a passing friar happens

for a moment to "compose" with cypress and crumbling archway.

Siena, once the successful rival of Florence in commerce, war, and politics, has, fortunately for the more vital interests which it represents, long desisted from such minor matters. Its worldly ruin has been complete for more than five hundred years; in truth the town has never recovered from the plague which, in the far-off days of 1348, carried off 80,000 of its population. Grassy mounds within the city walls mark the shrinking of the town since the date of their erection, and Mr. Murray gives its present population at less than 23,000. The free Ghibelline Republic which, on that memorable 4th of September 1260, defeated, with the help of Pisa, at Monte Aperto, the combined forces of the Guelf party in Tuscany, has now, after centuries of servitude to Spaniard and Austrian, to be content with the somewhat pinchbeck dignity of an Italian Prefettura. At least the architectural degradation which has overtaken Florence at the hands of her modern rulers has been as yet, in great measure, spared to Siena. Even the railway has had the grace to conceal its presence in the folds of olive which enwrap the base of the hill on which the city is set.

Once inside the rose-coloured walls, as we pass up the narrow, roughly paved streets between lines of palaces, some grim and massive like Casa Tolomei, built in 1205, others delicate specimens of Italian Gothic like the Palazzo

Saracini, others again illustrating the combination of grace and strength which marked the domestic architecture of the Renaissance at its prime, like the Palazzo Piccolomini, we find ourselves in a world very remote indeed from anything with which the experience of our own utilitarian century makes us familiar. And yet, as we rub our eyes, unmistakably a world of facts, though of facts, as it were, visibly interpreted by the deeper truth of an art whose insistent presence is on all sides of us. Here is Casa Tolomei, a huge cube of rough-hewn stone stained to the colour of tarnished silver with age, once the home of that Madonna Pia whose story lives for ever in the verse of Dante. Who shall distinguish between her actual tale of days and the immortal life given her by the poet? In her moment of suffering at least she has been made eternal. And not far from that ancient fortress-home, in a winding alley that can hardly be called a street, is another house of medieval Siena—no palace this time, but a small tradesman's dwelling. In the fourteenth century it belonged to Ser Giacomo Benincasa, a dyer. Part of it has now been converted into a chapel, over the door of which are inscribed the words: *Sponsae Xti Katerinae Domus.* Here, on March 5, 1347, being Palm Sunday, was born Giacomo's daughter Caterina, who still lives one of the purest glories of the Christian Church under the name of St. Catherine of Siena. More than 500 years have passed since the daughter of the Siennese dyer entered into the rest of that sublime and touching symbolism under which the Church half veils and half reveals her teaching as to the destiny of man. Another case, but how profoundly more significant than that of poor Madonna Pia, of the intertwining of the world of fact with the deeper truth of art.

St. Catherine was born at the same time as a twin-sister, who did not survive. Her parents, Giacomo and Lapa Benincasa, were simple towns-people, prosperous, and apparently deserving their reputation for piety. Lapa, the daughter of one Mucio Piagenti, a now wholly forgotten poet, bore twenty-five children to her husband, of whom thirteen only appear to have grown up. This large family lived together in the manner still obtaining in Italy, in the little house, till the death of Giacomo in 1368.

There are stirring pages enough in Christian hagiology. Who can read unmoved of the struggles towards his ideal of an Augustine or a Loyola, or of the heroic courage of a Theresa, affirming against all human odds the divinity of her mission, and justifying, after years of labour, her incredible assertions by the steadfastness of her will? There are other pages in the lives of the saints, less dramatic, it may be, but breathing, nevertheless, a naïve grace and poetry all their own : the childhood of those servants of Christ who have borne His yoke from the dawn of their days forms their charming theme. Here the blasting illuminations of the Revelation are toned down to a soft and tender glow, in which the curves and lines of natural humanity do but seem more pathetically human. The hymn at Lauds for the Feast of the Holy Innocents represents those unconscious martyrs as playing with their palms and crowns under the very altar of Heaven :—

> " Vos prima Christi victima
> Grex immolatorum tener
> Aram sub ipsam simplices
> Palma et coronis luditis ! "

And so these other saintly babies play at hermits or monasteries instead of the soldiers and house-keeping beloved of more secular-minded infants. Heaven condescends to their pious revels: we are told of the Blessed Hermann Joseph, the Premonstratensian, that his infantile sports were joyously shared by the Divine Child Himself. He would be a morose pedant indeed who should wish to rationalise this white mythology. The tiny Catherine was no exception to the rest of her canonised brothers and sisters. At the age of five it was her custom on the staircase to kneel and repeat a " Hail Mary " at each step, a devotion so pleasing to the angels, that they would frequently carry her up or down without letting her feet touch the ground, much to the alarm of her mother, who confided to Father Raymond of Capua, the Dominican confessor of the family, her fears of an accident. Nor were these phenomena the only reward of her infant piety. From the day that she could walk she became very popular among her numerous relatives and her parents' friends, who gave her the pet name of Euphrosyne, to signify the grief-dispelling effect of her conversation, and who were constantly inviting her to their houses on some pretext or other. Sent one morning on an errand to the house of her married sister Bonaventura, she was favoured with a beautiful vision which, as it has an important symbolical bearing on the great task of her after-life, I will relate in Father Raymond's words, slightly abridging their prolixity.

"So it happened that Catherine, being arrived at the age of six, went one day with her brother Stephen, who was a little older than herself, to the house of their sister Bonaventura, who was married to one Niccolò, as has been mentioned above, in order to carry something or give some message from their mother Lapa. Their mother's errand accomplished, while they were on the way back from their sister's house to their own and were passing along a certain valley, called by the people Valle Piatta, the holy child, lifting her eyes, saw on the opposite side above the Church of the Preaching Friars a most beautiful room, adorned with regal magnificence, in which was seated, on an imperial throne, Jesus Christ, the Saviour of the world, clothed in pontifical vestments, and wearing on His head a papal tiara ; with Him were the princes of the Apostles, Peter and Paul, and the holy evangelist John. Astounded at such a sight, Catherine stood still,

and with fixed and immovable look, gazed, full
of love, on her Saviour, who, appearing in so
marvellous a manner, in order sweetly to gain her
love to Himself, fixed on her the eyes of His
Majesty, and, with a tender smile, lifted over her
His right hand, and, making the sign of the
Holy Cross in the manner of a bishop, left with
her the gift of His eternal benediction. The
grace of this gift was so efficacious, that Catherine,
beside herself, and transformed into Him upon
whom she gazed with such love, forgetting not
only the road she was on, but also herself,
although naturally a timid child, stood still for a
space with lifted and immovable eyes in the
public road, where men and beasts were continually passing, and would certainly have continued
to stand there as long as the vision lasted, had
she not been violently diverted by others. But
while the Lord was working these marvels, the
child Stephen, leaving her standing still, continued his way down hill, thinking that she was
following, but, seeing her immovable in the
distance and paying no heed to his calls, he
returned and pulled her with his hands, saying:
'What are you doing here? why do you not
come?' Then Catherine, as if waking from a
heavy sleep, lowered her eyes and said: 'Oh, if
you had seen what I see, you would not distract
me from so sweet a vision!' and lifted her eyes
again on high; but the vision had entirely dis-
appeared, according to the will of Him who had
granted it, and she, not being able to endure this

without pain, began with tears to reproach herself for having turned her eyes to earth." Such was the "call" of St. Catherine of Siena, and, to a mind intent on mystical significance, the appearance of Christ, in the semblance of His Vicar, may fitly appear to symbolise the great mission of her after-life to the Holy See.

* *

Much might be said of the action of Catherine on her generation. Few individuals perhaps have ever led so active a life or have succeeded in leaving so remarkable an imprint of their personality on the events of their time. Catherine the Peacemaker reconciles warring factions of her native city and heals an international feud between Florence and the Holy See. Catherine the Consoler pours the balm of her gentle spirit into the lacerated souls of the suffering wherever she finds them, in the condemned cell or in the hospital ward. She is one of the most voluminous of letter-writers, keeping up a constant correspondence with a band of disciples, male and female, all over Italy, and last, but not least, with the distant Pope at Avignon.

Her lot was cast on evil days for the Church and the Peninsula. The trecento, the apogee of the middle ages was over. Francis and Dominic had come and gone, and though Franciscans and Dominicans remained and numbered saints among their ranks, still the first fervour of the original inspiration was a brightness that had fled. The

moral state of the secular clergy was, according
to Catherine herself, too often one of the deepest
degradation, while, in the absence of the Pontiff,
the States of the Church were governed by papal
legates, mostly men of blood and lust, who ground
the starving people under their heel.   Assuredly
it was not from Christian bishops who would
have disgraced Islam that their subjects could
learn the path of peace.   The Pope's residence
at Avignon, the Babylonish Captivity, as it was
called, may have seemed, at the time when his
departure from Rome was resolved upon, a wise
measure of temporary retreat before the anarchy
which was raging round the city of St. Peter.
But not many years passed before it became
evident that Philip the Fair, the astute adviser to
whose counsel—and possibly more than counsel—
Clement had submitted in leaving Rome, was the
only one who profited by the exile of the Pope.
Whatever the truth may be about the details of
Clement's election, so far as his subserviency to
the French king went, he might have remained
Archbishop of Bordeaux to the end of his days.
He accepted for his relations costly presents from
Philip; he placed the papal authority at his
service in the gravely suspicious matter of the
suppression of the Templars.   Gradually the
Holy See in exile lost its œcumenical character
and became more and more the vassal of the
French crown.   Such a decline in its position
could not fail to affect even its doctrinal prestige.
It was well enough in theory to apply to the

situation such maxims as *Ubi Petrus ibi Ecclesia*, or, as the Avignonese doctors paraphrased it, *Ubi Papa ibi Roma;* but, in practice, Christendom grew shy of a French Pope, living under the eye and power of the French king. The Romans, who had always treated the Pope badly, were furious when at last they had driven him away, and gratified their spite by insulting their exiled rulers. Nothing could exceed their contempt for the Popes of Avignon, who, as a matter of fact, though weak and compliant, were in their personal characters worthy ecclesiastics. They gave no credit to John XXII. for his genuine zeal in the cause of learning, or the energy with which he restored ecclesiastical studies in the Western Schools. For Benedict XII., a retiring and abstemious student, they invented the phrase: *bibere papaliter*—to drink like the Pope. Clement VI. they called *poco religioso*, forgetting his noble charity at the time of the plague, and also the fact that Rome herself had produced not a few popes whose lives furnished a singular commentary on the ethics of the Gospel.

The real danger ahead to Christendom was the possibility of an Italian anti-Pope who should fortify his position by recourse to the heretical elements scattered through the peninsula. Those elements were grave and numerous. The Fraticelli or Spiritual Franciscans, although crushed for the time by the iron hand of Pope Boniface, rather flourished than otherwise under persecution. These dangerous heretics had inherited a garbled version of the mysticism of Joachim of Flora, which constituted a doctrine perhaps more radically revolutionary than that of any heretics before or since. It amounted to belief in a new revelation of the Spirit, which was to supersede the dispensation of the Son as that had taken the place of the dispensation of the Father. According to the Eternal Gospel of Gerard of San Donnino, who had derived it, not without much adroit manipulation, from the writings of Abbot Joachim, the Roman Church was on the eve of destruction, and it was the duty of the *Spirituali*, the saints who had received the new dispensation, to fly from the contamination of her communion. An anti-Pope who should have rallied to his allegiance these elements of schism would have been a dangerous rival to a French Pope residing in distant Avignon, however legitimate his title. Nor was there wanting out-side Italy matter for grave anxiety. Germs of heresy were fermenting north of the Alps; the preaching of Wycliffe, the semi-Islamism of the Hungarian Beghards, the Theism of the Patarini of Dalmatia, the erotic mysticism of the Adamites of Paris, indicated a widespread anarchy in the minds of Christians. Moreover, the spiritual diffi-culties of the Pope were complicated by his tempo-ral preoccupations. For good or ill, it had come to be essential to the action of the Holy See that the successor of the penniless fisherman should have his place among the princes of the earth.

B

The papal monarchy had come about, as most things come about in this world, by what seems to have been the inevitable force of circumstances. The decay of the Imperial power in Italy due to the practical abandonment of the Western Empire—for the ruler of Constantinople lived at too great a distance to be an effective Emperor of the West—had resulted in a natural increase of secular importance to the See of Rome. To the genius of Pope Gregory I., one of the few men whom their fellows have named both Saint and Great, was due the development of the political situation thus created in Italy.

Chief and greatest of bishops in his day was St. Gregory the Great. Seldom, if ever, has the papal dignity been sustained with such lofty enthusiasm, such sagacious political insight. Himself a Roman of Rome, *Romano di Roma*, as those who possess that privilege still call themselves to-day, the instinct of government was his by hereditary right. He had the defects as well as the qualities of the statesman. His theological writings, which are voluminous and verbose, are marked rather by a sort of canonised common sense than by exalted flights of spirituality. His missionary enterprise was characterised by a shrewd and gracious condescension to the limitations of human nature. Thus he counsels St. Augustine, who had consulted him as to the best means of extirpating the pagan customs of our English forefathers, to deal gently with these ancient survivals. He ruled that the celebration of the Festivals of the Saints should if possible be held at the times and places at which the people had been in the habit of meeting together to worship the gods. They would thus come to associate the new religion with their traditional merry-makings, and their conversion would be gradually, and as it were unconsciously, effected. It was a kindly and statesmanlike thought. In this way Gregory may truly be looked upon as the founder of popular Catholicism, that "pensive use and wont religion," not assuredly in the entirety of its details Christian, but at least profoundly Catholic, as weaving together in the web of its own secular experience of man so large a proportion of the many-coloured threads that have at any time attached his hopes and fears to the mysterious unknown which surrounds him. No miracle is needed to explain the political ascendency which such a man inevitably came to acquire in an Italy deserted by the Empire, and, but for him and the organisation which depended on him, at the mercy of the invading Lombard. More and more, people came to look on the Pope as their temporal ruler no less than as their spiritual father. In many cases, indeed, his was the only government they knew. Kings and nobles had conferred much property on the Roman Church. By the end of the sixth century the Bishop of Rome held, by the right of such donations to his See, large tracts of country, not only in Italy, but also in Sicily, Corsica,

Gaul, and even Asia and Africa. Gregory successfully defended his Italian property against the
invaders, and came to the relief of the starving
population with corn from Sicily and Africa,
thus laying deep in the hearts of the people the
foundations of the secular power of the Papacy.

It would be an unnecessary digression from
our subject to work out in detail the stages by
which the Pope came to take his place first as
the Italian vicar of a distant emperor, and at
length, as the result of astute statecraft and the
necessities of the case, among the princes of
Europe, as their chief and arbiter. So much as
has been said was, however, necessary for the
comprehension of the task with which Catherine
measured, for the time, successfully her strength.
It was given to the Popolana of Siena, by the
effect of her eloquence in persuading the waver-
ing will of the Pope to return to his See, to
bring about what was, for the moment, the
only possible solution of that Roman question,
which, hanging perpetually round the skirts of
the Bride of Christ, seems at every step to impede her victorious advance.

* *

Nevertheless, it is neither the intrinsic importance nor the social consequences of her actions
that constitute the true greatness of St. Catherine.
Great ends may be pursued by essentially small
means, in an aridity and narrowness of temper
that goes far to discount their actual achieve-

ment. History, and in particular the history of the Church, is not wanting in such instances. Savonarola set great ends before himself—the freedom of his country and the regeneration of the state; but the spirit in which he pursued them excludes him from that Pantheon of gracious souls in which humanity enshrines its true benefactors. "Soul, as a quality of style, is a fact," and the soul of St. Catherine's *gesta* expressed itself in a "style" so winning, so sweetly reasonable, as to make her the dearest of friends to all who had the privilege of intimate association with her, and a permanent source of refreshment to the human spirit. She intuitively perceived life under the highest possible forms, the forms of Beauty and Love. Truth and Goodness were, she thought, means for the achievement of those two supreme ends. The sheer beauty of the soul "in a state of Grace" is a point on which she constantly dwells, hanging it as a bait before those whom she would induce to turn from evil. Similarly the ugliness of sin, as much as its wickedness, should warn us of its true nature. Love, that love of man for man which, in deepest truth, *is*, in the words of the writer of the First Epistle of St. John, God Himself, is, at once, the highest achievement of man and his supreme and satisfying beatitude. The Symbols of Catholic theology were to her the necessary and fitting means of transit, so to speak. See, in the following pages, the fine allegory of the Bridge of the Sacred

Humanity, of the soul in *viâ* on its dusty pilgrimage towards those gleaming heights of vision. "Truth" was to her the handmaid of the spiritualised imagination, not, as too often in these days of the twilight of the soul, its tyrant and its gaoler. Many of those who pass lives of unremitting preoccupation with the problems of truth and goodness are wearied and cumbered with much serving. We honour them, and rightly; but if they have nothing but this to offer us, our hearts do not run to meet them, as they fly to the embrace of those rare souls who inhabit a serener, more pellucid atmosphere. Among these spirits of the air, St. Catherine has taken a permanent and foremost place. She is among the few guides of humanity who have the perfect manner, the irresistible attractiveness, of that positive purity of heart, which not only sees God, but diffuses Him, as by some natural law of refraction, over the hearts of men. The Divine nuptials, about which the mystics tell us so much, have been accomplished in her, Nature and Grace have lain down together, and the mysteries of her religion seem but the natural expression of a perfectly balanced character, an unquenchable love and a deathless will.

*_**

The Dialogue of St. Catherine of Siena was dictated to her secretaries by the Saint in ecstasy. Apart from the extraordinary circumstances of its production, this work has a special interest.

The composition of the Siennese dyer's daughter, whose will, purified and sublimated by prayer, imposed itself on popes and princes, is an almost unique specimen of what may be called "ecclesiastical" mysticism; for its special value lies in the fact that from first to last it is nothing more than a mystical exposition of the creeds taught to every child in the Catholic poor-schools. Her insight is sometimes very wonderful. How subtle, for instance, is the analysis of the state of the "worldly man" who loves God for his own pleasure or profit! The special snares of the devout are cut through by the keen logic of one who has experienced and triumphed over them. Terrible, again, is the retribution prophesied to the "unworthy ministers of the Blood."

And so every well-known form of Christian life, healthy or parasitic, is treated of, detailed, analysed incisively, remorselessly, and then subsumed under the general conception of God's infinite loving-kindness and mercy.

The great mystics have usually taken as their starting-point what, to most, is the goal hardly to be reached; their own treatment of the preliminary stages of spirituality is frequently conventional and *jejune*. Compare, for instance, the first book with the two succeeding ones, of Ruysbrock's *Ornement des Noces spirituelles*, that unique breviary of the Christian Platonician. Another result of their having done so is that, with certain noble exceptions, the literature of this subject has fallen into the hands of a class of writers, or rather purveyors, well-intentioned no doubt, but not endowed with the higher spiritual and mental faculties, whom it is not unfair to describe as the *feuilletonistes* of piety. Such works, brightly bound, are appropriately exposed for sale in the Roman shop-windows, among the gaudy *objets de religion* they so much resemble. To keep healthy and raise the tone of devotional literature is surely an eighth spiritual work of mercy. St. Philip Neri's advice in the matter was to prefer those writers whose names were preceded by the title of Saint. In the *Dialogo* we have a great saint, one of the most extraordinary women who ever lived, treating, in a manner so simple and familiar as at times to become almost colloquial, of the elements of practical Christianity. Passages occur frequently of lofty eloquence, and also of such literary perfection that this book is held by critics to be one of the classics of the age and land which produced Boccaccio and Petrarch. To-day, in the streets of Siena, the same Tuscan idiom can be heard, hardly altered since the days of St. Catherine.

One word as to the translation. I have almost always followed the text of Gigli, a learned Siennese ecclesiastic, who edited the complete works of St. Catherine in the last century. His is the latest edition printed of the *Dialogo*. Once or twice I have preferred the *cinquecento* Venetian editor. My aim has been to translate as literally as possible, and at the same time to preserve the characteristic rhythm of the sentences, so suggestive in its way of the sing-song articulation of the Siennese of to-day. St. Catherine has no style as such; she introduces a metaphor and forgets it; the sea, a vine, and a plough will often appear in the same sentence, sometimes in the same phrase. In such cases I have occasionally taken the liberty of adhering to the first simile when the confusion of metaphor in the original involves hopeless obscurity of expression.

VIAREGGIO, *September* 1906.

A TREATISE OF
DIVINE PROVIDENCE

*How a soul, elevated by desire of the honour of God,
and of the salvation of her neighbours, exercising
herself in humble prayer, after she had seen the
union of the soul, through love, with God, asked
of God four requests.*

THE soul, who is lifted by a very great and
yearning desire for the honour of God and the
salvation of souls, begins by exercising herself,
for a certain space of time, in the ordinary
virtues, remaining in the cell of self-knowledge,
in order to know better the goodness of God
towards her. This she does because knowledge
must precede love, and only when she has attained
love, can she strive to follow and to clothe herself with the truth. But, in no way, does the
creature receive such a taste of the truth, or so
brilliant a light therefrom, as by means of humble
and continuous prayer, founded on knowledge of
herself and of God; because prayer, exercising
her in the above way, unites with God the soul
that follows the footprints of Christ Crucified,
and thus, by desire and affection, and union of
love, makes her another Himself. Christ would

seem to have meant this, when He said: *To him who will love Me and will observe My commandment, will I manifest Myself; and he shall be one thing with Me and I with him.* In several places we find similar words, by which we can see that it is, indeed, through the effect of love, that the soul becomes another Himself. That this may be seen more clearly, I will mention what I remember having heard from a handmaid of God, namely, that, when she was lifted up in prayer, with great elevation of mind, God was not wont to conceal, from the eye of her intellect, the love which He had for His servants, but rather to manifest it; and, that among other things, He used to say: "Open the eye of thy intellect, and gaze into Me, and thou shalt see the beauty of My rational creature. And look at those creatures who, among the beauties which I have given to the soul, creating her in My image and similitude, are clothed with the nuptial garment (that is, the garment of love), adorned with many virtues, by which they are united with Me through love. And yet I tell thee, if thou shouldest ask Me, who these are, I should reply " (said the sweet and amorous Word of God) "they are another Myself, inasmuch as they have lost and denied their own will, and are clothed with Mine, are united to Mine, are conformed to Mine." It is therefore true, indeed, that the soul unites herself with God by the affection of love.

So, that soul, wishing to know and follow the truth more manfully, and lifting her desires first for herself—for she considered that a soul could not be of use, whether in doctrine, example, or prayer, to her neighbour, if she did not first profit herself, that is, if she did not acquire virtue in herself—addressed four requests to the Supreme and Eternal Father. The first was for herself; the second for the reformation of the Holy Church; the third a general prayer for the whole world, and in particular for the peace of Christians who rebel, with much lewdness and persecution, against the Holy Church; in the fourth and last, she besought the Divine Providence to provide for things in general, and in particular, for a certain case with which she was concerned.

How the desire of this soul grew when God showed her the neediness of the world.

This desire was great and continuous, but grew much more, when the First Truth showed her the neediness of the world, and in what a tempest of offence against God it lay. And she had understood this the better from a letter, which she had received from the spiritual Father of her soul, in which he explained to her the penalties and intolerable dolour caused by offences against God, and the loss of souls, and the persecutions of Holy Church.

All this lighted the fire of her holy desire with grief for the offences, and with the joy of the lively hope, with which she waited for God to provide against such great evils. And, since the soul seems, in such communion, sweetly to bind herself fast within herself and with God, and knows better His truth, inasmuch as the soul is then in God, and God in the soul, as the fish is in the sea, and the sea in the fish, she desired the arrival of the morning (for the morrow was a feast of Mary) in order to hear Mass. And, when the morning came, and the hour of the Mass, she sought with anxious desire her accustomed place; and, with a great knowledge of herself, being ashamed of her own imperfection, appearing to herself to be the cause of all the evil that was happening throughout the world, conceiving a hatred and displeasure against herself, and a feeling of holy justice, with which knowledge, hatred, and justice, she purified the stains which seemed to her to cover her guilty soul, she said: "O Eternal Father, I accuse myself before Thee, in order that Thou mayest punish me for my sins in this finite life, and, inasmuch as my sins are the cause of the sufferings which my neighbour must endure, I implore Thee, in Thy kindness, to punish them in my person."

How finite works are not sufficient for punishment or recompense without the perpetual affection of love.

Then, the Eternal Truth seized and drew more strongly to Himself her desire, doing as He did in the Old Testament, for when the

sacrifice was offered to God, a fire descended
and drew to Him the sacrifice that was acceptable to Him; so did the sweet Truth to that
soul, in sending down the fire of the clemency
of the Holy Spirit, seizing the sacrifice of
desire that she made of herself, saying: " Dost
thou not know, dear daughter, that all the sufferings, which the soul endures, or can endure, in
this life, are insufficient to punish one smallest
fault, because the offence, being done to Me, who
am the Infinite Good, calls for an infinite satisfaction? However, I wish that thou shouldest
know, that not all the pains that are given to
men in this life are given as punishments, but
as corrections, in order to chastise a son when he
offends; though it is true that both the guilt and
the penalty can be expiated by the desire of the
soul, that is, by true contrition, not through the
finite pain endured, but through the infinite
desire; because God, who is infinite, wishes for
infinite love and infinite grief. Infinite grief I
wish from My creature in two ways: in one way,
through her sorrow for her own sins, which she
has committed against Me her Creator; in the
other way, through her sorrow for the sins which
she sees her neighbours commit against Me. Of
such as these, inasmuch as they have infinite
desire, that is, are joined to Me by an affection
of love, and therefore grieve when they offend
Me, or see Me offended, their every pain, whether
spiritual or corporeal, from wherever it may come,
receives infinite merit, and satisfies for a guilt

which deserved an infinite penalty, although their works are finite and done in finite time; but, inasmuch as they possess the virtue of desire, and sustain their suffering with desire, and contrition, and infinite displeasure against their guilt, their pain is held worthy. Paul explained this when he said : *If I had the tongues of angels, and if I knew the things of the future and gave my body to be burned, and have not love, it would be worth nothing to me.* The glorious Apostle thus shows that finite works are not valid, either as punishment or recompense, without the condiment of the affection of love."

How desire and contrition of heart satisfies, both for the guilt and the penalty in oneself and in others ; and how sometimes it satisfies for the guilt only, and not the penalty.

"I have shown thee, dearest daughter, that the guilt is not punished in this finite time by any pain which is sustained purely as such. And I say, that the guilt is punished by the pain which is endured through the desire, love, and contrition of the heart ; not by virtue of the pain, but by virtue of the desire of the soul ; inasmuch as desire and every virtue is of value, and has life in itself, through Christ crucified, My only begotten Son, in so far as the soul has drawn her love from Him, and virtuously follows His virtues, that is, His Footprints. In this way, and in no other, are virtues of value, and in this way, pains satisfy for the fault, by the sweet and intimate love acquired in the knowledge of My goodness, and in the bitterness and contrition of heart acquired by knowledge of one's self and one's own thoughts. And this knowledge generates a hatred and displeasure against sin, and against the soul's own sensuality, through which, she deems herself worthy of pains and unworthy of reward."

The sweet Truth continued : "See how, by contrition of the heart, together with love, with true patience, and with true humility, deeming themselves worthy of pain and unworthy of reward, such souls endure the patient humility in which consists the above-mentioned satisfaction. Thou askest me, then, for pains, so that I may receive satisfaction for the offences, which are done against Me by My Creatures, and thou further askest the will to know and love Me, who am the Supreme Truth. Wherefore I reply that this is the way, if thou wilt arrive at a perfect knowledge and enjoyment of Me, the Eternal Truth, that thou shouldest never go outside the knowledge of thyself, and, by humbling thyself in the valley of humility, thou wilt know Me and thyself, from which knowledge thou wilt draw all that is necessary. No virtue, my daughter, can have life in itself except through charity, and humility, which is the foster-mother and nurse of charity. In self-knowledge, then, thou wilt humble thyself, seeing that, in thyself, thou dost not even exist ; for thy very being, as thou wilt learn, is derived from Me, since I have loved both thee and others before you were in existence; and that, through the ineffable love which I had for you, wishing to re-create you to Grace, I have washed you, and re-created you in the Blood of My only-begotten Son, spilt with so great a fire of love. This Blood teaches the truth to him, who, by self-knowledge, dissipates the cloud of self-love, and in no other way can he learn. Then the soul will inflame herself in this knowledge of Me with an ineffable love, through which love she continues in constant pain; not, however, a pain which afflicts or dries up the soul, but one which rather fattens her; for since she has known My truth, and her own faults, and the ingratitude of men, she endures intolerable suffering, grieving because she loves Me; for, if she did not love Me, she would not be obliged to do so; whence it follows immediately, that it is right for thee, and My other servants who have learnt My truth in this way, to sustain, even unto death, many tribulations and injuries and insults in word and deed, for the glory and praise of My Name; thus wilt thou endure and suffer pains. Do thou, therefore, and My other servants, carry yourselves with true patience, with grief for your sins, and with love of virtue for the glory and praise of My Name. If thou actest thus, I will satisfy for thy sins, and for those of My other servants, inasmuch as the pains which thou wilt endure will be sufficient, through the virtue

of love, for satisfaction and reward, both in thee
and in others. In thyself thou wilt receive the
fruit of life, when the stains of thy ignorance are
effaced, and I shall not remember that thou ever
didst offend Me. In others I will satisfy through
the love and affection which thou hast to Me,
and I will give to them according to the disposition with which they will receive My gifts.
In particular, to those who dispose themselves,
humbly and with reverence, to receive the doctrine of My servants, will I remit both guilt and
penalty, since they will thus come to true knowledge and contrition for their sins. So that, by
means of prayer, and their desire of serving Me,
they receive the fruit of grace, receiving it humbly
in greater or less degree, according to the extent
of their exercise of virtue and grace in general.
I say then, that, through thy desires, they will
receive remission for their sins. See, however,
the condition, namely, that their obstinacy should
not be so great in their despair as to condemn
them through contempt of the Blood, which,
with such sweetness, has restored them.

" What fruit do they receive ?

" The fruit which I destine for them, constrained by the prayers of My servants, is that
I give them light, and that I wake up in them
the hound of conscience, and make them smell
the odour of virtue, and take delight in the conversation of My servants.

"Sometimes I allow the world to show them
what it is, so that, feeling its diverse and various

passions, they may know how little stability it has, and may come to lift their desire beyond it, and seek their native country, which is the Eternal Life.   And so I draw them by these, and by many other ways, for the eye cannot see, nor the tongue relate, nor the heart think, how many are the roads and ways which I use, through love alone, to lead them back to grace, so that My truth may be fulfilled in them.   I am constrained to do so by that inestimable love of Mine, by which I created them, and by the love, desire, and grief of My servants, since I am no despiser of their tears, and sweat, and humble prayers; rather I accept them, inasmuch as I am He who give them this love for the good of souls and grief for their loss.   But I do not, in general, grant to these others, for whom they pray, satisfaction for the penalty due to them, but, only for their guilt, since they are not disposed, on their side, to receive, with perfect love, My love, and that of My servants.   They do not receive their grief with bitterness, and perfect contrition for the sins they have committed, but with imperfect love and contrition, wherefore they have not, as others, remission of the penalty, but only of the guilt; because such complete satisfaction requires proper dispositions on both sides, both in him that gives and him that receives.   Wherefore, since they are imperfect, they receive imperfectly the perfection of the desires of those who offer them to Me, for their sakes, with suffering; and, inasmuch as I told thee that they do receive remission, this is indeed the truth, that, by that way which I have told thee, that is, by the light of conscience, and by other things, satisfaction is made for their guilt; for, beginning to learn, they vomit forth the corruption of their sins, and so receive the gift of grace.

"These are they who are in a state of ordinary charity, wherefore, if they have trouble, they receive it in the guise of correction, and do not resist over much the clemency of the Holy Spirit, but, coming out of their sin, they receive the life of grace. But if, like fools, they are un-grateful, and ignore Me and the labours of My servants done for them, that which was given them, through mercy, turns to their own ruin and judgment, not through defect of mercy, nor through defect of him who implored the mercy for the ingrate, but solely through the man's own wretchedness and hardness, with which, with the hands of his free will, he has covered his heart, as it were, with a diamond, which, if it be not broken by the Blood, can in no way be broken. And yet, I say to thee, that, in spite of his hardness of heart, he can use his free will while he has time, praying for the Blood of My Son, and let him with his own hand apply It to the diamond over his heart and shiver it, and he will receive the imprint of the Blood which has been paid for him. But, if he delays until the time be past, he has no remedy, because he has not used the dowry which I gave him, giving him memory so as to

remember My benefits, intellect, so as to see and
know the truth, affection, so that he should love
Me, the Eternal Truth, whom he would have
known through the use of his intellect. This is
the dowry which I have given you all, and which
ought to render fruit to Me, the Father; but, if
a man barters and sells it to the devil, the devil,
if he choose, has a right to seize on everything
that he has acquired in this life. And, filling his
memory with the delights of sin, and with the
recollection of shameful pride, avarice, self-love,
hatred, and unkindness to his neighbours (being
also a persecutor of My servants), with these
miseries, he has obscured his intellect by his disordinate will. Let such as these receive the
eternal pains, with their horrible stench, inasmuch
as they have not satisfied for their sins with contrition and displeasure of their guilt. Now,
therefore, thou hast understood how suffering
satisfies for guilt by perfect contrition, not
through the finite pain; and such as have this
contrition in perfection satisfy not only for the
guilt, but also for the penalty which follows
the guilt, as I have already said when speaking
in general; and if they satisfy for the guilt alone,
that is, if, having abandoned mortal sin, they
receive grace, and have not sufficient contrition
and love to satisfy for the penalty also, they
go to the pains of Purgatory, passing through
the second and last means of satisfaction.

"So thou seest that satisfaction is made, through
the desire of the soul united to Me, who am the

Infinite Good, in greater or less degree, according to the measure of love, obtained by the desire and prayer of the recipient. Wherefore, with that very same measure with which a man measures to Me, dost he receive in himself the measure of My goodness. Labour, therefore, to increase the fire of thy desire, and let not a moment pass without crying to Me with humble voice, or without continual prayers before Me for thy neighbours. I say this to thee and to the father of thy soul, whom I have given thee on earth. Bear yourselves with manful courage, and make yourselves dead to all your own sensuality."

How very pleasing to God is the willing desire to suffer for Him.

"Very pleasing to Me, dearest daughter, is the willing desire to bear every pain and fatigue, even unto death, for the salvation of souls, for the more the soul endures, the more she shows that she loves Me; loving Me she comes to know more of My truth, and the more she knows, the more pain and intolerable grief she feels at the offences committed against Me. Thou didst ask Me to sustain thee, and to punish the faults of others in thee, and thou didst not remark that thou wast really asking for love, light, and knowledge of the truth, since I have already told thee that, by the increase of love, grows grief and pain, wherefore he that grows in love grows in grief. Therefore, I say

to you all, that you should ask, and it will be
given you, for I deny nothing to him who asks
of Me in truth. Consider that the love of
divine charity is so closely joined in the soul
with perfect patience, that neither can leave the
soul without the other. For this reason (if the
soul elect to love Me) she should elect to endure
pains for Me in whatever mode or circumstance
I may send them to her. Patience cannot be
proved in any other way than by suffering, and
patience is united with love as has been said.
Therefore bear yourselves with manly courage,
for, unless you do so, you will not prove yourselves to be spouses of My Truth, and faithful
children, nor of the company of those who relish
the taste of My honour, and the salvation of
souls."

How every virtue and every defect is obtained by means of our neighbour.

"I wish also that thou shouldest know that
every virtue is obtained by means of thy neighbour, and likewise, every defect; he, therefore,
who stands in hatred of Me, does an injury to
his neighbour, and to himself, who is his own
chief neighbour, and this injury is both general
and particular. It is general because you are
obliged to love your neighbour as yourself, and
loving him, you ought to help him spiritually,
with prayer, counselling him with words, and
assisting him both spiritually and temporally,

according to the need in which he may be, at least with your goodwill if you have nothing else. A man therefore, who does not love, does not help him, and thereby does himself an injury; for he cuts off from himself grace, and injures his neighbour, by depriving him of the benefit of the prayers and of the sweet desires that he is bound to offer for him to Me. Thus, every act of help that he performs should proceed from the charity which he has through love of Me. And every evil also, is done by means of his neighbour, for, if he do not love Me, he cannot be in charity with his neighbour; and thus, all evils derive from the soul's deprivation of love of Me and her neighbour; whence, inasmuch as such a man does no good, it follows that he must do evil. To whom does he evil? First of all to himself, and then to his neighbour, not against Me, for no evil can touch Me, except in so far as I count done to Me that which he does to himself. To himself he does the injury of sin, which deprives him of grace, and worse than this he cannot do to his neighbour. Him he injures in not paying him the debt, which he owes him, of love, with which he ought to help him by means of prayer and holy desire offered to Me for him. This is an assistance which is owed in general to every rational creature; but its usefulness is more particular when it is done to those who are close at hand, under your eyes, as to whom, I say, you are all obliged to help one another by word and doctrine, and the example of good works, and in every other respect in which your neighbour may be seen to be in need ; counselling him exactly as you would yourselves, without any passion of self-love ; and he (a man not loving God) does not do this, because he has no love towards his neighbour ; and, by not doing it, he does him, as thou seest, a special injury. And he does him evil, not only by not doing him the good that he might do him, but by doing him a positive injury and a constant evil. In this way sin causes a physical and a mental injury. The mental injury is already done when the sinner has conceived pleasure in the idea of sin, and hatred of virtue, that is, pleasure from sensual self-love, which has deprived him of the affection of love which he ought to have towards Me, and his neighbour, as has been said. And, after he has conceived, he brings forth one sin after another against his neighbour, according to the diverse ways which may please his perverse sensual will. Sometimes it is seen that he brings forth cruelty, and that both in general and in particular.

"His general cruelty is to see himself and other creatures in danger of death and damnation through privation of grace, and so cruel is he that he reminds neither himself nor others of the love of virtue and hatred of vice. Being thus cruel he may wish to extend his cruelty still further, that is, not content with not giving an example of virtue, the villain also usurps the office of the demons, tempting, according to his power, his fellow-creatures to abandon virtue for vice; this is cruelty towards his neighbours, for he makes himself an instrument to destroy life and to give death. Cruelty towards the body has its origin in cupidity, which not only prevents a man from helping his neighbour, but causes him to seize the goods of others, robbing the poor creatures; sometimes this is done by the arbitrary use of power, and at other times by cheating and fraud, his neighbour being forced to redeem, to his own loss, his own goods, and often indeed his own person.

"Oh, miserable vice of cruelty, which will deprive the man who practises it of all mercy, unless he turn to kindness and benevolence towards his neighbour!

"Sometimes the sinner brings forth insults on which often follows murder; sometimes also impurity against the person of his neighbour, by which he becomes a brute beast full of stench, and in this case he does not poison one only, but whoever approaches him, with love or in conversation, is poisoned.

"Against whom does pride bring forth evils? Against the neighbour, through love of one's own reputation, whence comes hatred of the neighbour, reputing one's self to be greater than he; and in this way is injury done to him. And if a man be in a position of authority, he produces also injustice and cruelty and becomes a retailer of the flesh of men. Oh, dearest daughter, grieve for the offence against Me, and weep over these corpses, so that, by prayer, the bands of their death may be loosened!

"See now, that, in all places and in all kinds of people, sin is always produced against the neighbour, and through his medium; in no other way could sin ever be committed either secret or open. A secret sin is when you deprive your neighbour of that which you ought to give him; an open sin is where you perform positive acts of sin, as I have related to thee. It is, therefore, indeed the truth that every sin done against Me, is done through the medium of the neighbour."

How virtues are accomplished by means of our neighbour, and how it is that virtues differ to such an extent in creatures.

"I have told thee how all sins are accomplished by means of thy neighbour, through the principles which I exposed to thee, that is, because men are deprived of the affection of love, which gives light to every virtue. In the same way self-love, which destroys charity and affection towards the neighbour, is the principle and foundation of every evil. All scandals, hatred, cruelty, and every sort of trouble proceed from this perverse root of self-love, which has poisoned the entire world, and weakened the mystical body of the Holy Church, and the universal body of the believers in the Christian religion; and, therefore, I said to thee, that it was in the neighbour, that is to say in the love of him, that all virtues were founded; and, truly indeed did I say to thee, that charity gives life to all the virtues, because no virtue can be obtained without charity, which is the pure love of Me.

"Wherefore, when the soul knows herself, as we have said above, she finds humility and hatred of her own sensual passion, for she learns the perverse law, which is bound up in her members, and which ever fights against the spirit. And, therefore, arising with hatred of her own sensuality, crushing it under the heel of reason, with great earnestness, she discovers in herself the bounty of My goodness, through the many benefits which she has received from Me, all of which she considers again in herself. She attributes to Me, through humility, the knowledge which she has obtained of herself, knowing that, by My grace, I have drawn her out of darkness and lifted her up into the light of true knowledge. When she has recognised My goodness, she loves it without any medium, and yet at the same time with a medium, that is to say, without the medium of herself or of any advantage accruing to herself, and with the medium of virtue, which she has conceived through love of Me, because she sees that, in no other way, can she become grateful and acceptable to Me, but by conceiving, hatred of sin and love of virtue; and, when she has thus conceived by the affection of love, she immediately is delivered of fruit for her neighbour, because, in no other way, can she act out the truth she has conceived in herself, but, loving Me in truth, in the same truth she serves her neighbour.

"And it cannot be otherwise, because love of Me and of her neighbour are one and the same thing, and, so far as the soul loves Me, she loves her neighbour, because love towards him issues from Me. This is the means which I have given you, that you may exercise and prove your virtue therewith; because, inasmuch as you can do Me no profit, you should do it to your neighbour. This proves that you possess Me by grace in your soul, producing much fruit for your neighbour and making prayers to Me, seeking with sweet and amorous desire My honour and the salvation of souls. The soul, enamoured of My truth, never ceases to serve the whole world in general, and more or less in a particular case according to the disposition of the recipient and the ardent desire of the donor, as I have shown above, when I declared to thee that the endurance of suffering alone, without desire, was not sufficient to punish a fault.

"When she has discovered the advantage of this unitive love in Me, by means of which, she truly loves herself, extending her desire for the salvation of the whole world, thus coming to the aid of its neediness, she strives, inasmuch as she has done good to herself by the conception of virtue, from which she has drawn the life of grace, to fix her eye on the needs of her neighbour in particular. Wherefore, when she has discovered, through the affection of love, the state of all rational creatures in general, she helps those who are at hand, according to the various graces which I have entrusted to her to administer; one she helps with doctrine, that is, with words, giving sincere counsel without any respect of persons, another with the example of a good life, and this indeed all give to their neighbour, the edification of a holy and honourable life. These are the virtues, and many others, too many to enumerate, which are brought forth in the love of the neighbour; but, although I have given them in such a different way, that is to say not all to one, but to one, one virtue, and to another, another, it so happens that it is impossible to have one, without having them all, because all the virtues are bound together. Wherefore, learn, that, in many cases I give one virtue, to be as it were the chief of the others, that is to say, to one I will give principally love, to another justice, to another humility, to one a lively faith, to another prudence or temperance, or patience, to another fortitude. These, and many other virtues, I place, indifferently, in the souls of many creatures; it happens, therefore, that the particular one so placed in the soul becomes the principal object of its virtue; the soul disposing herself, for her chief conversation, to this rather than to other virtues, and, by the effect of this virtue, the soul draws to herself all the other virtues, which, as has been said, are all bound together in the affection of love; and so with many gifts and graces of virtue, and not only in the case of spiritual things but also of temporal. I use the word temporal for the things necessary to the physical life of man; all these I have given indifferently, and I have not placed them all in one soul, in order that man should, perforce, have material for love of his fellow. I could easily have created men possessed of all that they should need both for body and soul, but I wish that one should have need of the other, and that they should be My ministers to administer the graces and the gifts that they have received from Me. Whether man will or no, he cannot help making an act of love. It is true, however, that that act, unless made through love of Me, profits him nothing so far as grace is concerned. See then, that I have made men My ministers, and placed them in diverse stations and various ranks, in order that they may make use of the virtue of love.

"Wherefore, I show you that in My house are many mansions, and that I wish for no other thing than love, for in the love of Me is fulfilled and completed the love of the neighbour, and the law observed. For he, only, can be of use in his state of life, who is bound to Me with this love."

How virtues are proved and fortified by their contraries.

"Up to the present, I have taught thee how a man may serve his neighbour, and manifest, by that service, the love which he has towards Me.

" Now I wish to tell thee further, that a man proves his patience on his neighbour, when he receives injuries from him.

"Similarly, he proves his humility on a proud man, his faith on an infidel, his true hope on one who despairs, his justice on the unjust, his kindness on the cruel, his gentleness and benignity on the irascible. Good men produce and prove all their virtues on their neighbour, just as perverse men all their vices; thus, if thou consider well, humility is proved on pride in this way. The humble man extinguishes pride, because a proud man can do no harm to a humble one; neither can the infidelity of a wicked man, who neither loves Me, nor hopes in Me, when brought forth against one who is faithful to Me, do him any harm; his infidelity does not diminish the faith or the hope of him who has conceived his faith and hope through love of Me, it rather fortifies it, and proves it in the love he feels for his neighbour. For, he sees that the infidel is unfaithful, because he is without hope in Me, and in My servant, because he does not love Me, placing his faith and hope rather in his own sensuality, which is all that he loves. My faithful servant does not leave him because he does not faithfully love Me, or because he does not constantly seek, with hope in Me, for his salvation, inasmuch as he sees clearly the causes of his infidelity and lack of hope. The virtue of faith is proved in these and other ways. Wherefore, to those, who need the proof of it, My servant proves his faith in himself and in his neighbour, and so, justice is not diminished by the wicked man's injustice, but is rather proved, that is to say, the justice of a just man. Similarly, the virtues of patience, benignity, and kindness manifest themselves in a time of wrath by the same sweet patience in My servants, and envy, vexation, and hatred demonstrate their love, and hunger and desire for the salvation of souls. I say, also, to thee, that, not only is virtue proved in those who render good for evil, but, that many times a good man gives back fiery coals of love, which dispel the hatred and rancour of heart of the angry, and so from hatred often comes benevolence, and that this is by virtue of the love and perfect patience which is in him, who sustains the anger of the wicked, bearing and supporting his defects. If thou wilt observe the virtues of fortitude and perseverance, these virtues are proved by the long endurance of the injuries and detractions of wicked men, who, whether by injuries or by flattery, constantly endeavour to turn a man aside from following the road and the doctrine of truth. Wherefore, in all these things, the virtue of fortitude conceived within the soul, perseveres with strength, and, in addition proves itself externally upon the neighbour, as I have said to thee; and, if fortitude were not able to make that good proof of itself, being tested by many contrarieties, it would not be a serious virtue founded in truth."

A TREATISE OF DISCRETION

How the affection should not place reliance chiefly on penance, but rather on virtues; and how discretion receives life from humility, and renders to each man his due.

"THESE are the holy and sweet works which I seek from My servants; these are the proved intrinsic virtues of the soul, as I have told thee. They not only consist of those virtues which are done by means of the body, that is, with an exterior act, or with diverse and varied penances, which are the instruments of virtue; works of penance performed alone without the above-mentioned virtues would please Me little; often, indeed, if the soul perform not her penance with discretion, that is to say, if her affection be placed principally in the penance she has undertaken, her perfection will be impeded; she should rather place reliance on the affection of love, with a holy hatred of herself, accompanied by true humility and perfect patience, together with the other intrinsic virtues of the soul, with hunger and desire for My honour and the salvation of souls. For these virtues demonstrate that the will is dead, and continually slays its own sensuality through the affection of love of virtue. With this dis-

cretion, then, should the soul perform her penance,
that is, she should place her principal affection
in virtue rather than in penance. Penance should
be but the means to increase virtue according to
the needs of the individual, and according to
what the soul sees she can do in the measure of
her own possibility. Otherwise, if the soul place
her foundation on penance she will contaminate
her own perfection, because her penance will not
be done in the light of knowledge of herself and
of My goodness, with discretion, and she will
not seize hold of My truth; neither loving that
which I love, nor hating that which I hate.
This virtue of discretion is no other than a
true knowledge which the soul should have of
herself and of Me, and in this knowledge is
virtue rooted. Discretion is the only child of
self-knowledge, and, wedding with charity, has
indeed many other descendants, as a tree which
has many branches; but that which gives life
to the tree, to its branches, and its root, is
the ground of humility, in which it is planted,
which humility is the foster-mother and nurse
of charity, by whose means this tree remains in
the perpetual calm of discretion. Because otherwise the tree would not produce the virtue of discretion, or any fruit of life, if it were not planted
in the virtue of humility, because humility proceeds from self-knowledge. And I have already
said to thee, that the root of discretion is a real
knowledge of self and of My goodness, by which
the soul immediately, and discreetly, renders to

each one his due. Chiefly to Me in rendering praise and glory to My Name, and in referring to Me the graces and the gifts which she sees and knows she has received from Me; and rendering to herself that which she sees herself to have merited, knowing that she does not even exist of herself, and attributing to Me, and not to herself, her being, which she knows she has received by grace from Me, and every other grace which she has received besides.

"And she seems to herself to be ungrateful for so many benefits, and negligent, in that she has not made the most of her time, and the graces she has received, and so seems to herself worthy of suffering; wherefore she becomes odious and displeasing to herself through her guilt. And this founds the virtue of discretion on knowledge of self, that is, on true humility, for, were this humility not in the soul, the soul would be indiscreet, indiscretion being founded on pride, as discretion is on humility.

"An indiscreet soul robs Me of the honour due to Me, and attributes it to herself, through vainglory, and that which is really her own she imputes to Me, grieving and murmuring concerning My mysteries, with which I work in her soul and in those of My other creatures; wherefore everything in Me and in her neighbour is cause of scandal to her. Contrariwise those who possess the virtue of discretion. For, when they have rendered what is due to Me and to themselves, they proceed to render to their neighbour

their principal debt of love, and of humble and
continuous prayer, which all should pay to each
other, and further, the debt of doctrine, and
example of a holy and honourable life, counselling and helping others according to their needs
for salvation, as I said to thee above. Whatever
rank a man be in, whether that of a noble, a
prelate, or a servant, if he have this virtue,
everything that he does to his neighbour is done
discreetly and lovingly, because these virtues are
bound and mingled together, and both planted
in the ground of humility which proceeds from
self-knowledge."

*A parable showing how love, humility, and discretion
are united; and how the soul should conform
herself to this parable.*

"Dost thou know how these three virtues
stand together? It is, as if a circle were drawn
on the surface of the earth, and a tree, with an
off-shoot joined to its side, grew in the centre of
the circle. The tree is nourished in the earth
contained in the diameter of the circle, for if
the tree were out of the earth it would die, and
give no fruit. Now, consider, in the same way,
that the soul is a tree existing by love, and that
it can live by nothing else than love; and, that
if this soul have not in very truth the divine
love of perfect charity, she cannot produce fruit
of life, but only of death. It is necessary then,
that the root of this tree, that is the affection

of the soul, should grow in, and issue from the circle of true self-knowledge which is contained in Me, who have neither beginning nor end, like the circumference of the circle, for, turn as thou wilt within a circle, inasmuch as the circumference has neither end nor beginning, thou always remainest within it.

"This knowledge of thyself and of Me is found in the earth of true humility, which is as wide as the diameter of the circle, that is as the knowledge of self and of Me (for, otherwise, the circle would not be without end and beginning, but would have its beginning in knowledge of self, and its end in confusion, if this knowledge were not contained in Me). Then the tree of love feeds itself on humility, bringing forth from its side the off-shoot of true discretion, in the way that I have already told thee, from the heart of the tree, that is the affection of love which is in the soul, and the patience, which proves that I am in the soul and the soul in Me. This tree then, so sweetly planted, produces fragrant blossoms of virtue, with many scents of great variety, inasmuch as the soul renders fruit of grace and of utility to her neighbour, according to the zeal of those who come to receive fruit from My servants; and to Me she renders the sweet odour of glory and praise to My Name, and so fulfils the object of her creation.

"In this way, therefore, she reaches the term of her being, that is Myself, her God, who am Eternal Life. And these fruits cannot be taken from her without her will, inasmuch as they are all flavoured with discretion, because they are all united, as has been said above."

How penance and other corporal exercises are to be taken as instruments for arriving at virtue, and not as the principal affection of the soul; and of the light of discretion in various other modes and operations.

"These are the fruits and the works which I seek from the soul, the proving, namely, of virtue in the time of need. And yet some time ago, if thou remember, when thou wert desirous of doing great penance for My sake, asking, 'What can I do to endure suffering for Thee, oh Lord?' I replied to thee, speaking in thy mind, 'I take delight in few words and many works.' I wished to show thee that he who merely calls on me with the sound of words, saying: 'Lord, Lord, I would do something for Thee,' and he, who desires for My sake to mortify his body with many penances, and not his own will, did not give Me much pleasure; but that I desired the manifold works of manly endurance with patience, together with the other virtues, which I have mentioned to thee above, intrinsic to the soul, all of which must be in activity in order to obtain fruits worthy of grace. All other works, founded on any other principle than this, I judge to be a mere calling with words, because they are finite works, and I, who am Infinite, seek infinite works, that is an infinite perfection of love.

"I wish therefore that the works of penance, and of other corporal exercises, should be observed merely as means, and not as the fundamental affection of the soul. For, if the principal affection of the soul were placed in penance, I should receive a finite thing like a word, which, when it has issued from the mouth, is no more, unless it have issued with affection of the soul, which conceives and brings forth virtue in truth; that is, unless the finite operation, which I have called a word, should be joined with the affection or love, in which case it would be grateful and pleasant to Me. And this is because such a work would not be alone, but accompanied by true discretion, using corporal works as means, and not as the principal foundation; for it would not be becoming that that principal foundation should be placed in penance only, or in any exterior corporal act, such works being finite, since they are done in finite time, and also because it is often profitable that the creature omit them, and even that she be made to do so.

"Wherefore, when the soul omits them through necessity, being unable through various circumstances to complete an action which she has begun, or, as may frequently happen, through obedience at the order of her director, it is well; since, if she continued then to do them, she not only would receive no merit, but would offend Me; thus thou seest that they are merely finite.

She ought, therefore, to adopt them as a means, and not as an end. For, if she takes them as an end she will be obliged, some time or other, to leave them, and will then remain empty. This, My trumpeter, the glorious Paul, taught you when he said in his epistle, that you should mortify the body and destroy self-will, knowing, that is to say, how to keep the rein on the body, macerating the flesh whenever it should wish to combat the spirit, but the will should be dead and annihilated in everything, and subject to My will, and this slaying of the will is that due which, as I told thee, the virtue of discretion renders to the soul, that is to say, hatred and disgust of her own offences and sensuality, which are acquired by self-knowledge. This is the knife which slays and cuts off all self-love founded in self-will. These then are they who give Me not only words but manifold works, and in these I take delight. And then I said that I desired few words, and many actions; by the use of the word 'many' I assign no particular number to thee, because the affection of the soul, founded in love, which gives life to all the virtues and good works, should increase infinitely, and yet I do not, by this, exclude words, I merely said that I wished few of them, showing thee that every actual operation, as such, was finite, and therefore I called them of little account; but they please Me when they are performed as the instruments of virtue, and not as a principal end in themselves.

"However, no one should judge that he has greater perfection, because he performs great penances, and gives himself in excess to the slaying of his body, than he who does less, inasmuch as neither virtue nor merit consists therein; for otherwise he would be in an evil case, who, from some legitimate reason, was unable to do actual penance. Merit consists in the virtue of love alone, flavoured with the light of true discretion, without which the soul is worth nothing. And this love should be directed to Me endlessly, boundlessly, since I am the Supreme and Eternal Truth. The soul can therefore place neither laws nor limits to her love for Me; but her love for her neighbour, on the contrary, is ordered in certain conditions. The light of discretion (which proceeds from love, as I have told thee) gives to the neighbour a conditioned love, one that, being ordered aright, does not cause the injury of sin to self in order to be useful to others, for, if one single sin were committed to save the whole world from Hell, or to obtain one great virtue, the motive would not be a rightly ordered or discreet love, but rather indiscreet, for it is not lawful to perform even one act of great virtue and profit to others, by means of the guilt of sin. Holy discretion ordains that the soul should direct all her powers to My service with a manly zeal, and, that she should love her neighbour with such devotion that she would lay down a thousand times, if it were possible, the life of her body for the salvation of souls, enduring pains and torments so that her neighbour may have the life of grace, and giving her temporal substance for the profit and relief of his body.

" This is the supreme office of discretion which proceeds from charity. So thou seest how discreetly every soul, who wishes for grace, should pay her debts, that is, should love Me with an infinite love and without measure, but her neighbour with measure, with a restricted love, as I have said, not doing herself the injury of sin in order to be useful to others. This is St. Paul's counsel to thee when he says that charity ought to be concerned first with self, otherwise it will never be of perfect utility to others. Because, when perfection is not in the soul, everything which the soul does for itself and for others is imperfect. It would not, therefore, be just that creatures, who are finite and created by Me, should be saved through offence done to Me, who am the Infinite Good. The more serious the fault is in such a case, the less fruit will the action produce; therefore, in no way shouldest thou ever incur the guilt of sin.

"And this true love knows well, because she carries with herself the light of holy discretion, that light which dissipates all darkness, takes away ignorance, and is the condiment of every instrument of virtue. Holy discretion is a prudence which cannot be cheated, a fortitude which cannot be beaten, a perseverance from end to end, stretching from Heaven to earth, that is, from

knowledge of Me to knowledge of self, and from
love of Me to love of others. And the soul
escapes dangers by her true humility, and, by her
prudence, flies all the nets of the world and its
creatures, and, with unarmed hands, that is through
much endurance, discomfits the devil and the flesh
with this sweet and glorious light; knowing, by
it, her own fragility, she renders to her weakness
its due of hatred.

"Wherefore she has trampled on the world,
and placed it under the feet of her affection,
despising it, and holding it vile, and thus becoming lord of it, holding it as folly. And the
men of the world cannot take her virtues from
such a soul, but all their persecutions increase
her virtues and prove them, which virtues have
been at first conceived by the virtue of love,
as has been said, and then are proved on her
neighbour, and bring forth their fruit on him.
Thus have I shown thee, that, if virtue were
not visible and did not shine in the time of
trial, it would not have been truly conceived;
for, I have already told thee, that perfect virtue
cannot exist and give fruit except by means of
the neighbour, even as a woman, who has conceived a child, if she do not bring it forth, so
that it may appear before the eyes of men,
deprives her husband of his fame of paternity.
It is the same with Me, who am the Spouse of
the soul, if she do not produce the child of
virtue, in the love of her neighbour, showing
her child to him who is in need, both in general

and in particular, as I have said to thee before, so I declare now that, in truth, she has not conceived virtue at all; and this is also true of the vices, all of which are committed by means of the neighbour."

How this soul grew by means of the divine response, and how her sorrows grew less, and how she prayed to God for the Holy Church, and for her own people.

"Then that soul, thirsting and burning with the very great desire that she had conceived on learning the ineffable love of God, shown in His great goodness, and, seeing the breadth of His charity, that, with such sweetness, He had deigned to reply to her request and to satisfy it, giving hope to the sorrow which she had conceived, on account of offences against God, and the damage of the Holy Church, and through His own mercy, which she saw through self-knowledge, diminished, and yet, at the same time, increased her sorrow.

"For, the Supreme and Eternal Father, in manifesting the way of perfection, showed her anew her own guilt, and the loss of souls, as has been said more fully above. Also because in the knowledge which the soul obtains of herself, she knows more of God, and knowing the goodness of God in herself, the sweet mirror of God, she knows her own dignity and indignity. Her dignity is that of her creation, seeing that

she is the image of God, and this has been given
her by grace, and not as her due. In that same
mirror of the goodness of God, the soul knows
her own indignity, which is the consequence of
her own fault. Wherefore, as a man more
readily sees spots on his face when he looks in
a mirror, so, the soul who, with true knowledge
of self, rises with desire, and gazes with the eye
of the intellect at herself in the sweet mirror of
God, knows better the stains of her own face,
by the purity which she sees in Him.

"Wherefore, because light and knowledge
increased in that soul in the aforesaid way, a
sweet sorrow grew in her, and at the same time,
her sorrow was diminished by the hope which
the Supreme Truth gave her, and, as fire grows
when it is fed with wood, so grew the fire in
that soul to such an extent that it was no longer
possible for the body to endure it without the
departure of the soul ; so that, had she not been
surrounded by the strength of Him who is the
Supreme Strength, it would not have been possible for her to have lived any longer. This soul
then, being purified by the fire of divine love,
which she found in the knowledge of herself
and of God, and her hunger for the salvation
of the whole world, and for the reformation of
the Holy Church, having grown with her hope
of obtaining the same, rose with confidence
before the Supreme Father, showing Him the
leprosy of the Holy Church, and the misery of
the world, saying, as if with the words of Moses,

'My Lord, turn the eyes of Thy mercy upon Thy people, and upon the mystical body of the Holy Church, for Thou wilt be the more glorified if Thou pardonest so many creatures, and givest to them the light of knowledge, since all will render Thee praise when they see themselves escape through Thy infinite goodness from the clouds of mortal sin, and from eternal damnation; and then Thou wilt not only be praised by my wretched self, who have so much offended Thee, and who am the cause and the instrument of all this evil, for which reason I pray Thy divine and eternal love to take Thy revenge on me, and to do mercy to Thy people, and never will I depart from before Thy presence until I see that thou grantest them mercy. For what is it to me if I have life, and Thy people death, and the clouds of darkness cover Thy spouse, when it is my own sins, and not those of Thy other creatures, that are the principal cause of this? I desire, then, and beg of Thee, by Thy grace, that Thou have mercy on Thy people, and I adjure Thee that Thou do this by Thy uncreated love which moved Thee Thyself to create man in Thy image and similitude, saying, "Let us make man in our own image," and this Thou didst, oh eternal Trinity, that man might participate in everything belonging to Thee, the most high and eternal Trinity.'

"Wherefore Thou gavest him memory in order to receive Thy benefits, by which he participates in the power of the Eternal Father; and intellect that he might know, seeing Thy goodness, and so might participate in the wisdom of Thine only-begotten Son; and will, that he might love that which his intellect has seen and known of Thy truth, thus participating in the clemency of Thy Holy Spirit. What reason hadst Thou for creating man in such dignity? The inestimable love with which Thou sawest Thy creature in Thyself, and didst become enamoured of him, for Thou didst create him through love, and didst destine him to be such that he might taste and enjoy Thy Eternal Good. I see therefore that through his sin he lost this dignity in which Thou didst originally place him, and by his rebellion against Thee, fell into a state of war with Thy kindness, that is to say, we all became Thy enemies.

"Therefore, Thou, moved by that same fire of love with which Thou didst create him, didst willingly give man a means of reconciliation, so that after the great rebellion into which he had fallen, there should come a great peace; and so Thou didst give him the only-begotten Word, Thy Son, to be the Mediator between us and Thee. He was our Justice, for He took on Himself all our offences and injustices, and performed Thy obedience, Eternal Father, which Thou didst impose on Him, when Thou didst clothe Him with our humanity, our human nature and likeness. Oh, abyss of love! What heart can help breaking when it sees such dignity as Thine descend to such lowliness as

our humanity? We are Thy image, and Thou
hast become ours, by this union which Thou
hast accomplished with man, veiling the Eternal
Deity with the cloud of woe, and the corrupted
clay of Adam. For what reason? — Love.
Wherefore, Thou, O God, hast become man, and
man has become God. By this ineffable love of
Thine, therefore, I constrain Thee, and implore
Thee that Thou do mercy to Thy creatures."

*How God grieves over the Christian people, and
particularly over His ministers; and touches
on the subject of the Sacrament of Christ's
Body, and the benefit of the Incarnation.*

Then God, turning the eye of His mercy
towards her, allowing Himself to be constrained
by her tears, and bound by the chain of her holy
desire, replied with lamentation—"My sweetest
daughter, thy tears constrain Me, because they
are joined with My love, and fall for love of Me,
and thy painful desires force Me to answer thee;
but marvel, and see how My spouse has defiled
her face, and become leprous, on account of her
filthiness and self-love, and swollen with the pride
and avarice of those who feed on their own sin.

"What I say of the universal body and the
mystical body of the Holy Church (that is to
say the Christian religion) I also say of My
ministers, who stand and feed at the breasts of
Holy Church; and, not only should they feed
themselves, but it is also their duty to feed and

hold to those breasts the universal body of Christian people, and also any other people who should wish to leave the darkness of their infidelity, and bind themselves as members to My Church. See then with what ignorance and darkness, and ingratitude, are administered, and with what filthy hands are handled this glorious milk and blood of My spouse, and with what presumption and irreverence they are received. Wherefore, that which really gives life, often gives, through the defects of those who receive it, death; that is to say, the precious Blood of My only-begotten Son, which destroyed death and darkness, and gave life and truth, and confounded falsehood. For I give this Blood and use It for salvation and perfection in the case of that man who disposes himself properly to receive it, for It gives life and adorns the soul with every grace, in proportion to the disposition and affection of him who receives It; similarly It gives death to him who receives It unworthily, living in iniquity and in the darkness of mortal sin; to him, I say, It gives death and not life; not through defect of the Blood, nor through defect of the minister, though there might be great evil in him, because his evil would not spoil nor defile the Blood nor diminish Its grace and virtue, nor does an evil minister do harm to him to whom he gives the Blood, but to himself he does the harm of guilt, which will be followed by punishment, unless he correct himself with contrition and repentance. I say then that the Blood does harm to him who receives it unworthily, not through defect of the Blood, nor of the minister, but through his own evil disposition and defect inasmuch as he has befouled his mind and body with such impurity and misery, and has been so cruel to himself and his neighbour. He has used cruelty to himself, depriving himself of grace, trampling under the feet of his affection the fruit of the Blood which he had received in Holy Baptism, when the stain of original sin was taken from him by virtue of the Blood, which stain he drew from his origin, when he was generated by his father and mother.

"Wherefore I gave My Word, My only-begotten Son, because the whole stuff of human generation was corrupted through the sin of the first man Adam. Wherefore, all of you, vessels made of this stuff, were corrupted and not disposed to the possession of eternal life—so I, with My dignity, joined Myself to the baseness of your human generation, in order to restore it to grace which you had lost by sin; for I was incapable of suffering, and yet, on account of guilt, My divine justice demanded suffering. But man was not sufficient to satisfy it, for, even if he had satisfied to a certain extent, he could only have satisfied for himself, and not for other rational creatures, besides which, neither for himself, nor for others, could man satisfy, his sin having been committed against Me, who am the Infinite Good. Wishing, however, to restore man, who was enfeebled, and could not satisfy for the above reason, I sent My Word, My own Son, clothed in your own very

nature, the corrupted clay of Adam, in order that
He might endure suffering in that self-same
nature in which man had offended, suffering in
His body even to the opprobrious death of the
Cross, and so He satisfied My justice and My
divine mercy. For My mercy willed to make
satisfaction for the sin of man and to dispose
him to that good for which I had created him.
This human nature, joined with the divine nature,
was sufficient to satisfy for the whole human race,
not only on account of the pain which it sustained in its finite nature, that is in the flesh of
Adam, but by virtue of the Eternal Deity, the
divine and infinite nature joined to it. The two
natures being thus joined together, I received and
accepted the sacrifice of My only-begotten Son,
kneaded into one dough with the divine nature,
by the fire of divine love which was the fetter
which held him fastened and nailed to the Cross
in this way. Thus human nature was sufficient
to satisfy for guilt, but only by virtue of the
divine nature. And in this way was destroyed
the stain of Adam's sin, only the mark of it
remaining behind, that is an inclination to sin,
and to every sort of corporeal defect, like the
cicatrice which remains when a man is healed of
a wound. In this way the original fault of Adam
was able still to cause a fatal stain; wherefore
the coming of the great Physician, that is to say,
of My only-begotten Son, cured this invalid, He
drinking this bitter medicine, which man could
not drink on account of his great weakness, like

a foster-mother who takes medicine instead of
her suckling, because she is grown up and strong,
and the child is not fit to endure its bitterness.
He was man's foster-mother, enduring, with the
greatness and strength of the Deity united with
your nature, the bitter medicine of the painful
death of the Cross, to give life to you little ones
debilitated by guilt. I say therefore that the
mark alone of original sin remains, which sin
you take from your father and your mother
when you were generated by them. But this
mark is removed from the soul, though not
altogether, by Holy Baptism, which has the
virtue of communicating the life of grace by
means of that glorious and precious Blood.
Wherefore, at the moment that the soul receives
Holy Baptism, original sin is taken away from
her, and grace is infused into her, and that inclination to sin, which remains from the original
corruption, as has been said, is indeed a source of
weakness, but the soul can keep the bridle on it
if she choose. Then the vessel of the soul is
disposed to receive and increase in herself grace,
more or less, according as it pleases her to dispose herself willingly with affection, and desire
of loving and serving Me ; and, in the same way,
she can dispose herself to evil as to good, in spite
of her having received grace in Holy Baptism.
Wherefore when the time of discretion is come,
the soul can, by her free will, make choice either
of good or evil, according as it pleases her will ;
and so great is this liberty that man has, and so

strong has this liberty been made by virtue of
this glorious Blood, that no demon or creature
can constrain him to one smallest fault without
his free consent.   He has been redeemed from
slavery, and made free in order that he might
govern his own sensuality, and obtain the end
for which he was created.   Oh, miserable man,
who delights to remain in the mud like a brute,
and does not learn this great benefit which he has
received from Me!   A benefit so great, that the
poor wretched creature full of such ignorance
could receive no greater."

*How sin is more gravely punished after the Passion of
Christ than before ; and how God promises to do
mercy to the world, and to the Holy Church, by
means of the prayers and sufferings of His servants.*

"And I wish thee to know, My daughter,
that, although I have re-created and restored to
the life of grace, the human race, through the
Blood of My only-begotten Son, as I have said,
men are not grateful, but, going from bad to
worse, and from guilt to guilt, even persecuting
Me with many injuries, taking so little account
of the graces which I have given them, and continue to give them, that, not only do they not
attribute what they have received to grace, but
seem to themselves on occasion to receive injuries
from Me, as if I desired anything else than their
sanctification.

"I say to thee that they will be more hard-hearted, and worthy of more punishment, and will, indeed, be punished more severely, now that they have received redemption in the Blood of My Son, than they would have been before that redemption took place—that is, before the stain of Adam's sin had been taken away. It is right that he who receives more should render more, and should be under great obligations to Him from whom he receives more.

"Man, then, was closely bound to Me through his being which I have given him, creating him in My own image and similitude ; for which reason, he was bound to render Me glory, but he deprived Me of it, and wished to give it to himself. Thus he came to transgress My obedience imposed on him, and became My enemy. And I, with My humility, destroyed his pride, humiliating the divine nature, and taking your humanity, and, freeing you from the service of the devil, I made you free. And, not only did I give you liberty, but, if you examine, you will see that man has become God, and God has become man, through the union of the divine with the human nature. This is the debt which they have incurred—that is to say, the treasure of the Blood, by which they have been procreated to grace. See, therefore, how much more they owe after the redemption than before. For they are now obliged to render Me glory and praise by following in the steps of My Incarnate Word, My only-begotten Son, for then they repay Me the debt of love both of Myself and of their neighbour, with true and genuine virtue, as I have said to thee above, and if they do not do it, the greater their debt, the greater will be the offence they fall into, and therefore, by divine justice, the greater their suffering in eternal damnation.

"A false Christian is punished more than a pagan, and the deathless fire of divine justice consumes him more, that is, afflicts him more, and, in his affliction, he feels himself being consumed by the worm of conscience, though, in truth, he is not consumed, because the damned do not lose their being through any torment which they receive. Wherefore I say to thee, that they ask for death and cannot have it, for they cannot lose their being; the existence of grace they lose, through their fault, but not their natural existence. Therefore guilt is more gravely punished after the Redemption of the Blood than before, because man received more ; but sinners neither seem to perceive this, nor to pay any attention to their own sins, and so become My enemies, though I have reconciled them, by means of the Blood of My Son. But there is a remedy with which I appease My wrath—that is to say, by means of My servants, if they are jealous to constrain Me by their desire. Thou seest, therefore, that thou hast bound Me with this bond which I have given thee, because I wished to do mercy to the world.

"Therefore I give My servants hunger and desire for My honour, and the salvation of souls, so that, constrained by their tears, I may mitigate the fury of My divine justice. Take, therefore, thy tears and thy sweat, drawn from the fountain of My divine love, and, with them, wash the face of My spouse.

"I promise thee, that, by this means, her beauty will be restored to her, not by the knife nor by cruelty, but peacefully, by humble and continued prayer, by the sweat and the tears shed by the fiery desire of My servants, and thus will I fulfil thy desire if thou, on thy part, endure much, casting the light of thy patience into the darkness of perverse man, not fearing the world's persecutions, for I will protect thee, and My Providence shall never fail thee in the slightest need."

How the road to Heaven being broken through the disobedience of Adam, God made of His Son a Bridge by which man could pass.

"Wherefore I have told thee that I have made a Bridge of My Word, of My only-begotten Son, and this is the truth. I wish that you, My children, should know that the road was broken by the sin and disobedience of Adam, in such a way, that no one could arrive at Eternal Life. Wherefore men did not render Me glory in the way in which they ought to have, as they did not participate in that Good for which I had created them, and My truth was not fulfilled. This truth is that I have created man to My own image and similitude, in order that he might have Eternal Life, and might partake of Me, and taste My supreme and eternal sweetness and goodness.

But, after sin had closed Heaven and bolted the doors of mercy, the soul of man produced thorns and prickly brambles, and My creature found in himself rebellion against himself.

"And the flesh immediately began to war against the Spirit, and, losing the state of innocency, became a foul animal, and all created things rebelled against man, whereas they would have been obedient to him, had he remained in the state in which I had placed him. He, not remaining therein, transgressed My obedience, and merited eternal death in soul and body. And, as soon as he had sinned, a tempestuous flood arose, which ever buffets him with its waves, bringing him weariness and trouble from himself, the devil, and the world. Every one was drowned in the flood, because no one, with his own justice alone, could arrive at Eternal Life. And so, wishing to remedy your great evils, I have given you the Bridge of My Son, in order that, passing across the flood, you may not be drowned, which flood is the tempestuous sea of this dark life. See, therefore, under what obligations the creature is to Me, and how ignorant he is, not to take the remedy which I have offered, but to be willing to drown."

How God induces the soul to look at the greatness of this Bridge, inasmuch as it reaches from earth to Heaven.

"Open, my daughter, the eye of thy intellect, and thou wilt see the accepted and the ignorant, the imperfect, and also the perfect who follow Me in truth, so that thou mayest grieve over the damnation of the ignorant, and rejoice over the perfection of My beloved servants.

"Thou wilt see further how those bear themselves who walk in the light, and those who walk in the darkness. I also wish thee to look at the Bridge of My only-begotten Son, and see the greatness thereof, for it reaches from Heaven to earth, that is, that the earth of your humanity is joined to the greatness of the Deity thereby. I say then that this Bridge reaches from Heaven to earth, and constitutes the union which I have made with man.

"This was necessary, in order to reform the road which was broken, as I said to thee, in order that man should pass through the bitterness of the world, and arrive at life; but the Bridge could not be made of earth sufficiently large to span the flood and give you Eternal Life, because the earth of human nature was not sufficient to satisfy for guilt, to remove the stain of Adam's sin. Which stain corrupted the whole human race and gave out a stench, as I have said to thee above. It was, therefore, necessary to join human nature with the height of My nature, the Eternal Deity, so that it might be sufficient to satisfy for the whole human race, so that human nature should sustain the punishment, and that the Divine nature, united with the human, should make acceptable the sacrifice of My only Son, offered to Me to take death from you and to give you life.

"So the height of the Divinity, humbled to the earth, and joined with your humanity, made the Bridge and reformed the road. Why was this done? In order that man might come to his true happiness with the angels. And observe, that it is not enough, in order that you should have life, that My Son should have made you this Bridge, unless you walk thereon."

How this soul prays God to show her those who cross by the aforesaid Bridge, and those who do not.

Then this soul exclaimed with ardent love,— "Oh, inestimable Charity, sweet above all sweetness! Who would not be inflamed by such great love? What heart can help breaking at such tenderness? It seems, oh, Abyss of Charity, as if thou wert mad with love of Thy creature, as if Thou couldest not live without him, and yet Thou art our God who hast no heed of us, Thy greatness does not increase through our good, for Thou art unchangeable, and our evil causes Thee no harm, for Thou art the Supreme and Eternal Goodness. What moves Thee to do us such mercy through pure love, and on account of no debt that Thou owedst us, or need that Thou hadst of us? We are rather Thy guilty and malignant debtors. Wherefore, if I understand aright, Oh, Supreme and Eternal Truth, I am the thief and Thou hast been punished for me. For I see Thy Word, Thy Son, fastened and nailed to the Cross, of which Thou hast made me a Bridge, as Thou hast shown me, Thy miserable servant, for which reason, my heart is bursting, and yet cannot burst, through the hunger and the desire which it has conceived towards Thee. I remember, my Lord, that Thou wast willing to show me who are those who go by the Bridge and those who do not; should it please Thy goodness to manifest this to me, willingly would I see and hear it."

How this Bridge has three steps, which signify the three states of the soul; and how, being lifted on high, yet it is not separated from the earth; and how these words are to be understood: " If I am lifted up from the earth, I will draw all things unto Me."

Then the Eternal God, to enamour and excite that soul still more for the salvation of souls, replied to her, and said : " First, as I have shown thee that for which thou didst wish, and ask Me, I will now explain to thee the nature of this Bridge. I have told thee, My daughter, that the Bridge reaches from Heaven to earth; this is through the union which I have made with man, whom I formed of the clay of the earth. Now learn that this Bridge, My only-begotten Son, has three steps, of which two were made with the wood of the most Holy Cross, and the third still retains the great bitterness He tasted, when He was given gall and vinegar to drink. In these three steps you will recognise three states of the soul, which I will explain to thee below. The feet of the soul, signifying her affection, are the first step, for the feet carry the body as the affection carries the soul. Wherefore these pierced Feet are steps by which thou canst arrive at His Side, Which manifests to thee the secret of His Heart, because the soul, rising on the steps of her affection, commences to taste the love of His Heart, gazing into that open Heart of My Son, with the eye of the intellect, and finds It consumed with ineffable love. I say consumed, because He does not love you for His own profit, because you can be of no profit to Him, He being one and the same thing with Me. Then the soul is filled with love, seeing herself so much loved. Having passed the second step, the soul reaches out to the third—that is—to the Mouth, where she finds peace from the terrible war she has been waging with her sin. On the first step, then, lifting her feet from the affections of the earth, the soul strips herself of vice ; on the second she fills herself with love and virtue ; and on the third she tastes peace. So the Bridge has three steps, in order that, climbing past the first and the second, you may reach the last, which is lifted on high, so that the water, running beneath, may not touch it ; for, in My Son, was no venom of sin. This Bridge is lifted on high, and yet, at the same time, joined to the earth. Dost thou know when it was lifted on high ? When My Son was lifted up on the wood of the most Holy

Cross, the Divine nature remaining joined to the lowliness of the earth of your humanity.

"For this reason I said to thee that, being lifted on high, He was not lifted out of the earth, for the Divine nature is united and kneaded into one thing with it. And there was no one who could go on the Bridge until It had been lifted on high, wherefore He said,—'*Si exaltatus fuero a terra omnia traham ad me ipsum*,' that is, '*If I am lifted on high I will draw all things to Me*.'   My Goodness, seeing that in no other way could you be drawn to Me, I sent Him in order that He should be lifted on high on the wood of the Cross, making of it an anvil on which My Son, born of human generation, should be re-made, in order to free you from death, and to restore you to the life of grace; wherefore He drew everything to Himself by this means, namely, by showing the ineffable love, with which I love you, the heart of man being always attracted by love.   Greater love, then, I could not show you, than to lay down My life for you; perforce, then, My Son was treated in this way by love, in order that ignorant man should be unable to resist being drawn to Me.

"In very truth, then, My Son said, that, being lifted on high, He would draw all things to Him.   And this is to be understood in two ways.   Firstly, that, when the heart of man is drawn by the affection of love, as I have said, it is drawn together with all the powers of his soul, that is, with the Memory, the Intellect, and the

Will; now, when these three powers are har-
moniously joined together in My Name, all the
other operations which the man performs, whether
in deed or thought, are pleasing, and joined together by the effect of love, because love is lifted
on high, following the Sorrowful Crucified One;
so My Truth said well, ' *If I am lifted on high*,'
&c., meaning, that if the heart and the powers of
the soul are drawn to Him, all the actions are
also drawn to Him.   Secondly, everything has
been created for the service of man, to serve the
necessities of rational creatures, and the rational
creature has not been made for them, but for Me,
in order to serve Me with all his heart, and with
all his affection.   See, then, that man being drawn,
everything else is drawn with him, because everything else has been made for him.   It was therefore necessary that the Bridge should be lifted
on high, and have steps, in order that it might
be climbed with greater facility."

*How this Bridge is built of stones which signify
virtues; and how on the Bridge is a hostelry
where food is given to the travellers; and how
he who goes over the Bridge goes to life, while
he who goes under It goes to perdition and death.*

"This Bridge is built of stones, so that, if the
rain come, it may not impede the traveller.   Dost
thou know what these stones are?   They are the
stones of true and sincere virtues.   These stones
were not built into the walls before the Passion

of My Son, and therefore even those who attempted to walk by the road of virtue were prevented from arriving at their journey's end, because Heaven was not yet unlocked with the key of the Blood, and the rain of Justice did not let them pass; but, after the stones were made, and built up on the Body of My sweet Son, My Word, of whom I have spoken to thee, He, who was Himself the Bridge, moistened the mortar for its building with His Blood. That is, His Blood was united with the mortar of divinity, and with the fortitude, and the fire of love; and, by My power, these stones of the virtues were built into a wall, upon Him as the foundation, for there is no virtue which has not been proved in Him, and from Him all virtues have their life. Wherefore no one can have the virtue given by a life of grace, but from Him, that is, without following the footsteps of His doctrine. He has built a wall of the virtues, planting them as living stones, and cementing them with His Blood, so that every believer may walk speedily, and without any servile fear of the rain of Divine justice, for he is sheltered by the mercy which descended from Heaven in the Incarnation of this My Son. How was Heaven opened? With the key of His Blood; so thou seest that the Bridge is walled and roofed with Mercy. His also is the Hostelry in the Garden of the Holy Church, which keeps and ministers the Bread of Life, and gives to drink of the Blood, so that My creatures, journeying on their pilgrimage, may not, through weariness, faint by the way ; and for this reason My love has ordained that the Blood and the Body of My only-begotten Son, wholly God and wholly man, may be ministered to you. The pilgrim, having passed the Bridge, arrives at the door which is part of the Bridge, at which all must enter, wherefore He says: '*I am the Way, the Truth, and the Life, he who follows Me does not walk in darkness, but in light.*' And in another place My Truth says, '*That no man can come to Me if not by Him,*' and so indeed it is. Therefore He says of Himself that He is the Road, and this is the truth, and I have already shown thee that He is a Road in the form of the Bridge. And He says that He is the Truth, and so He is, because He is united with Me who am the Truth, and he who follows Him, walks in the Truth, and in Life, because he who follows this Truth receives the life of grace, and cannot faint from hunger, because the Truth has become your food, nor fall in the darkness, because He is light without any falsehood. And, with that Truth, He confounded and destroyed the lie that the Devil told to Eve, with which he broke up the road to Heaven, and the Truth brought the pieces together again, and cemented them with His Blood. Wherefore, those who follow this road are the sons of the Truth, because they follow the Truth, and pass through the door of Truth and find themselves united to Me, who am the Door and the Road and at the same time Infinite Peace.

"But he, who walks not on this road, goes under the Bridge, in the river where there are no stones, only water, and since there are no supports in the water, no one can travel that way without drowning; thus have come to pass the sins, and the condition of the world. Wherefore, if the affection is not placed on the stones, but is placed, with disordinate love, on creatures, loving them, and being kept by them far from Me, the soul drowns, for creatures are like water that continually runs past, and man also passes continually like the river, although it seems to him that he stands still and the creatures that he loves pass by, and yet he is passing himself continually to the end of his journey—death! And he would fain retain himself (that is his life, and the things that he loves), but he does not succeed, either, through death, by which he has to leave them, or through my disposition, by which these created things are taken from the sight of My creatures. Such as these follow a lie, walking on the road of falsehood, and are sons of the Devil, who is the Father of Lies; and, because they pass by the door of falsehood, they receive eternal damnation. So then thou seest, that I have shown thee both Truth and Falsehood, that is, My road which is Truth, and the Devil's which is Falsehood."

*How travelling on both of these roads, that is the
Bridge and the River, is fatiguing; and of
the delight which the soul feels in travelling by
the Bridge.*

"These are the two roads, and both are hard to
travel. Wonder, then, at the ignorance and blindness of man, who, having a Road made for him,
which causes such delight to those who use It,
that every bitterness becomes sweet, and every
burden light, yet prefers to walk over the water.
For those who cross by the Bridge, being still in
the darkness of the body, find light, and, being
mortal, find immortal life, tasting, through love,
the light of Eternal Truth which promises refreshment to him who wearies himself for Me,
who am grateful and just, and render to every
man according as he deserves. Wherefore every
good deed is rewarded, and every fault is punished.
The tongue would not be sufficient to relate the
delight felt by him who goes on this road, for,
even in this life, he tastes and participates in that
good which has been prepared for him in eternal
life. He, therefore, is a fool indeed, who despises
so great a good, and chooses rather to receive in
this life, the earnest money of Hell, walking by
the lower road with great toil, and without any
refreshment or advantage. Wherefore, through
their sins, they are deprived of Me, who am the
Supreme and Eternal Good. Truly then hast
thou reason for grief, and I will that thou and
My other servants remain in continual bitter-

ness of soul at the offence done to Me, and in compassion for the ignorant, and the loss of those who, in their ignorance, thus offend Me. Now thou hast seen and heard about this Bridge, how it is, and this I have told thee in order to explain My words, that My only-begotten Son was a Bridge. And thus, thou seest that He is the Truth, made in the way that I have shown thee, that is—by the union of height and lowliness."

How this Bridge, having reached to Heaven on the day of the Ascension, did not for that reason leave the earth.

" When My only-begotten Son returned to Me, forty days after the resurrection, this Bridge, namely Himself, arose from the earth, that is, from among the conversation of men, and ascended into Heaven by virtue of the Divine Nature and sat at the right hand of Me, the Eternal Father, as the angels said, on the day of the Ascension, to the disciples, standing like dead men, their hearts lifted on high, and ascended into Heaven with the wisdom of My Son—' *Do not stand here any longer, for He is seated at the right hand of the Father!* ' When He, then, had thus ascended on high, and returned to Me the Father, I sent the Master, that is the Holy Spirit, who came to you with My power and the wisdom of My Son, and with His own clemency, which is the essence of the Holy Spirit. He is one thing

with Me, the Father, and with My Son. And
He built up the road of the doctrine which My
Truth had left in the world. Thus, though the
bodily presence of My Son left you, His doctrine
remained, and the virtue of the stones founded
upon this doctrine, which is the way made for
you by this Bridge. For first, He practised this
doctrine and made the road by His actions, giving
you His doctrine by example rather than by
words ; for He practised, first Himself, what He
afterwards taught you, then the clemency of the
Holy Spirit made you certain of the doctrine,
fortifying the minds of the disciples to confess
the truth, and to announce this road, that is, the
doctrine of Christ crucified, reproving, by this
means, the world of its injustice and false judgment, of which injustice and false judgment, I
will in time discourse to you at greater length.

"This much I have said to thee in order that
there might be no cloud of darkness in the mind
of your hearers, that is, that they may know that
of this Body of Christ I made a Bridge by the
union of the divine with the human nature, for
this is the truth.

"This Bridge, taking its point of departure
in you, rose into Heaven, and was the one road
which was taught you by the example and life of
the Truth. What has now remained of all this,
and where is the road to be found ? I will tell
thee, that is, I will rather tell those who might
fall into ignorance on this point. I tell thee
that this way of His doctrine, of which I have

spoken to thee, confirmed by the Apostles, declared by the blood of the martyrs, illuminated by the light of doctors, confessed by the confessors, narrated in all its love by the Evangelists, all of whom stand as witnesses to confess the Truth, is found in the mystical body of the Holy Church. These witnesses are like the light placed on a candlestick, to show forth the way of the Truth which leads to life with a perfect light, as I have said to thee, and, as they themselves say to thee, with proof, since they have proved in their own cases, that every person may, if he will, be illuminated to know the Truth, unless he choose to deprive his reason of light by his inordinate self-love. It is, indeed, the truth that His doctrine is true, and has remained like a lifeboat to draw the soul out of the tempestuous sea and to conduct her to the port of salvation.

"Wherefore, first I gave you the Bridge of My Son living and conversing in very deed amongst men, and when He, the living Bridge, left you, there remained the Bridge and the road of His doctrine, as has been said, His doctrine being joined with My power and with His wisdom, and with the clemency of the Holy Spirit. This power of Mine gives the virtue of fortitude to whoever follows this road, wisdom gives him light, so that, in this road, he may recognise the truth, and the Holy Spirit gives him love, which consumes and takes away all sensitive love out of the soul, leaving there only the love of virtue. Thus, in both ways, both actually and through His doctrine, He is the Way, the Truth, and the Life; that is, the Bridge which leads you to the height of Heaven. This is what He meant when He said, '*I came from the Father, and I return to the Father, and shall return to you*'; that is to say, 'My Father sent Me to you, and made Me your Bridge, so that you might be saved from the river and attain to life.' Then He says, '*I will return to you, I will not leave you orphans, but will send you the Paraclete*'—as if My Truth should say, 'I will go to the Father and return; that is, that when the Holy Spirit shall come, who is called the Paraclete, He will show you more clearly, and will confirm you in the way of truth, that I have given you.' He said that He would return, and He did return, because the Holy Spirit came not alone, but with the power of the Father, and the wisdom of the Son, and the clemency of His own Essence.

"See then how He returns, not in actual flesh and blood, but, as I have said, building the road of His doctrine, with His power, which road cannot be destroyed or taken away from him who wishes to follow it, because it is firm and stable, and proceeds from Me, who am immoveable.

"Manfully, then, should you follow this road, without any cloud of doubt, but with the light of faith which has been given you as a principle in Holy Baptism.

"Now I have fully shown to you the Bridge

as it actually is, and the doctrine, which is one
and the same thing with it. And I have shown
it to the ignorant, in order that they may see
where this road of Truth is, and where stand
those who teach it; and I have explained that
they are the Apostles, Martyrs, Confessors,
Evangelists, and Holy Doctors, placed like
lanterns in the Holy Church.

"And I have shown how My Son, returning
to Me, none the less, returned to you, not in
His bodily presence, but by His power, when
the Holy Spirit came upon the disciples, as I
have said. For in His bodily presence He will
not return until the last Day of Judgment, when
He will come again with My Majesty and Divine
Power to judge the world, to render good to
the virtuous, and reward them for their labours,
both in body and soul, and to dispense the evil
of eternal death to those who have lived wickedly
in the world.

"And now I wish to tell thee that which I,
the Truth, promised thee, that is, to show thee
the perfect, the imperfect, and the supremely
perfect; and the wicked, who, through their
iniquities, drown in the river, attaining to punishment and torment; wherefore I say to you,
My dearest sons, walk over the Bridge, and not
underneath it, because underneath is not the
way of truth, but the way of falsehood, by which
walk the wicked, of whom I will presently speak
to you. These are those sinners for whom I
beg you to pray to Me, and for whom I ask in

addition your tears and sweat, in order that they may receive mercy from Me."

*How this soul wondering at the mercy of God, relates
many gifts and graces given to the human race.*

Then this soul, as it were, like one intoxicated, could not contain herself, but standing before the face of God, exclaimed, "How great is the Eternal Mercy with which Thou coverest the sins of Thy creatures! I do not wonder that Thou sayest of those who abandon mortal sin and return to Thee, '*I do not remember that you have ever offended Me.*' Oh, ineffable Mercy! I do not wonder that Thou sayest this to those who are converted, when Thou sayest of those who persecute Thee, 'I wish you to pray for such, in order that I may do them mercy.' Oh, Mercy, who proceedest from Thy Eternal Father, the Divinity who governest with Thy power the whole world, by Thee were we created, in Thee were we re-created in the Blood of Thy Son. Thy Mercy preserves us, Thy Mercy caused Thy Son to do battle for us, hanging by His arms on the wood of the Cross, life and death battling together; then life confounded the death of our sin, and the death of our sin destroyed the bodily life of the Immaculate Lamb. Which was finally conquered? Death! By what means? Mercy! Thy Mercy gives light and life, by which Thy clemency is known in all Thy creatures, both the just and the unjust. In the height of Heaven Thy Mercy shines, that is, in Thy saints. If I turn to the earth, it abounds with Thy Mercy. In the darkness of Hell Thy Mercy shines, for the damned do not receive the pains they deserve; with Thy Mercy Thou temperest Justice. By Mercy Thou hast washed us in the Blood, and by Mercy Thou wishest to converse with Thy creatures. Oh, Loving Madman! was it not enough for Thee to become Incarnate, that Thou must also die? Was not death enough, that Thou must also descend into Limbo, taking thence the holy fathers to fulfil Thy Mercy and Thy Truth in them? Because Thy goodness promises a reward to them that serve Thee in truth, didst Thou descend to Limbo, to withdraw from their pain Thy servants, and give them the fruit of their labours. Thy Mercy constrains Thee to give even more to man, namely, to leave Thyself to him in food, so that we, weak ones, should have comfort, and the ignorant commemorating Thee, should not lose the memory of Thy benefits. Wherefore every day Thou givest Thyself to man, representing Thyself in the Sacrament of the Altar, in the body of Thy Holy Church. What has done this? Thy Mercy. Oh, Divine Mercy! My heart suffocates in thinking of thee, for on every side to which I turn my thought, I find nothing but mercy. Oh, Eternal Father! Forgive my ignorance, that I presume thus to chatter to Thee, but the love of Thy Mercy will be my excuse before the Face of Thy loving-kindness."

*Of the baseness of those who pass by the river under
    the Bridge; and how the soul, that passes
    underneath, is called by God the tree of death,
    whose roots are held in four vices.*

After this soul had refreshed a little her heart
in the mercy of God, by these words, she humbly
waited for the fulfilment of the promise made
to her, and God continuing His discourse said :
" Dearest daughter, thou hast spoken before Me
of My mercy, because I gave it thee to taste and
to see in the word which I spoke to thee when
I said : 'these are those for whom I pray you to
intercede with Me,' but know, that My mercy
is without any comparison, far more than thou
canst see, because thy sight is imperfect, and My
mercy perfect and infinite, so that there can be
no comparison between the two, except what
may be between a finite and an infinite thing.
But I have wished that thou shouldest taste this
mercy, and also the dignity of man, which I
have shown thee above, so that thou mightest
know better the cruelty of those wicked men
who travel below the Bridge. Open the eye of
thy intellect, and wonder at those who voluntarily drown themselves, and at the baseness to
which they are fallen by their fault, from which
cause, they have first become weak, and this was
when they conceived mortal sin in their minds,
for they then bring it forth, and lose the life
of grace. And, as a corpse which can have no
feeling or movement of itself, but only when it

is moved and lifted by others, so those, who are
drowned in the stream of disordinate love of the
world, are dead to grace. Wherefore because
they are dead their memory takes no heed of
My mercy. The eye of their intellect sees not
and knows not My Truth, because their feeling
is dead, that is, their intellect has no object
before it but themselves, with the dead love of
their own sensuality, and so their will is dead
to My will because it loves nothing but dead
things. These three powers then being dead,
all the soul's operations both in deed and thought
are dead as far as grace is concerned. For the
soul cannot defend herself against her enemies,
nor help herself through her own power, but
only so far as she is helped by Me. It is true
indeed, that every time that this corpse, in whom
only free-will has remained (which remains as
long as the mortal body lives), asks My help,
he can have it, but never can he help himself;
he has become insupportable to himself, and,
wishing to govern the world, is governed by
that which is not, that is by sin, for sin in itself
is nothing, and such men have become the servants and slaves of sin. I have made them trees
of love with the life of grace which they received
in Holy Baptism; and they have become trees
of death, because they are dead, as I have already
said to thee. Dost thou know how this tree
finds such roots? In the height of pride, which
is nourished by their own sensitive self-love.
Its branch is their own impatience, and its off-

shoot indiscretion : these are the four principal
vices which destroy the soul of him who is a
tree of death, because he has not drawn life
from grace.   Inside the tree is nourished the
worm of conscience, which, while man lives in
mortal sin, is blinded by self-love, and therefore
felt but little ; the fruits of this tree are mortal,
for they have drawn their nourishment, which
should have been humility, from the roots of
pride, and the miserable soul is full of ingratitude, whence proceeds every evil.   But if she
were grateful for the benefits she has received,
she would know Me, and knowing Me would
know herself, and so would remain in My love :
but she, as if blind, goes groping down the river,
and she does not see that the water does not
support her."

*How the fruits of this tree are as diverse as are the
sins ; and first, of the sin of sensuality.*

"The fruits of this death-giving tree, are as
diverse as sins are diverse.   See that some of
these fruits are the food of beasts who live im-
purely, using their body and their mind like a
swine who wallows in mud, for in the same way
they wallow in the mire of sensuality.   Oh, ugly
soul, where hast thou left thy dignity ?   Thou
wast made sister to the angels, and now thou art
become a brute beast.   To such misery come
sinners, notwithstanding that they are sustained
by Me, who am Supreme Purity, notwithstanding

that the very devils, whose friends and servants they have become, cannot endure the sight of such filthy actions. Neither does any sin, abominable as it may be, take away the light of the intellect from man, so much as does this one. This the philosophers knew, not by the light of grace, because they had it not, but because nature gave them the light to know that this sin obscured the intellect, and for that reason they preserved themselves in continence the better to study. Thus also they flung away their riches in order that the thought of them should not occupy their heart. Not so does the ignorant and false Christian, who has lost grace by sin."

How the fruit of others is avarice; and of the evils that proceed from it.

"A fruit of the earth belongs to some others, who are covetous misers, acting like the mole, who always feeds on earth till death, and when they arrive at death they find no remedy. Such as these, with their meanness, despise My generosity, selling time to their neighbour. They are cruel usurers, and robbers of their neighbour; because in their memory they have not the remembrance of My mercy, for if they had it they would not be cruel to themselves or to their neighbour; on the contrary, they would be compassionate and merciful to themselves, practising the virtues on their neighbour and succouring him charitably. Oh, how many are the evils

that come of this cursed sin of avarice, how
many homicides and thefts, and how much pillage
with unlawful gain, and cruelty of heart and
injustice! It kills the soul and makes her the
slave of riches, so that she cares not to observe
My commandments.

"A miser loves no one except for his own
profit. Avarice proceeds from and feeds pride,
the one follows from the other, because the miser
always carries with him the thought of his own
reputation, and thus avarice, which is immediately combined with pride, full of its own
opinions, goes on from bad to worse. It is a
fire which always germinates the smoke of vainglory and vanity of heart, and boasting in that
which does not belong to it. It is a root which
has many branches, and the principal one is that
which makes a man care for his own reputation,
from whence proceeds his desire to be greater
than his neighbour. It also brings forth the
deceitful heart that is neither pure nor liberal,
but is double, making a man show one thing
with his tongue, while he has another in his
heart, and making him conceal the truth and
tell lies for his own profit. And it produces
envy, which is a worm that is always gnawing,
and does not let the miser have any happiness
out of his own or others' good. How will
these wicked ones in so wretched a state give
of their substance to the poor, when they rob
others? How will they draw their foul soul
out of the mire, when they themselves put it

there? Sometimes even do they become so brutish, that they do not consider their children and relations, and cause them to fall with them into great misery. And, nevertheless, in My mercy I sustain them, I do not command the earth to swallow them up, that they may repent of their sins. Would they then give their life for the salvation of souls, when they will not give their substance? Would they give their affections when they are gnawed with envy? Oh, miserable vices that destroy the heaven of the soul. Heaven I call her (the soul) because so I made her, living in her at first by grace, and hiding Myself within her, and making of her a mansion through affection of love. Now she has separated herself from Me, like an adulteress, loving herself, and creatures more than Me, and has made a god of herself, persecuting Me with many and diverse sins. And this she does because she does not consider the benefit of the Blood that was shed with so great Fire of Love."

How some others hold positions of authority, and bring forth fruits of injustice.

"There are others who hold their heads high by their position of authority, and who bear the banner of injustice—using injustice against Me, God, and against their neighbour, and against themselves — to themselves by not paying the debt of virtue, and towards Me by not paying the debt of honour in glorifying and praising My Name, which debt they are bound to pay.   But they, like thieves, steal what is Mine, and give it to the service of their own sensuality.   So that they commit injustice towards Me and towards themselves, like blind and ignorant men who do not recognise Me in themselves on account of self-love, like the Jews and the ministers of the Law who, with envy and self-love, blinded themselves so that they did not recognise the Truth, My only-begotten Son, and rendered not His due to the Eternal Truth, who was amongst them, as said My Truth : ' *The Kingdom of God is among you.*'   But they knew it not, because, in the aforesaid way, they had lost the light of reason, and so they did not pay their debt of honour and glory to Me, and to Him, who was one thing with Me, and like blind ones committed injustice, persecuting Him with much ignominy, even to the death of the Cross.

"Thus are such as these unjust to themselves, to Me, and to their neighbour, unjustly selling the flesh of their dependants, and of any person who falls into their hands."

How through these and through other defects, one falls into false judgment; and of the indignity to which one comes.

" By these and by other sins men fall into false judgment, as I will explain to you below.   They are continually being scandalised by My works, which are all just, and all performed in truth through love and mercy. With this false judgment, and with the poison of envy and pride, the works of My Son were slandered and unjustly judged, and with lies did His enemies say: '*This man works by virtue of Beelzebub.*' Thus wicked men, standing in self-love, impurity, pride, and avarice, and founded in envy, and in perverse rashness with impatience, are for ever scandalised at Me and at My servants, whom they judge to be feignedly practising the virtues, because their heart is rotten, and, having spoilt their taste, good things seem evil to them, and bad things, that is to say disorderly living, seem good to them. Oh, how blind is the human generation in that it considers not its own dignity! From being great thou hast become small, from a ruler thou hast become a slave, and that in the vilest service that can be had, because thou art the servant and slave of sin, and art become like unto that which thou dost serve.

"Sin is nothing. Thou, then, hast become nothing; it has deprived thee of life, and given thee death. This life and power were given you by the Word, My only-begotten Son, the glorious Bridge, He drawing you from out of your servitude when you were servants of the devil, Himself becoming as a servant to take you out of servitude, imposing on Himself obedience to do away the disobedience òf Adam, and humbling Himself to the shameful death of the Cross to confound pride. By His death He destroyed every vice, so that no one could say that any vice remained that was not punished and beaten out with pains, as I said to thee above, when I said that of His Body He had made an anvil. All the remedies are ready to save men from eternal death, and they despise the Blood, and have trampled It under the feet of their disordinate affection; and it is for this injustice and false judgment that the world is reproved, and will be reproved on the Last Day of Judgment.

"This was meant by My Truth when He said: '*I will send the Paraclete, who will reprove the world for injustice and false judgment.*' And it was reproved when I sent the Holy Spirit on the Apostles."

Of the words that Christ said: "I will send the Holy Spirit, who will reprove the world of injustice and of false judgment;" and how one of these reproofs is continuous.

"There are three reproofs. One was given when the Holy Spirit came upon the disciples, who, as it is said, being fortified by My power, and illuminated by the wisdom of My beloved Son, received all in the plenitude of the Holy Spirit. Then the Holy Spirit, who is one thing with Me and with My Son, reproved the world by the mouth of the Apostles, with the doctrine of My Truth. They and all others, who are descended from them, following the truth which they understand through the same means, reprove the world.

"This is that continuous reproof that I make to the world by means of the Holy Scriptures, and My servants, putting the Holy Spirit on their tongues to announce My truth, even as the Devil puts himself on the tongues of his servants, that is to say, of those who pass through the river in iniquity. This is that sweet reproof that I have fixed for ever, in the aforesaid way, out of My most great affection of love for the salvation of souls. And they cannot say 'I had no one who reproved me,' because the truth is revealed to them showing them vice and virtue. And I have made them see the fruit of virtue, and the hurtfulness of vice, to give them love and holy fear with hatred of vice and love of virtue, and this truth has not been shown them by an angel, so that they cannot say, 'the angel is a blessed spirit who cannot offend, and feels not the vexations of the flesh as we do, neither the heaviness of our body,' because the Incarnate Word of My Truth has been given to them with your mortal flesh.

"Who were the others who followed this Word? Mortal creatures, susceptible of pain like you, having the same opposition of the flesh to the Spirit, as had the glorious Paul, My standard-bearer, and many other saints who, by one thing or another, have been tormented. Which torments I permitted for the increase of grace and virtue in their souls. Thus, they were born in sin like you, and nourished with a like food, and I am God now as then. My power is not weakened, and cannot become weak. So that I can and will succour him who wishes to be succoured by Me. Man wants My succour when he comes out of the river, and walks by the Bridge, following the doctrine of My Truth. Thus no one has any excuse, because both reproof and truth are constantly given to them. Wherefore, if they do not amend while they have time, they will be condemned by the second condemnation which will take place at the extremity of death, when My Justice will cry to them, 'Rise, ye dead, and come to judgment!' That is to say, ' Thou, who art dead to grace, and hast reached the moment of thy corporal death, arise and come before the Supreme Judge with thy injustice and false judgment, and with the extinguished light of faith which thou didst receive burning in Holy Baptism (and which thou hast blown out with the wind of pride), and with the vanity of thy heart, with which thou didst set thy sails to winds which were contrary to thy salvation, for with the wind of self-esteem, didst thou fill the sail of self-love.' Thus didst thou hasten down the stream of the delights and dignities of the world at thy own will, following thy fragile flesh and the temptations of the devil, who, with the sail of thy own will set, has led thee along the underway which is a running stream, and so has brought thee with himself to eternal damnation."

Of the second reproof of injustice, and of false
judgment, in general and in particular.

"This second reproof, dearest daughter, is indeed a condemnation, for the soul has arrived at
the end, where there can be no remedy, for she is
at the extremity of death, where is the worm
of conscience, which I told thee was blinded
self-love. Now at the time of death, since she
cannot get out of My hands, she begins to see,
and therefore is gnawed with remorse, seeing that
her own sin has brought her into so great evil.
But if the soul have light to know and grieve for
her fault, not on account of the pain of Hell
that follows upon it, but on account of pain at
her offence against Me, who am Supreme and
Eternal Good, still she can find mercy. But if
she pass the Bridge of death without light, and
alone, with the worm of conscience, without the
hope of the Blood, and bewailing herself more
on account of her first condemnation than on
account of My displeasure, she arrives at eternal
damnation. And then she is reproved cruelly by
My Justice of injustice and of false judgment,
and not so much of general injustice and false
judgment which she has practised generally in
all her works, but much more on account of
the particular injustice and false judgment which
she practises at the end, in judging her misery
greater than My mercy. This is that sin which
is neither pardoned here nor there, because the
soul would not be pardoned, depreciating My

mercy. Therefore is this last sin graver to
Me than all the other sins that the soul has
committed. Wherefore the despair of Judas
displeased Me more, and was more grave to
My Son than was his betrayal of Him. So
that they are reproved of this false judgment,
which is to have held their sin to be greater
than My mercy, and, on that account, are they
punished with the devils, and eternally tortured
with them. And they are reproved of injustice
because they grieve more over their condemnation than over My displeasure, and do not render
to Me that which is Mine, and to themselves
that which is theirs. For to Me, they ought to
render love, and to themselves bitterness, with
contrition of heart, and offer it to Me, for the
offence they have done Me. And they do the
contrary because they give to themselves love,
pitying themselves, and grieving on account of
the pain they expect for their sin; so thou seest
that they are guilty of injustice and false judgment, and are punished for the one and the other
together. Wherefore, they, having depreciated
My mercy, I with justice send them, with their
cruel servant, sensuality, and the cruel tyrant
the Devil, whose servants they made themselves
through their own sensuality, so that, together,
they are punished and tormented, as together
they have offended Me. Tormented, I say, by
My ministering devils whom My judgment has
appointed to torment those who have done
evil."

*Of the four principal torments of the damned, from
    which follow all the others; and particularly
    of the foulness of the Devil.*

"My daughter, the tongue is not sufficient to
narrate the pain of these poor souls. As there
are three principal vices, namely : self-love,
whence proceeds the second, that is love of
reputation, whence proceeds the third, that is
pride, with injustice and cruelty, and with other
filthiness and iniquitous sins, that follow upon
these. So I say to thee, that in Hell, the souls
have four principal torments, out of which proceed all the other torments. The first is, that
they see themselves deprived of the vision of
Me, which is such pain to them, that, were it
possible, they would rather choose the fire, and
the tortures and torments, and to see Me, than
to be without the torments and not to see Me.

"This first pain revives in them, then, the
second, the worm of Conscience, which gnaws
unceasingly, seeing that the soul is deprived of
Me, and of the conversation of the angels,
through her sin, made worthy of the conversation and sight of the devils, which vision of
the Devil is the third pain and redoubles to
them their every toil. As the saints exult in the
sight of Me, refreshing themselves with joyousness in the fruit of their toils borne for Me
with such abundance of love, and displeasure
of themselves, so does the sight of the Devil
revive these wretched ones to torments, because

in seeing him they know themselves more, that is to say, they know that, by their own sin, they have made themselves worthy of him. And so the worm of Conscience gnaws more and more, and the fire of this Conscience never ceases to burn. And the sight is more painful to them, because they see him in his own form, which is so horrible that the heart of man could not imagine it. And if thou remember well, thou knowest that I showed him to thee in his own form for a little space of time, hardly a moment, and thou didst choose (after thou hadst returned to thyself) rather to walk on a road of fire, even until the Day of Judgment, than to see him again. With all this that thou hast seen, even thou dost not know well how horrible he is, because, by Divine justice, he appears more horrible to the soul that is deprived of Me, and more or less according to the gravity of her sin. The fourth torment that they have is the fire. This fire burns and does not consume, for the being of the soul cannot be consumed, because it is not a material thing that fire can consume. But I, by Divine justice, have permitted the fire to burn them with torments, so that it torments them, without consuming them, with the greatest pains in diverse ways according to the diversity of their sins, to some more, and to some less, according to the gravity of their fault. Out of these four torments issue all others, such as cold and heat and gnashing of the teeth and many others. Now because

they did not amend themselves after the first
reproof that they had of injustice and false judgment, neither in the second, which was that, in
death, they would not hope in Me, nor grieve
for the offence done to Me, but only for their
own pain, have they thus so miserably received
Eternal Punishment."

Of the third reproof which is made on the Day of Judgment.

"Now it remains to tell of the third reproof
which is on the Last Day of Judgment. Already
I have told thee of two, and now, so that thou
mayest see how greatly man deceives himself, I
will tell thee of the third—of the General Judgment, when the pain of the miserable soul is
renewed and increased by the union that the
soul will make with the body, with an intolerable reproof, which will generate in it confusion
and shame. Know that, in the Last Day of
Judgment, when will come the Word—My Son,
with My Divine Majesty to reprove the world
with Divine Power, He will not come like a
poor one, as when He was born, coming in the
womb of the Virgin, and being born in a stable
amongst the animals, and then dying between
two thieves. Then I concealed My power in
Him, letting Him suffer pain and torment like
man, not that My divine nature was therefore
separated from human nature, but I let Him
suffer like man to satisfy for your guilt. He

will not come thus in that last moment, but He will come, with power, to reprove in His Own Person, and will render to every one his due, and there will be no one in that Day who will not tremble. To the miserable ones who are damned, His aspect will cause such torment and terror that the tongue cannot describe it. To the just it will cause the fear of reverence with great joy; not that His face changes, because He is unchangeable, being one thing with Me according to the divine nature, and, according to the human nature, His face was unchangeable, after it took the glory of the Resurrection. But, to the eye of the damned, it will appear such, on account of their terrible and darkened vision, that, as the sun which is so bright, appears all darkness to the infirm eye, but to the healthy eye light (and it is not the defect of the light that makes it appear other to the blind than to the illuminated one, but the defect of the eye which is infirm), so will the condemned ones see His countenance in darkness, in confusion, and in hatred, not through defect of My Divine Majesty, with which He will come to judge the world, but through their own defect."

How the damned cannot desire any good.

"And their hatred is so great that they cannot will or desire any good, but they continually blaspheme Me. And dost thou know why they

cannot desire good? Because the life of man
ended, free-will is bound. Wherefore they cannot
merit, having lost, as they have, the time to do
so. If they finish their life, dying in hatred
with the guilt of mortal sin, their souls, by
divine justice, remain for ever bound with the
bonds of hatred, and for ever obstinate in that
evil, in which, therefore, being gnawed by themselves, their pains always increase, especially the
pains of those who have been the cause of
damnation to others, as that rich man, who was
damned, demonstrated to you when he begged
the favour that Lazarus might go to his brothers,
who were in the world, to tell them of his pains.
This, certainly, he did not do out of love or
compassion for his brothers, for he was deprived
of love and could not desire good, either for
My honour or their salvation, because, as I have
already told thee, the damned souls cannot do
any good to their neighbour, and they blaspheme
Me, because their life ended in hatred of Me
and of virtue. But why then did he do it?
He did it because he was the eldest, and had
nourished them up in the same miseries in which
he had lived, so that he was the cause of their
damnation, and he saw pain increased to himself,
on account of their damnation when they should
arrive in torment together with him, to be gnawed
for ever by hatred, because in hatred they finished
their lives."

Of the glory of the Blessed.

"Similarly, the just soul, for whom life finishes in the affection of charity and the bonds of love, cannot increase in virtue, time having come to nought, but she can always love with that affection with which she comes to Me, and that measure that is measured to her. She always desires Me, and loves Me, and her desire is not in vain—being hungry, she is satisfied, and being satisfied, she has hunger, but the tediousness of satiety and the pain of hunger are far from her. In love, the Blessed rejoice in My eternal vision, participating in that good that I have in Myself, every one according to his measure, that is that, with that measure of love, with which they have come to Me, is it measured to them. Because they have lived in love of Me and of the neighbour, united together with the general love, and the particular, which, moreover, both proceed from the same love. And they rejoice and exult, participating in each other's good with the affection of love, besides the universal good that they enjoy altogether. And they rejoice and exult with the angels with whom they are placed, according to their diverse and various virtues in the world, being all bound in the bonds of love. And they have a special participation with those whom they closely loved with particular affection in the world, with which affection they grew in grace, increasing virtue, and the one was the occasion to the other of manifesting the glory

and praise of My name, in themselves and in
their neighbour ; and, in the life everlasting, they
have not lost their love, but have it still, participating closely, with more abundance, the one
with the other, their love being added to the
universal good, and I would not that thou
shouldest think that they have this particular
good, of which I have told thee, for themselves
alone, for it is not so, but it is shared by all
the proved citizens, My beloved sons, and all
the angels—for, when the soul arrives at eternal
life, all participate in the good of that soul, and
the soul in their good. Not that her vessel or
theirs can increase, nor that there be need to fill
it, because it is full, but they have an exultation,
a mirthfulness, a jubilee, a joyousness in themselves, which is refreshed by the knowledge that
they have found in that soul. They see that,
by My mercy, she is raised from the earth with
the plenitude of grace, and therefore they exult
in Me in the good of that soul, which good she
has received through My goodness.

"And that soul rejoices in Me, and in the
souls, and in the blessed spirits, seeing and
tasting in them the beauty and the sweetnes
of My love. And their desires for ever cry
out to Me, for the salvation of the whole world.
And because their life ended in the love of the
neighbour, they have not left it behind, but, with
it, they will pass through the Door, My only-
begotten Son in the way that I will relate to
thee. So thou seest that in those bonds of love

in which they finished their life, they go on and remain eternally. They are conformed so entirely to My will, that they cannot desire except what I desire, because their free-will is bound in the bond of love, in such a way that, time failing them, and, dying in a state of grace, they cannot sin any more. And their will is so united with Mine, that a father or a mother seeing their son, or a son seeing his father or his mother in Hell, do not trouble themselves, and even are contented to see them punished as My enemies. Wherefore in nothing do they disagree with Me, and their desires are all satisfied. The desire of the blessed is to see My honour in you wayfarers, who are pilgrims, for ever running on towards the term of death. In their desire for My honour, they desire your salvation, and always pray to Me for you, which desire is fulfilled by Me, when you ignorant ones do not resist My mercy. They have a desire too, to regain the gifts of their body, but this desire does not afflict them, as they do not actually feel it, but they rejoice in tasting the desire, from the certainty they feel of having it fulfilled. Their desire does not afflict them, because, though they have it not yet fulfilled, no bliss is thereby lacking to them. Wherefore they feel not the pain of desire. And think not, that the bliss of the body after the resurrection gives more bliss to the soul, for, if this were so, it would follow that, until they had the body, they had imperfect bliss, which cannot be, because no perfection is lacking to them. So it is not the body that gives bliss to the soul, but the soul will give bliss to the body, because the soul will give of her abundance, and will re-clothe herself on the Last Day of Judgment, in the garments of her own flesh which she had quitted. For, as the soul is made immortal, stayed and stablished in Me, so the body in that union becomes immortal, and, having lost heaviness, is made fine and light. Wherefore, know that the glorified body can pass through a wall, and that neither water nor fire can injure it, not by virtue of itself, but by virtue of the soul, which virtue is of Me, given to her by grace, and by the ineffable love with which I created her in My image and likeness. The eye of thy intellect is not sufficient to see, nor thy ear to hear, nor thy tongue to tell of the good of the Blessed. Oh, how much delight they have in seeing Me, who am every good! Oh, how much delight they will have in being with the glorified body, though, not having that delight from now to the general Judgment, they have not, on that account, pain, because no bliss is lacking to them, the soul being satisfied in herself, and, as I have told thee, the body will participate in this bliss.

"I told thee of the happiness which the glorified body would take in the glorified humanity of My only-begotten Son, which gives you assurance of your resurrection. There, they exult in His wounds, which have remained fresh, and the Scars in His Body are preserved, and continually

H

cry for mercy for you, to Me, the Supreme and Eternal Father. And they are all conformed with Him, in joyousness and mirth, and you will all be conformed with Him, eye with eye, and hand with hand, and with the whole Body of the sweet Word My Son, and, dwelling in Me, you will dwell in Him, because He is one thing with Me. But their bodily eye, as I told thee, will delight itself in the glorified humanity of the Word, My only-begotten Son. Why so? Because their life finished in the affection of My love, and therefore will this delight endure for them eternally. Not that they can work any good, but they rejoice and delight in that good which they have brought with them, that is, they cannot do any meritorious act, by which they could merit anything, because in this life alone can they merit and sin, according as they please, with free-will.

"These then do not await, with fear, the Divine judgment, but with joy, and the Face of My Son will not seem to them terrible, or full of hatred, because they finished their lives in love and affection for Me, and good-will towards their neighbour. So thou seest then, that the transformation is not in His Face, when He comes to judge with My Divine Majesty, but in the vision of those who will be judged by Him. To the damned He will appear with hatred and with justice. And to the saved with love and mercy."

*How, after the General Judgment, the pain of
the damned will increase.*

"I have told thee of the dignity of the Righteous, so that thou mayest the better know the
misery of the damned. For this is another of
their pains, namely, the vision of the bliss of the
righteous, which is to them an increase of pain,
as, to the righteous, the damnation of the damned
is an increase of exultation in My goodness. As
light is seen better near darkness, and darkness
near light, so the sight of the Blessed increases
their pain. With pain they await the Last Day
of Judgment, because they see, following it, an
increase of pain to themselves. And so will it
be, because when that terrible voice shall say to
them, 'Arise, ye dead, and come to judgment,'
the soul will return with the body, in the just
to be glorified, and in the damned to be tortured
eternally. And the aspect of My Truth, and
of all the blessed ones will reproach them greatly,
and make them ashamed, and the worm of conscience will gnaw the pith of the tree, that is
the soul, and also the bark outside, which is the
body. They will be reproached by the Blood
that was shed for them, and by the works of
mercy, spiritual and temporal, which I did for
them by means of My Son, and which they
should have done for their neighbour, as is
contained in the Holy Gospel. They will be
reproved for their cruelty towards their neighbour, for their pride and self-love, for their

filthiness and avarice; and when they see the mercy that they have received from Me, their reproof will seem to be intensified in harshness. At the time of death, the soul only is reproved, but, at the General Judgment, the soul is reproved together with the body, because the body has been the companion and instrument of the soul—to do good and evil according as the free-will pleased. Every work, good or bad, is done by means of the body. And, therefore, justly, My daughter, glory and infinite good are rendered to My elect ones with their glorified body, rewarding them for the toils they bore for Me, together with the soul. And to the perverse ones will be rendered eternal pains by means of their body, because their body was the instrument of evil. Wherefore, being their body, restored, their pains will revive and increase at the aspect of My Son, their miserable sensuality with its filthiness, in the vision of their nature (that is, the humanity of Christ), united with the purity of My Deity, and of this mass of their Adam nature raised above all the choirs of Angels, and themselves, by their own fault, sunk into the depths of Hell. And they will see generosity and mercy shining in the blessed ones, who receive the fruit of the Blood of the Lamb, the pains that they have borne remaining as ornaments on their bodies, like the dye upon the cloth, not by virtue of the body but only out of the fulness of the soul, representing in the body the fruit of its labour, because it was

the companion of the soul in the working of
virtue. As in the mirror is represented the face
of the man, so in the body is represented the
fruit of bodily toils, in the way that I have
told thee.

"The pain and confusion of the darkened
ones, on seeing so great a dignity (of which they
are deprived), will increase, and their bodies will
appear the sign of the wickedness they have
committed, with pain and torture. And when
they hear that terrible speech, '*Go, cursed ones,
to the Eternal Fire,*' the soul and the body will
go to be with the Devil without any remedy or
hope—each one being wrapped up in diverse
filth of earth, according to his evil works. The
miser with the filth of avarice, wrapping himself
up with the worldly substance which he loved
disordinately, and the burning in the fire; the
cruel one with cruelty; the foul man with foulness and miserable concupiscence; the unjust
with his injustice; the envious with envy; and
the hater of his neighbour with hatred. And
inordinate self-love, whence were born all their
ills, will be burnt with intolerable pain, as the
head and principle of every evil, in company with
pride. So that body and soul together will be
punished in diverse ways. Thus miserably do
they arrive at their end who go by the lower
way, that is, by the river, not turning back to
see their sins and My Mercy. And they arrive
at the Gate of the Lie, because they follow the
doctrine of the Devil, who is the Father of

Lies; and this Devil is their Door, through which they go to Eternal Damnation, as has been said, as the elect and My sons, keeping by the way above, that is by the Bridge, follow the Way of Truth, and this Truth is the Door, and therefore said My Truth, '*No one can go to the Father but by Me.*' He is the Door and the Way through which they pass to enter the Sea Pacific. It is the contrary for those who have kept the Way of the Lie, which leads them to the water of death. And it is to this that the Devil calls them, and they are as blind and mad, and do not perceive it, because they have lost the light of faith. The Devil says, as it were, to them: 'Whosoever thirsts for the water of death, let him come and I will give it to him.'"

Of the use of temptations, and how every soul in her extremity sees her final place either of pain or of glory, before she is separated from the body.

"The Devil, dearest daughter, is the instrument of My Justice to torment the souls who have miserably offended Me. And I have set him in this life to tempt and molest My creatures, not for My creatures to be conquered, but that they may conquer, proving their virtue, and receive from Me the glory of victory. And no one should fear any battle or temptation of the Devil that may come to him, because I have made My creatures strong, and have given them strength of will, fortified in the Blood of my

Son, which will, neither Devil nor creature can move, because it is yours, given by Me. You therefore, with free arbitration, can hold it or leave it, according as you please. It is an arm, which, if you place it in the hands of the Devil, straightway becomes a knife, with which he strikes you and slays you. But if man do not give this knife of his will into the hands of the Devil, that is, if he do not consent to his temptations and molestations, he will never be injured by the guilt of sin in any temptation, but will even be fortified by it, when the eye of his intellect is opened to see My love which allowed him to be tempted, so as to arrive at virtue, by being proved. For one does not arrive at virtue except through knowledge of self, and knowledge of Me, which knowledge is more perfectly acquired in the time of temptation, because then man knows himself to be nothing, being unable to lift off himself the pains and vexations which he would flee ; and he knows Me in his will, which is fortified by My goodness, so that it does not yield to these thoughts. And he has seen that My love permits these temptations, for the devil is weak, and by himself can do nothing, unless I allow him. And I let him tempt, through love, and not through hatred, that you may conquer, and not that you may be conquered, and that you may come to a perfect knowledge of yourself, and of Me, and that virtue may be proved, for it is not proved except by its contrary. Thou seest, then, that he is my Minister to torture the damned in Hell, and in this life, to exercise and prove virtue in the soul. Not that it is the intention of the Devil to prove virtue in you (for he has not love), but rather to deprive you of it, and this he cannot do, if you do not wish it. Now thou seest, then, how great is the foolishness of men in making themselves feeble, when I have made them strong, and in putting themselves into the hands of the Devil. Wherefore, know, that at the moment of death, they, having passed their life under the lordship of the Devil (not that they were forced to do so, for as I told you they cannot be forced, but they voluntarily put themselves into his hands), and, arriving at the extremity of their death under this perverse lordship, they await no other judgment than that of their own conscience, and desperately, despairingly, come to eternal damnation. Wherefore Hell, through their hate, surges up to them in the extremity of death, and before they get there, they take hold of it, by means of their lord the Devil. As the righteous, who have lived in charity and died in love, if they have lived perfectly in virtue, illuminated with the light of faith, with perfect hope in the Blood of the Lamb, when the extremity of death comes, see the good which I have prepared for them, and embrace it with the arms of love, holding fast with pressure of love to Me, the Supreme and Eternal Good. And so they taste eternal life before they have left the mortal body, that is, before the soul be separated from the body. Others who have passed their lives, and have arrived at the last extremity of death with an ordinary charity (not in that great perfection), embrace My mercy with the same light of faith and hope that had those perfect ones, but, in them, it is imperfect, for, because they were imperfect, they constrained My mercy, counting My mercy greater than their sins. The wicked sinners do the contrary, for, seeing, with desperation, their destination, they embrace it with hatred, as I told thee. So that neither the one nor the other waits for judgment, but, in departing this life, they receive every one their place, as I have told thee, and they taste it and possess it before they depart from the body, at the extremity of death—the damned with hatred and with despair, and the perfect ones with love and the light of faith and with the hope of the Blood. And the imperfect arrive at the place of Purgatory, with mercy and the same faith."

How the Devil gets hold of souls, under pretence of some good: and, how those are deceived who keep by the river, and not by the aforesaid Bridge, for, wishing to fly pains, they fall into them; and of the vision of a tree, that this soul once had.

"I have told thee that the Devil invites men to the water of death, that is, to that which he has, and, blinding them with the pleasures and con-

ditions of the world, he catches them with the
hook of pleasure, under the pretence of good,
because in no other way could he catch them, for
they would not allow themselves to be caught
if they saw that no good or pleasure to themselves were to be obtained thereby.   For the
soul, from her nature, always relishes good,
though it is true that the soul, blinded by
self-love, does not know and discern what is
true good, and of profit to the soul and to the
body.   And, therefore, the Devil, seeing them
blinded by self-love, iniquitously places before
them diverse and various delights, coloured so
as to have the appearance of some benefit or
good ; and he gives to every one according to
his condition and those principal vices to which
he sees him to be most disposed—of one kind
to the secular, of another to the religious, and
others to prelates and noblemen, according to
their different conditions.   I have told thee this,
because I now speak to thee of those who drown
themselves in the river, and who care for nothing
but themselves, to love themselves to My injury,
and I will relate to thee their end.

"Now I want to show thee how they deceive
themselves, and how, wishing to flee troubles,
they fall into them.   For, because it seems to
them that following Me, that is, walking by
the way of the Bridge, the Word, My Son, is
great toil, they draw back, fearing the thorn.
This is because they are blinded and do not
know or see the Truth, as, thou knowest, I

showed thee in the beginning of thy life, when
thou didst pray Me to have mercy on the world,
and draw it out of the darkness of mortal sin.
Thou knowest that I then showed thee Myself
under the figure of a Tree, of which thou sawest
neither the beginning nor the end, so that thou
didst not see that the roots were united with the
earth of your humanity.   At the foot of the
Tree, if thou rememberest well, there was a
certain thorn, from which thorn all those who
love their own sensuality kept away, and ran
to a mountain of Lolla, in which thou didst
figure to thyself all the delights of the world.
That Lolla seemed to be of corn and was not,
and, therefore, as thou didst see, many souls
thereon died of hunger, and many, recognising
the deceits of the world, returned to the Tree
and passed the thorn, which is the deliberation
of the will.   Which deliberation, before it is
made, is a thorn which appears to man to
stand in the way of following the Truth.   And
conscience always fights on one side, and sensuality on the other; but as soon as he, with hatred
and displeasure of himself, manfully makes up
his mind, saying, 'I wish to follow Christ crucified,' he breaks at once the thorn, and finds
inestimable sweetness, as I showed thee then,
some finding more and some less, according to
their disposition and desire.   And thou knowest
that then I said to thee, 'I am your God, un-
moving and unchangeable,' and I do not draw
away from any creature who wants to come to

Me.   I have shown them the Truth, making
Myself visible to them, and I have shown them
what it is to love anything without Me.   But
they, as if blinded by the fog of disordinate love,
know neither Me nor themselves.   Thou seest
how deceived they are, choosing rather to die
of hunger than to pass a little thorn.   And
they cannot escape enduring pain, for no one
can pass through this life without a cross, far
less those who travel by the lower way.   Not
that My servants pass without pain, but their
pain is alleviated.   And because—by sin, as I
said to thee above—the world germinates thorns
and tribulations, and because this river flows with
tempestuous waters, I gave you the Bridge, so
that you might not be drowned.

"I have shown thee how they are deceived by
a disordinate fear, and how I am your God,
immovable, who am not an Acceptor of persons
but of holy desire.   And this I have shown thee
under the figure of the Tree, as I told thee."

*How, the world having germinated thorns, who those
are whom they do not harm ; although no one
passes this life without pain.*

"Now I want to show thee to whom the
thorns and tribulations, that the world germinated through sin, do harm, and to whom
they do not.   And as, so far, I have shown
thee the damnation of sinners, together with
My goodness, and have told thee how they are

deceived by their own sensuality, now I wish
to tell thee how it is only they themselves who
are injured by the thorns. No one born passes
this life without pain, bodily or mental. Bodily
pain My servants bear, but their minds are free,
that is, they do not feel the weariness of the
pain; for their will is accorded with Mine, and
it is the will that gives trouble to man. Pain
of mind and of body have those, of whom I
have narrated to thee, who, in this life, taste
the earnest money of hell, as My servants taste
the earnest money of eternal life. Knowest thou
what is the special good of the blessed ones?
It is having their desire filled with what they
desire; wherefore desiring Me, they have Me,
and taste Me without any revolt, for they have
left the burden of the body, which was a law
that opposed the spirit, and came between it
and the perfect knowledge of the Truth, preventing it from seeing Me face to face. But
after the soul has left the weight of the body,
her desire is full, for, desiring to see Me, she
sees Me, in which vision is her bliss; and seeing
she knows, and knowing she loves, and loving
she tastes Me, Supreme and Eternal Good, and,
in tasting Me, she is satisfied, and her desire is
fulfilled, that is, the desire she had to see and
know Me; wherefore desiring she has, and
having she desires. And as I told thee pain is
far from the desire, and weariness from the satisfaction of it. So thou seest that My servants
are blessed principally in seeing and in knowing

Me, in which vision and knowledge their will is fulfilled, for they have that which they desired to have, and so are they satisfied. Wherefore I told thee that the tasting of eternal life consisted especially in having that which the will desires, and thus being satisfied; but know that the will is satisfied in seeing and knowing Me, as I have told thee. In this life then, they taste the earnest money of eternal life, tasting the above, with which I have told thee they will be satisfied.

"But how have they the earnest money in this present life? I reply to thee, they have it in seeing My goodness in themselves, and in the knowledge of My Truth, which knowledge, the intellect (which is the eye of the soul) illuminated in Me, possesses. This eye has the pupil of the most holy faith, which light of faith enables the soul to discern, to know, and to follow the way and the doctrine of My Truth—the Word Incarnate; and without this pupil of faith she would not see, except as a man who has the form of the eye, but who has covered the pupil (which causes the eye to see) with a cloth. So the pupil of the intellect is faith, and if the soul has covered it with the cloth of infidelity, drawn over it by self-love, she does not see, but only has the form of the eye without the light, because she has hidden it. Thus thou seest, that in seeing they know, and in knowing they love, and in loving they deny and lose their self-will. Their own will lost, they clothe themselves in

Mine, and I will nothing but your sanctification.
At once they set to, turning their back to the
way below, and begin to ascend by the Bridge,
and pass over the thorns, which do not hurt
them, their feet being shod with the affection
of My love. For I told thee that My servants
suffered corporally but not mentally, because the
sensitive will, which gives pain and afflicts the
mind of the creature, is dead. Wherefore, the
will not being there, neither is there any pain.
They bear everything with reverence, deeming
themselves favoured in having tribulation for
My sake, and they desire nothing but what I
desire. If I allow the Devil to trouble them,
permitting temptations to prove them in virtue,
as I told thee above, they resist with their will
fortified in Me, humiliating themselves, and
deeming themselves unworthy of peace and quiet
of mind and deserving of pain, and so they
proceed with cheerfulness and self-knowledge,
without painful affliction. And if tribulations
on man's account, or infirmity, or poverty, or
change of worldly condition, or loss of children,
or of other much loved creatures (all of which
are thorns that the earth produced after sin)
come upon them, they endure them all with the
light of reason and holy faith, looking to Me,
who am the Supreme Good, and who cannot
desire other than good, for which I permit
these tribulations through love, and not through
hatred. And they that love Me recognise this,
and, examining themselves, they see their sins,

and understand by the light of faith, that good must be rewarded and evil punished. And they see that every little sin merits infinite pain, because it is against Me, who am Infinite Good, wherefore they deem themselves favoured because I wish to punish them in this life, and in this finite time; they drive away sin with contrition of heart, and with perfect patience do they merit, and their labours are rewarded with infinite good. Hereafter they know that all labour in this life is small, on account of the shortness of time. Time is as the point of a needle and no more; and, when time has passed labour is ended, therefore thou seest that the labour is small. They endure with patience, and the thorns they pass through do not touch their heart, because their heart is drawn out of them and united to Me by the affection of love. It is a good truth then that these do taste eternal life, receiving the earnest money of it in this life, and that, though they walk on thorns, they are not pricked, because as I told thee, they have known My Supreme Goodness, and sought for it where it was to be found, that is in the Word, My only-begotten Son."

How this soul was in great bitterness, on account of the blindness of those who are drowned below in the river.

Then that soul, tormented by desire, considering her own imperfections and those of others, was saddened to hear of and to see the great blindness of creatures, notwithstanding the great goodness of GOD, in having placed nothing in this life, no matter in what condition, that could be an impediment to the salvation of creatures, but rather arranged for the exercising and proving of virtue in them. And, notwithstanding all this, she saw them, through self-love and disordinate affection, go under by the river and arrive at eternal damnation, and many who were in the river and had begun to come out, turn back again, scandalised at her, because they had heard of the sweet goodness of GOD, who had deigned to manifest Himself to her. And, for this, she was in bitterness, and fixing the eye of her intellect on the Eternal Father, she said : "Oh, Inestimable Love, great is the delusion of Thy creatures. I would that, when it is pleasing to Thy Goodness, Thou wouldst more clearly explain to me the three steps figured in the Body of Thy only Son, and what method should be used so as to come entirely out of the depths and to keep the way of Thy Truth, and who are those who ascend the stair-case."

How the three steps figured in the Bridge, that is, in the Son of GOD, signify the three powers of the soul.

Then the Divine Goodness, regarding with the eye of His mercy, the hunger and desire of that soul, said : "Oh, My most delightful daughter,

I

I am not a Despiser, but the Fulfiller of holy desire, and therefore I will show and declare to thee that which thou askest Me. Thou askest Me to explain to thee the figure of three steps, and to tell thee what method they who want to come out of the river must use, to be able to ascend the Bridge. And, although above, in relating to thee the delusion and blindness of men, tasting in this life the earnest-money of Hell, and, as martyrs of the Devil, receiving damnation, I showed thee the methods they should use ; nevertheless, now I will declare it to thee more fully, satisfying thy desire. Thou knowest that every evil is founded in self-love, and that self-love is a cloud that takes away the light of reason, which reason holds in itself the light of faith, and one is not lost without the other. The soul I created in My image and similitude, giving her memory, intellect, and will. The intellect is the most noble part of the soul, and is moved by the affection, and nourishes it, and the hand of love—that is, the affection—fills the memory with the remembrance of Me and of the benefits received, which it does with care and gratitude, and so one power spurs on another, and the soul is nourished in the life of grace.

" The soul cannot live without love, but always wants to love something, because she is made of love, and, by love, I created her. And therefore I told thee that the affection moved the intellect, saying, as it were, '*I will love, because the food on which I feed is love.*' Then the intellect, feeling itself awakened by the affection, says, as it were, 'If thou wilt love, I will give thee that which thou canst love.' And at once it arises, considering carefully the dignity of the soul, and the indignity into which she has fallen through sin. In the dignity of her being it tastes My inestimable goodness, and the increate charity with which I created her, and, in contemplating her misery, it discovers and tastes My mercy, and sees how, through mercy, I have lent her time and drawn her out of darkness. Then the affection nourishes itself in love, opening the mouth of holy desire, with which it eats hatred and displeasure of its own sensuality, united with true humility and perfect patience, which it drew from holy hatred. The virtues conceived, they give birth to themselves perfectly and imperfectly, according as the soul exercises perfection in herself, as I will tell thee below. So, on the contrary, if the sensual affection wants to love sensual things, the eye of the intellect set before itself for its sole object transitory things, with self-love, displeasure of virtue, and love of vice, whence she draws pride and impatience, and the memory is filled with nothing but that which the affection presents to it. This love so dazzles the eye of the intellect that it can discern and see nothing but such glittering objects. It is the very brightness of the things that causes the intellect to perceive them and the affection to love them; for had worldly things no such brightness there would be no sin, for man, by his nature, cannot desire anything but good, and vice, appearing to him thus, under colour of the soul's good, causes him to sin. But, because the eye, on account of its blindness, does not discern, and knows not the truth, it errs, seeking good and delights there where they are not.

"I have already told thee that the delights of the world, without Me, are venomous thorns, and, that the vision of the intellect is deluded by them, and the affection of the will is deluded into loving them, and the memory into retaining remembrance of them. The unity of these powers of the soul is so great that I cannot be offended by one without all the others offending Me at the same time, because the one presents to the other, as I told thee, good or evil, according to the pleasure of the free will. This free will is bound to the affection, and it moves as it pleases, either with the light of reason or without it. Your reason is attached to Me when your will does not, by disordinate love, cut it off from Me; you have also in you the law of perversity, that continually fights against the Spirit. You have, then, two parts in you—sensuality and reason. Sensuality is appointed to be the servant, so that, with the instrument of the body, you may prove and exercise the virtues. The soul is free, liberated from sin by the Blood of My Son, and she cannot be dominated unless she consent with her will, which is controlled by her free choice, and when this free choice agrees with the will, it becomes one thing with it. And I tell thee truly, that, when the soul undertakes to gather together, with the hand of free choice, her powers in My Name, then are assembled all the actions, both spiritual and temporal, that the creature can do, and free choice gets rid of sensuality and binds itself with reason. I, then, by grace, rest in the midst of them; and this is what My truth, the Word Incarnate, meant, when He said : ' *When there are two or three or more gathered together in My name, there am I in the midst of them.*' And this is the truth. I have already told thee that no one could come to Me except by Him, and therefore did I make of Him a Bridge with three steps. And those three steps figure, as I will narrate to thee below, the three states of the soul."

How if the three aforesaid powers are not united, there cannot be perseverance, without which no man arrives at his end.

" I have explained to thee the figure of the three steps, in general, as the three powers of the soul, and no one who wishes to pass by the Bridge and doctrine of My Truth can mount one without the other, and the soul cannot persevere except by the union of her three powers. Of which I told thee above, when thou askedst Me, how the voyagers could come out of the river. There are two goals, and, for the attainment of either, perseverance is needful—they are vice and virtue. If thou desire to arrive at life, thou must persevere in virtue, and if thou would have eternal death, thou must persevere in vice. Thus it is with perseverance that they who want life arrive at Me who am Life, and with perseverance that they who taste the water of death arrive at the Devil."

An exposition on Christ's words: "Whosoever thirsteth, let him come to Me and drink."

"You were all invited, generally and in particular, by My Truth, when He cried in the Temple, saying: '*Whosoever thirsteth, let him come to Me and drink, for I am the Fountain of the Water of Life.*' He did not say '*Go to the Father and drink,*' but He said '*Come to Me.*' He spoke thus, because in Me, the Father, there can be no pain, but in My Son there can be pain. And you, while you are pilgrims and wayfarers in this mortal life, cannot be without pain, because the earth, through sin, brought forth thorns. And why did He say '*Let him come to Me and drink*'? Because whoever follows His doctrine, whether in the most perfect way or by dwelling in the life of common charity, finds to drink, tasting the fruit of the Blood, through the union of the Divine nature with the human nature. And you, finding yourselves in Him, find yourselves also in Me, who am the Sea Pacific, because I am one thing with Him, and He with Me. So that you are invited to the

Fountain of Living Water of Grace, and it is
right for you, with perseverance, to keep by
Him who is made for you a Bridge, not being
turned back by any contrary wind that may arise,
either of prosperity or adversity, and to persevere
till you find Me, who am the Giver of the Water
of Life, by means of this sweet and amorous
Word, My only-begotten Son. And why did
He say: '*I am the Fountain of Living Water*'?
Because He was the Fountain which contained
Me, the Giver of the Living Water, by means
of the union of the Divine with the human
nature. Why did He say '*Come to Me and
drink*'? Because you cannot pass this mortal
life without pain, and in Me, the Father, there
can be no pain, but in Him there can be pain,
and therefore of Him did I make for you a
Bridge. No one can come to Me except by
Him, as He told you in the words: '*No one
can come to the Father except by Me.*'

"Now thou hast seen to what way thou
shouldest keep, and how, namely with perseverance, otherwise thou shalt not drink, for
perseverance receives the crown of glory and
victory in the life everlasting."

*The general method by which every rational creature
    can come out of the sea of the world, and go by
    the aforesaid holy Bridge.*

"I will now return to the three steps, which
you must climb in order to issue from the river

without drowning, and attain to the Living Water, to which you are invited, and to desire My Presence in the midst of you. For in this way, in which you should follow, I am in your midst, reposing, by grace, in your souls. In order to have desire to mount the steps, you must have thirst, because only those who thirst are invited : '*Whosoever thirsteth, let him come to Me and drink.*' He who has no thirst will not persevere, for either fatigue causes him to stop, or pleasure, and he does not care to carry the vessel with which he may get the water, and neither does he care for the company, and alone he cannot go, and he turns back at the smallest prick of persecution, for he loves it not. He is afraid because he is alone; were he accompanied he would not fear, and had he ascended the three steps he would not have been alone, and would, therefore, have been secure. You must then have thirst and gather yourselves together, as it is said, '*two or three or more.*'

"Why is it said '*two or three or more*'? Because there are not two without three, nor three without two, neither three nor two without more. The number one is excluded, for, unless a man has a companion, I cannot be in the midst; this is no indifferent trifle, for he who is wrapped up in self-love is solitary.

"Why is he solitary? Because he is separated from My grace and the love of his neighbour, and being, by sin, deprived of Me, he turns to that which is nought, because I am He that is.

So that he who is solitary, that is, who is alone in self-love, is not mentioned by My Truth and is not acceptable to Me. He says then: '*If there be two or three or more gathered together in My name, I will be in the midst of them.*' I said to thee that two were not without three, nor three without two, and so it is. Thou knowest that the commandments of the Law are completely contained in two, and if these two are not observed the Law is not observed. The two commandments are to love Me above everything, and thy neighbour as thyself, which two are the beginning, the middle and the end of the Law. These two cannot be gathered together in My Name, without three, that is without the congregation of the powers of the soul, the memory, the intellect, and the will; the memory to retain the remembrance of My benefits and My goodness, the intellect to gaze into the ineffable love, which I have shown thee by means of My only-begotten Son, whom I have placed as the object of the vision of your intellect, so that, in Him, you behold the fire of My charity, and the will to love and desire Me, who am your End. When these virtues and powers of the soul are congregated together in My Name, I am in the midst of them by grace, and a man, who is full of My love and that of his neighbour, suddenly finds himself the companion of many and royal virtues. Then the appetite of the soul is disposed to thirst. Thirst, I say, for virtue, and the honour of My Name and salvation of souls,

and his every other thirst is spent and dead, and
he then proceeds securely without any servile
fear, having ascended the first step of the affection, for the affection, stripped of self-love,
mounts above itself and above transitory things,
or, if he will still hold them, he does so according to My will—that is, with a holy and true
fear, and love of virtue. He then finds that he
has attained to the second step—that is, to the
light of the intellect, which is, through Christ
crucified, mirrored in cordial love of Me, for
through Him have I shown My love to man.
He finds peace and quiet, because the memory
is filled with My love. Thou knowest that an
empty thing, when touched, resounds, but not
so when it is full. So memory, being filled with
the light of the intellect, and the affection with
love, on being moved by the tribulations or
delights of the world, will not resound with
disordinate merriment or with impatience, because they are full of Me, who am every good.

"Having climbed the three steps, he finds that
the three powers of the soul have been gathered
together by his reason in My Name. And his
soul, having gathered together the two commandments, that is love of Me and of the neighbour,
finds herself accompanied by Me, who am her
strength and security, and walks safely because
I am in the midst of her. Wherefore then he
follows on with anxious desire, thirsting after the
way of Truth, in which way he finds the Fountain of the Water of Life, through his thirst for

My honour and his own salvation and that of his neighbour, without which thirst he would not be able to arrive at the Fountain. He walks on, carrying the vessel of the heart, emptied of every affection and disordinate love of the world, but filled immediately it is emptied with other things, for nothing can remain empty, and, being without disordinate love for transitory things, it is filled with love of celestial things, and sweet Divine love, with which he arrives at the Fountain of the Water of Life, and passes through the Door of Christ crucified, and tastes the Water of Life, finding himself in Me, the Sea Pacific."

How this devoted soul looking in the Divine mirror saw the creatures going in diverse ways.

Then that soul, tormented with intense desire, gazing into the sweet Divine mirror, saw creatures setting out to attain their end in diverse ways and with diverse considerations. She saw that many began to mount, feeling themselves pricked by servile fear, that is, fearing their own personal pain, and she saw others, practising this first state, arriving at the second state, but few she saw who arrived at the greatest perfection.

How servile fear is not sufficient, without the love of virtue, to give eternal life; and how the law of fear and that of love are united.

Then the goodness of God, wishing to satisfy the desire of that soul, said, "Dost thou see those? They have arisen with servile fear from the vomit of mortal sin, but, if they do not arise with love of virtue, servile fear alone is not sufficient to give eternal life. But love with holy fear is sufficient, because the law is founded in love and holy fear. The old law was the law of fear, that was given by Me to Moses, by which law they who committed sin suffered the penalty of it. The new law is the law of love, given by the Word of My only-begotten Son, and is founded in love alone. The new law does not break the old law, but rather fulfils it, as said My Truth, '*I come not to destroy the law, but to fulfil it.*' And He united the law of fear with that of love. Through love was taken away the imperfection of the fear of the penalty, and the perfection of holy fear remained, that is, the fear of offending, not on account of one's own damnation, but of offending Me, who am Supreme Good. So that the imperfect law was made perfect with the law of love. Wherefore, after the car of the fire of My only-begotten Son came and brought the fire of My charity into your humanity with abundance of mercy, the penalty of the sins committed by humanity was taken away, that is, he who offended was no longer punished suddenly, as was of old given and ordained in the law of Moses.

"There is, therefore, no need for servile fear; and this does not mean that sin is not punished, but that the punishment is reserved, unless, that is to say, the person punish himself in this life with perfect contrition. For, in the other life,

the soul is separated from the body, wherefore while man lives is his time for mercy, but
when he is dead comes the time of justice. He
ought, then, to arise from servile fear, and arrive
at love and holy fear of Me, otherwise there is no
remedy against his falling back again into the
river, and reaching the waters of tribulation, and
seeking the thorns of consolation, for all consolations are thorns that pierce the soul who loves
them disordinately."

*How, by exercising oneself in servile fear, which is the
state of imperfection, by which is meant the first
step of the holy Bridge, one arrives at the second
step, which is the state of perfection.*

"I told thee that no one could go by the
Bridge or come out of the river without climbing the three steps, which is the truth. There
are some who climb imperfectly, and some perfectly, and some climb with the greatest perfection. The first are those who are moved by
servile fear, and have climbed so far being imperfectly gathered together; that is to say, the
soul, having seen the punishment which follows
her sin, climbs; and gathers together her memory
to recollect her vice, her intellect to see the
punishment which she expects to receive for her
fault, and her will to move her to hate that fault.
And let us consider this to be the first step and
the first gathering together of the powers of the
soul, which should be exercised by the light of

the intellect with the pupil of the eye of holy
faith, which looks, not only at the punishment of
sin, but at the fruit of virtue, and the love which
I bear to the soul, so that she may climb with
love and affection, and stripped of servile fear.
And doing so, such souls will become faithful
and not unfaithful servants, serving Me through
love and not through fear, and if, with hatred of
sin, they employ their minds to dig out the root
of their self-love with prudence, constancy, and
perseverance they will succeed in doing so. But
there are many who begin their course climbing
so slowly, and render their debt to Me by such
small degrees, and with such negligence and
ignorance, that they suddenly faint, and every
little breeze catches their sails, and turns their
prow backwards. Wherefore, because they imperfectly climb to the first Step of the Bridge of
Christ crucified, they do not arrive at the second
step of His Heart."

Of the imperfection of those who love GOD for their own profit, delight, and consolation.

"Some there are who have become faithful
servants, serving Me with fidelity without servile
fear of punishment, but rather with love. This
very love, however, if they serve Me with a view
to their own profit, or the delight and pleasure
which they find in Me, is imperfect. Dost thou
know what proves the imperfection of this love?
The withdrawal of the consolations which they

found in Me, and the insufficiency and short duration of their love for their neighbour, which grows weak by degrees, and ofttimes disappears. Towards Me their love grows weak when, on occasion, in order to exercise them in virtue and raise them above their imperfection, I withdraw from their minds My consolation and allow them to fall into battles and perplexities. This I do so that, coming to perfect self-knowledge, they may know that of themselves they are nothing and have no grace, and accordingly in time of battle fly to Me, as their Benefactor, seeking Me alone, with true humility, for which purpose I treat them thus, without drawing from them consolation indeed, but not grace. At such a time these weak ones, of whom I speak, relax their energy, impatiently turning backwards, and sometimes abandon, under colour of virtue, many of their exercises, saying to themselves, *This labour does not profit me.* All this they do, because they feel themselves deprived of mental consolation. Such a soul acts imperfectly, for she has not yet unwound the bandage of spiritual self-love, for, had she unwound it she would see that, in truth, everything proceeds from Me, that no leaf of a tree falls to the ground without My providence, and that what I give and promise to My creatures, I give and promise to them for their sanctification, which is the good and the end for which I created them. My creatures should see and know that I wish nothing but their good, through the Blood of My only-

begotten Son, in which they are washed from
their iniquities. By this Blood they are enabled
to know My Truth, how, in order to give them
eternal life, I created them in My image and
likeness and re-created them to grace with the
Blood of My Son, making them sons of adop-
tion. But, since they are imperfect, they make
use of Me only for their own profit, relaxing
their love for their neighbour. Thus, those in
the first state come to nought through the fear
of enduring pain, and those in the second, because they slacken their pace, ceasing to render
service to their neighbour, and withdrawing their
charity if they see their own profit or consolation withdrawn from them : this happens because
their love was originally impure, for they gave
to their neighbour the same imperfect love which
they gave to Me, that is to say, a love based only
on desire of their own advantage. If, through a
desire for perfection, they do not recognise this
imperfection of theirs, it is impossible that they
should not turn back. For those who desire
Eternal Life, a pure love, prescinding from themselves, is necessary, for it is not enough for
eternal life to fly sin from fear of punishment, or
to embrace virtue from the motive of one's own
advantage. Sin should be abandoned because it
is displeasing to Me, and virtue should be loved
for My sake. It is true that, generally speaking,
every person is first called in this way, but this
is because the soul herself is at first imperfect,
from which imperfection she must advance to

perfection, either while she lives, by a generous love to Me with a pure and virtuous heart that takes no thought for herself, or, at least, in the moment of death, recognising her own imperfection, with the purpose, had she but time, of serving Me, irrespectively of herself. It was with this imperfect love that S. Peter loved the sweet and good Jesus, My only-begotten Son, enjoying most pleasantly His sweet conversation, but, when the time of trouble came, he failed, and so disgraceful was his fall, that, not only could he not bear any pain himself, but his terror of the very approach of pain caused him to fall, and deny the Lord, with the words, '*I have never known Him.*' The soul who has climbed this step with servile fear and mercenary love alone, falls into many troubles. Such souls should arise and become sons, and serve Me, irrespective of themselves, for I, who am the Rewarder of every labour, render to each man according to his state and his labour; wherefore, if these souls do not abandon the exercise of holy prayer and their other good works, but go on, with perseverance, to increase their virtues, they will arrive at the state of filial love, because I respond to them with the same love, with which they love Me, so that, if they love Me, as a servant does his master, I pay them their wages according to their deserts, but I do not reveal Myself to them, because secrets are revealed to a friend, who has become one thing with his friend, and not to a servant. Yet it is true, that a servant may

so advance by the virtuous love, which he bears
to his master, as to become a very dear friend,
and so do some of these of whom I have spoken,
but while they remain in the state of mercenary
love, I do not manifest Myself to them. If they,
through displeasure at their imperfection, and
love of virtue, dig up, with hatred, the root of
spiritual self-love, and mount to the throne of
conscience, reasoning with themselves, so as to
quell the motions of servile fear in their heart,
and to correct mercenary love by the light of the
holy faith, they will be so pleasing to Me, that
they will attain to the love of the friend. And
I will manifest Myself to them, as My Truth
said in these words: '*He who loves Me shall be
one thing with Me and I with him, and I will
manifest Myself to him and we will dwell together.*'
This is the state of two dear friends, for though
they are two in body, yet they are one in soul
through the affection of love, because love trans-
forms the lover into the object loved, and where
two friends have one soul, there can be no secret
between them, wherefore My Truth said: '*I will
come and we will dwell together,*' and this is the
truth."

*Of the way in which GOD manifests Himself
to the soul who loves Him.*

"Knowest thou how I manifest Myself to the
soul who loves Me in truth, and follows the
doctrine of My sweet and amorous Word? In

many is My virtue manifested in the soul in proportion to her desire, but I make three special
manifestations. The first manifestation of My
virtue, that is to say, of My love and charity in
the soul, is made through the Word of My Son,
and shown in the Blood, which He spilled with
such fire of love. Now this charity is manifested
in two ways; first, in general, to ordinary people,
that is to those who live in the ordinary grace
of God. It is manifested to them by the many
and diverse benefits which they receive from Me.
The second mode of manifestation, which is
developed from the first, is peculiar to those
who have become My friends in the way mentioned above, and is known through a sentiment
of the soul, by which they taste, know, prove,
and feel it. This second manifestation, however, is in men themselves; they manifesting
Me, through the affection of their love. For
though I am no Acceptor of creatures, I am
an Acceptor of holy desires, and Myself in the
soul in that precise degree of perfection which
she seeks in Me. Sometimes I manifest Myself
(and this is also a part of the second manifestation) by endowing men with the spirit of prophecy, showing them the things of the future.
This I do in many and diverse ways, according
as I see need in the soul herself and in other
creatures. At other times the third manifestation takes place. I then form in the mind the
presence of the Truth, My only-begotten Son,
in many ways, according to the will and the

desire of the soul. Sometimes she seeks Me
in prayer, wishing to know My power, and I
satisfy her by causing her to taste and see My
virtue. Sometimes she seeks Me in the wisdom
of My Son, and I satisfy her by placing His
wisdom before the eye of her intellect, sometimes in the clemency of the Holy Spirit and
then My Goodness causes her to taste the fire
of Divine charity, and to conceive the true and
royal virtues, which are founded on the pure
love of her neighbour."

Why Christ did not say " I will manifest My
Father," but " I will manifest Myself."

" Thou seest now how truly My Word spoke,
when He said : ' *He who loves Me shall be one*
thing with Me.' Because, by following His doctrine with the affection of love, you are united
with Him, and, being united with Him, you
are united with Me, because We are one thing
together. And so it is that I manifest Myself
to you, because We are one and the same thing
together. Wherefore if My Truth said, ' *I will*
manifest Myself to you,' He said the truth, because,
in manifesting Himself, He manifested Me, and,
in manifesting Me, He manifested Himself. But
why did He not say, ' *I will manifest My Father*
to you ' ? For three reasons in particular. First,
because He wished to show that He and I are
not separate from each other, on which account
He also made the following reply to S. Philip,

when he said to Him, '*Show us the Father, and it is enough for us.*' My Word said, '*Who sees Me sees the Father, and who sees the Father sees Me.*' This He said because He was one thing with Me, and that which He had, He had from Me, I having nothing from Him; wherefore, again, He said to Judas, '*My doctrine is not Mine, but My Father's who sent Me,*' because My Son proceeds from Me, not I from Him, though I with Him and He with Me are but one thing. For this reason He did not say '*I will manifest the Father,*' but '*I will manifest Myself,*' being one thing with the Father. The second reason was because, in manifesting Himself to you, He did not present to you anything He had not received from Me, the Father. These words, then, mean, the Father has manifested Himself to Me, because I am one thing with Him, and I will manifest to you, by means of Myself, Me and Him. The third reason was, because I, being invisible, could not be seen by you, until you should be separated from your bodies. Then, indeed, will you see Me, your GOD, and My Son, the Word, face to face. From now until after the general Resurrection, when your humanity will be conformed with the humanity of the Eternal Word, according to what I told thee in the treatise of the Resurrection, you can see Me, with the eye of the intellect alone, for, as I am, you cannot see Me now. Wherefore I veiled the Divine nature with your humanity, so that you might see Me through that medium. I, the Invisible,

made Myself, as it were, visible by sending you
the Word, My Son, veiled in the flesh of your
humanity. He manifested Me to you. Therefore it was that He did not say '*I will manifest
the Father to you*,' but rather, '*I will manifest
Myself to you*,' as if He should say, '*According
as My Father manifests Himself to Me, will I manifest Myself to you, for, in this manifestation of Himself,
He manifests Me.*' Now therefore thou under-
standest why He did not say '*I will manifest the
Father to you.*' Both, because such a vision is
impossible for you, while yet in the mortal body,
and because He is one thing with Me."

*How the soul, after having mounted the first step of
the Bridge, should proceed to mount the second.*

"Thou hast now seen how excellent is the
state of him who has attained to the love of a
friend ; climbing with the foot of affection, he
has reached the secret of the Heart, which is
the second of the three steps figured in the Body
of My Son. I have told thee what was meant
by the three powers of the soul, and now I will
show thee how they signify the three states,
through which the soul passes. Before treating
of the third state, I wish to show thee how a
man becomes a friend and how, from a friend,
he grows into a son, attaining to filial love, and
how a man may know if he has become a friend.
And first of how a man arrives at being a friend.
In the beginning, a man serves Me imperfectly

through servile fear, but, by exercise and perseverance, he arrives at the love of delight, finding his own delight and profit in Me. This is a necessary stage, by which he must pass, who would attain to perfect love, to the love that is of friend and son. I call filial love perfect, because thereby, a man receives his inheritance from Me, the Eternal Father, and because a son's love includes that of a friend, which is why I told thee that a friend grows into a son. What means does he take to arrive thereat? I will tell thee. Every perfection and every virtue proceeds from charity, and charity is nourished by humility, which results from the knowledge and holy hatred of self, that is, sensuality. To arrive thereat, a man must persevere, and remain in the cellar of self-knowledge in which he will learn My mercy, in the Blood of My only-begotten Son, drawing to Himself, with this love, My divine charity, exercising himself in the extirpation of his perverse self-will, both spiritual and temporal, hiding himself in his own house, as did Peter, who, after the sin of denying My Son, began to weep. Yet his lamentations were imperfect and remained so, until after the forty days, that is until after the Ascension. But when My Truth returned to Me, in His humanity, Peter and the others concealed themselves in the house, awaiting the coming of the Holy Spirit, which My Truth had promised them. They remained barred in from fear, because the soul always fears until she arrives at true love.

But when they had persevered in fasting and in
humble and continual prayer, until they had
received the abundance of the Holy Spirit, they
lost their fear, and followed and preached Christ
crucified. So also the soul, who wishes to arrive
at this perfection, after she has risen from the
guilt of mortal sin, recognising it for what it is,
begins to weep from fear of the penalty, whence
she rises to the consideration of My mercy, in
which contemplation, she finds her own pleasure
and profit. This is an imperfect state, and I, in
order to develop perfection in the soul, after the
forty days, that is after these two states, withdraw Myself from time to time, not in grace but
in feeling. My Truth showed you this when He
said to the disciples ' *I will go and will return to
you.*'

"Everything that He said was said primarily,
and in particular, to the disciples, but referred in
general to the whole present and future, to those,
that is to say, who should come after. He said
' *I will go and will return to you;* ' and so it was,
for, when the Holy Spirit returned upon the
disciples, He also returned, as I told you above,
for the Holy Spirit did not return alone, but
came with My power, and the wisdom of the
Son, who is one thing with Me, and with His
own clemency, which proceeds from Me the
Father, and from the Son. Now, as I told thee,
in order to raise the soul from imperfection, I
withdraw Myself from her sentiment, depriving
her of former consolations. When she was in

the guilt of mortal sin, she had separated herself from Me, and I deprived her of grace through her own guilt, because that guilt had barred the door of her desires. Wherefore the sun of grace did not shine, not through its own defect, but through the defect of the creature, who bars the door of desire. When she knows herself and her darkness, she opens the window and vomits her filth, by holy confession. Then I, having returned to the soul by grace, withdraw Myself from her by sentiment, which I do in order to humiliate her, and cause her to seek Me in truth, and to prove her in the light of faith, so that she come to prudence. Then, if she love Me without thought of self, and with lively faith and with hatred of her own sensuality, she rejoices in the time of trouble, deeming herself unworthy of peace and quietness of mind. Now comes the second of the three things of which I told thee, that is to say: how the soul arrives at perfection, and what she does when she is perfect. This is what she does. Though she perceives that I have withdrawn Myself, she does not, on that account, look back, but perseveres with humility in her exercises, remaining barred in the house of self-knowledge, and, continuing to dwell therein, awaits, with lively faith, the coming of the Holy Spirit, that is of Me, who am the fire of charity. How does she await me ? Not in idleness, but in watching and continued prayer, and not only with physical, but also with intellectual watching, that is, with the eye of her mind alert, and, watching with the light of faith, she extirpates, with hatred, the wandering thoughts of her heart, looking for the affection of My charity, and knowing that I desire nothing but her sanctification, which is certified to her in the Blood of My Son. As long as her eye thus watches, illumined by the knowledge of Me and of herself, she continues to pray with the prayer of holy desire, which is a continued prayer, and also with actual prayer, which she practises at the appointed times, according to the orders of Holy Church. This is what the soul does in order to rise from imperfection and arrive at perfection, and it is to this end, namely that she may arrive at perfection, that I withdraw from her, not by grace but by sentiment. Once more do I leave her, so that she may see and know her defects, so that, feeling herself deprived of consolation and afflicted by pain, she may recognise her own weakness, and learn how incapable she is of stability or perseverance, thus cutting down to the very root of spiritual self-love, for this should be the end and purpose of all her self-knowledge, to rise above herself, mounting the throne of conscience, and not permitting the sentiment of imperfect love to turn again in its death-struggle, but, with correction and reproof, digging up the root of self-love, with the knife of self-hatred and the love of virtue."

How an imperfect lover of GOD loves his neighbour also imperfectly, and of the signs of this imperfect love.

"And I would have thee know that just as every imperfection and perfection is acquired from Me, so is it manifested by means of the neighbour. And simple souls, who often love creatures with spiritual love, know this well, for, if they have received My love sincerely without any self-regarding considerations, they satisfy the thirst of their love for their neighbour equally sincerely. If a man carry away the vessel which he has filled at the fountain and then drink of it, the vessel becomes empty, but if he keep his vessel standing in the fountain, while he drinks, it always remains full. So the love of the neighbour, whether spiritual or temporal, should be drunk in Me, without any self-regarding considerations. I require that you should love Me with the same love with which I love you. This indeed you cannot do, because I loved you without being loved. All the love which you have for Me you owe to Me, so that it is not of grace that you love Me, but because you ought to do so. While I love you of grace, and not because I owe you My love. Therefore to Me, in person, you cannot repay the love which I require of you, and I have placed you in the midst of your fellows, that you may do to them that which you cannot do to Me, that is to say, that you may love your neighbour of free grace, without expecting any return from him, and what you do to him, I count as done to Me, which My Truth showed forth when He said to Paul, My persecutor—'*Saul, Saul, why persecutest thou Me?*' This He said, judging that Paul persecuted Him in His faithful. This love must be sincere, because it is with the same love with which you love Me, that you must love your neighbour. Dost thou know how the imperfection of spiritual love for the creature is shown? It is shown when the lover feels pain if it appear to him that the object of his love does not satisfy or return his love, or when he sees the beloved one's conversation turned aside from him, or himself deprived of consolation, or another loved more than he. In these and in many other ways can it be seen that his neighbourly love is still imperfect, and that, though his love was originally drawn from Me, the Fountain of all love, he took the vessel out of the water, in order to drink from it. It is because his love for Me is still imperfect, that his neighbourly love is so weak, and because the root of self-love has not been properly dug out. Wherefore I often permit such a love to exist, so that the soul may in this way come to the knowledge of her own imperfection, and for the same reason do I withdraw myself from the soul by sentiment, that she may be thus led to enclose herself in the house of self-knowledge, where is acquired every perfection. After which I return into her with more light and with more knowledge of My Truth. in proportion to the degree in which she refers to grace the power of slaying her own will. And she never ceases to cultivate the vine of her soul, and to root out the thorns of evil thoughts, replacing them with the stones of virtues, cemented together in the Blood of Christ crucified, which she has found on her journey across the Bridge of Christ, My only-begotten Son. For I told thee, if thou remember, that upon the Bridge, that is, upon the doctrine of My Truth, were built up the stones, based upon the virtue of His Blood, for it is in virtue of this Blood that the virtues give life."

A TREATISE OF PRAYER

Of the means which the soul takes to arrive at pure and generous love ; and here begins the Treatise of Prayer.

"When the soul has passed through the doctrine of Christ crucified, with true love of virtue and hatred of vice, and has arrived at the house of self-knowledge and entered therein, she remains, with her door barred, in watching and constant prayer, separated entirely from the consolations of the world. Why does she thus shut herself in? She does so from fear, knowing her own imperfections, and also from the desire, which she has, of arriving at pure and generous love. And because she sees and knows well that in no other way can she arrive thereat, she waits, with a lively faith for My arrival, through increase of grace in her. How is a lively faith to be recognised? By perseverance in virtue, and by the fact that the soul never turns back for anything, whatever it be, nor rises from holy prayer, for any reason except (note well) for obedience or charity's sake. For no other reason ought she to leave off prayer, for, during the time ordained for prayer, the Devil is wont to arrive in the soul, causing much more conflict and trouble than when the soul is not occupied in prayer. This he does in order that holy prayer may become tedious to the soul, tempting her often with these words: ' *This prayer avails thee nothing, for thou needest attend to nothing except thy vocal prayers.*' He acts thus in order that, becoming wearied and confused in mind, she may abandon the exercise of prayer, which is a weapon with which the soul can defend herself from every adversary, if grasped with the hand of love, by the arm of free choice in the light of the Holy Faith."

Here, touching something concerning the Sacrament of the Body of Christ, the complete doctrine is given; and how the soul proceeds from vocal to mental prayer, and a vision is related which this devout soul once received.

"Know, dearest daughter, how, by humble, continual, and faithful prayer, the soul acquires, with time and perseverance, every virtue. Wherefore should she persevere and never abandon prayer, either through the illusion of the Devil or her own fragility, that is to say, either on account of any thought or movement coming from her own body, or of the words of any creature. The Devil often places himself upon the tongues of creatures, causing them to chatter nonsensically, with the purpose of preventing the prayer of the soul. All of this she should pass by, by means of the virtue of perseverance. Oh, how sweet and pleasant to that soul and to Me is holy prayer, made in the house of knowledge of self and of Me, opening the eye of the intellect to the light of faith, and the affections to the abundance of My charity, which was made visible to you, through My visible only-begotten Son, who showed it to you with His blood! Which Blood inebriates the soul and clothes her with the fire of divine charity, giving her the food of the Sacrament [which is placed in the tavern of the mystical body of the Holy Church] that is to say, the food of the Body and Blood of My Son, wholly God and wholly man, administered to you by the hand of My vicar, who holds the key of the Blood. This is that tavern, which I mentioned to thee, standing on the Bridge, to provide food and comfort for the travellers and the pilgrims, who pass by the way of the doctrine of My Truth, lest they should faint through weakness. This food strengthens little or much, according to the desire of the recipient, whether he receives sacramentally or virtually. He receives sacramentally when he actually communicates with the Blessed Sacrament. He receives virtually when he communicates, both by desire of communion, and by contemplation of the Blood of Christ crucified, communicating, as it were, sacramentally, with the affection of love, which is to be tasted in the Blood which, as the soul sees, was shed through love. On seeing this the soul becomes inebriated, and blazes with holy desire and satisfies herself, becoming full of love for Me and for her neighbour. Where can this be acquired? In the house of self-knowledge with holy prayer, where imperfections are lost, even as Peter and the disciples, while they remained in watching and prayer, lost their imperfection and acquired perfection. By what means is this acquired? By perseverance seasoned with the most holy faith.

"But do not think that the soul receives such ardour and nourishment from prayer, if she pray only vocally, as do many souls whose prayers are rather words than love. Such as these give heed to nothing except to completing Psalms and saying many paternosters. And when they have once completed their appointed tale, they do not appear to think of anything further, but seem to place devout attention and love in merely vocal recitation, which the soul is not required to do, for, in doing only this, she bears but little fruit, which pleases Me but little. But if thou askest Me, whether the soul should abandon vocal prayer, since it does not seem to all that they are called to mental prayer, I should reply ' *No.*' The soul should advance by degrees, and I know well that, just as the soul is at first imperfect and afterwards perfect, so also is it with her prayer. She should nevertheless continue in vocal prayer, while she is yet imperfect, so as not to fall into idleness. But she should not say her vocal prayers without joining them to mental prayer, that is to say, that while she is reciting, she

L

should endeavour to elevate her mind in My love, with the consideration of her own defects and of the Blood of My only-begotten Son, wherein she finds the breadth of My charity and the remission of her sins. And this she should do, so that self-knowledge and the consideration of her own defects should make her recognise My goodness in herself and continue her exercises with true humility. I do not wish defects to be considered in particular, but in general, so that the mind may not be contaminated by the remembrance of particular and hideous sins. But, as I said, I do not wish the soul to consider her sins, either in general or in particular, without also remembering the Blood and the broadness of My mercy, for fear that otherwise she should be brought to confusion. And together with confusion would come the Devil, who has caused it, under colour of contrition and displeasure of sin, and so she would arrive at eternal damnation, not only on account of her confusion, but also through the despair which would come to her, because she did not seize the arm of My mercy. This is one of the subtle devices with which the Devil deludes My servants, and, in order to escape from his deceit, and to be pleasing to Me, you must enlarge your hearts and affections in My boundless mercy, with true humility. Thou knowest that the pride of the Devil cannot resist the humble mind, nor can any confusion of spirit be greater than the broadness of My good mercy, if the soul

will only truly hope therein. Wherefore it was,
if thou remember rightly, that, once, when the
Devil wished to overthrow thee, by confusion,
wishing to prove to thee that thy life had been
deluded, and that thou hadst not followed My
will, thou didst that which was thy duty, which
My goodness (which is never withheld from him
who will receive it) gave thee strength to do,
that is thou didst rise, humbly trusting in My
mercy, and saying : '*I confess to my Creator that
my life has indeed been passed in darkness, but I will
hide myself in the Wounds of Christ crucified, and
bathe myself in His Blood and so shall my iniquities
be consumed, and with desire will I rejoice in my
Creator.*' Thou rememberest that then the Devil
fled, and, turning round to the opposite side, he
endeavoured to inflate thee with pride, saying :
'*Thou art perfect and pleasing to God, and there is
no more need for thee to afflict thyself or to lament
thy sins.*' And once more I gave thee the light
to see thy true path, namely, humiliation of thyself, and thou didst answer the Devil with these
words : '*Wretch that I am, John the Baptist never
sinned and was sanctified in his mother's womb.
And I have committed so many sins, and have hardly
begun to know them with grief and true contrition,
seeing who God is, who is offended by me, and who
I am, who offend Him.*' Then the Devil, not
being able to resist thy humble hope in My
goodness, said to thee : '*Cursed that thou art, for
I can find no way to take thee. If I put thee down
through confusion, thou risest to Heaven on the wings*

of mercy, and if I raise thee on high, thou humblest thyself down to Hell, and when I go into Hell thou persecutest me, so that I will return to thee no more, because thou strikest me with the stick of charity.' The soul, therefore, should season the knowledge of herself with the knowledge of My goodness, and then vocal prayer will be of use to the soul who makes it, and pleasing to Me, and she will arrive, from the vocal imperfect prayer, exercised with perseverance, at perfect mental prayer; but if she simply aims at completing her tale, and, for vocal abandons mental prayer, she will never arrive at it.   Sometimes the soul will be so ignorant that, having resolved to say so many prayers vocally, and I, visiting her mind sometimes in one way, and sometimes in another, in a flash of self-knowledge or of contrition for sin, sometimes in the broadness of My charity, and sometimes by placing before her mind, in diverse ways, according to My pleasure and the desire of the soul, the presence of My Truth, she (the soul), in order to complete her tale, will abandon My visitation, that she feels, as it were, by conscience, rather than abandon that which she had begun.   She should not do so, for, in so doing, she yields to a deception of the Devil.   The moment she feels her mind disposed by My visitation, in the many ways I have told thee, she should abandon vocal prayer; then, My visitation past, if there be time, she can resume the vocal prayers which she had resolved to say, but if she has not time to complete them, she ought not on that account to be troubled or suffer annoyance and confusion of mind ; of course provided that it were not the Divine office which clerics and religious are bound and obliged to say under penalty of offending Me, for, they must, until death, say their office. But if they, at the hour appointed for saying it, should feel their minds drawn and raised by desire, they should so arrange as to say it before or after My visitation, so that the debt of rendering the office be not omitted. But, in any other case, vocal prayer should be immediately abandoned for the said cause. Vocal prayer, made in the way that I have told thee, will enable the soul to arrive at perfection, and therefore she should not abandon it, but use it in the way that I have told thee.

And so, with exercise in perseverance, she will taste prayer in truth, and the food of the Blood of My only-begotten Son, and therefore I told thee that some communicated virtually with the Body and Blood of Christ, although not sacramentally ; that is, they communicate in the affection of charity, which they taste by means of holy prayer, little or much, according to the affection with which they pray. They who proceed with little prudence and without method, taste little, and they who proceed with much, taste much. For the more the soul tries to loosen her affection from herself, and fasten it in Me with the light of the intellect, the more she knows ; and the more she knows, the more she loves, and, loving much, she tastes much.

Thou seest then, that perfect prayer is not attained to through many words, but through affection of desire, the soul raising herself to Me, with knowledge of herself and of My mercy, seasoned the one with the other. Thus she will exercise together mental and vocal prayer, for, even as the active and contemplative life is one, so are they. Although vocal or mental prayer can be understood in many and diverse ways, for I have told thee that a holy desire is a continual prayer, in this sense that a good and holy will disposes itself with desire to the occasion actually appointed for prayer in addition to the continual prayer of holy desire, wherefore vocal prayer will be made at the appointed time by the soul who remains firm in a habitual holy will, and will sometimes be continued beyond the appointed time, according as charity commands for the salvation of the neighbour, if the soul see him to be in need, and also her own necessities according to the state in which I have placed her. Each one, according to his condition, ought to exert himself for the salvation of souls, for this exercise lies at the root of a holy will, and whatever he may contribute, by words or deeds, towards the salvation of his neighbour, is virtually a prayer, although it does not replace a prayer which one should make oneself at the appointed season, as My glorious standard-bearer Paul said, in the words, ' *He who ceases not to work ceases not to pray.*' It was for this reason that I told thee that prayer was made in many ways, that is, that actual prayer may be united with mental prayer if made with the affection of charity, which charity is itself continual prayer. I have now told thee how mental prayer is reached by exercise and perseverance, and by leaving vocal prayer for mental when I visit the soul. I have also spoken to thee of common prayer, that is, of vocal prayer in general, made outside of ordained times, and of the prayers of good-will, and how every exercise, whether performed, in oneself or in one's neighbour, with good-will, is prayer. The enclosed soul should therefore spur herself on with prayer, and when she has arrived at friendly and filial love she does so. Unless the soul keep to this path, she will always remain tepid and imperfect, and will only love Me and her neighbour in proportion to the pleasure which she finds in My service."

Of the method by which the soul separates herself from imperfect love, and attains to perfect love, friendly and filial.

"Hitherto I have shown thee in many ways how the soul raises herself from imperfection and attains to perfection, which she does after she has attained to friendly and filial love. I tell thee that she arrives at perfect love by means of perseverance, barring herself into the House of Self-Knowledge, which knowledge of self requires to be seasoned with knowledge of Me, lest it bring the soul to confusion, for it would cause the soul to hate her own sensitive pleasure and the delight of her own consolations. But from this hatred, founded in humility, she will draw patience, with which she will become strong against the attacks of the Devil, against the persecutions of man, and towards Me, when, for her good, I withdraw delight from her mind. And if her sensuality, through malevolence, should lift its head against reason, the judgment of conscience should rise against it, and, with hatred of it, hold out reason against it, not allowing such evil emotions to get by it. Though sometimes the soul who lives in holy hatred corrects and reproves herself, not only for those things that are against reason, but also for things that in reality come from Me, which is what My sweet servant S. Gregory meant, when he said that a holy and pure conscience made sin where there was no sin, that is, that through purity of conscience, it saw sin where there was no sin.

"Now the soul who wishes to rise above imperfection should await My Providence in the House of Self-Knowledge, with the light of faith, as did the disciples, who remained in the house in perseverance and in watching, and in humble and continual prayer, awaiting the coming of the Holy Spirit. She should remain fasting and watching, the eye of her intellect fastened on the doctrine of My Truth, and she will become humble because she will know herself in humble and continual prayer and holy and true desire."

*Of the signs by which the soul knows she has
arrived at perfect love.*

"It now remains to be told thee how it can be
seen that souls have arrived at perfect love. This
is seen by the same sign that was given to the
holy disciples after they had received the Holy
Spirit, when they came forth from the house,
and fearlessly announced the doctrine of My
Word, My only-begotten Son, not fearing pain,
but rather glorying therein. They did not mind
going before the tyrants of the world, to announce to them the truth, for the glory and
praise of My Name. So the soul, who has
awaited Me in self-knowledge as I have told
thee, receives Me, on My return to her, with
the fire of charity, in which charity, while still
remaining in the house with perseverance, she
conceives the virtues by affection of love, participating in My power; with which power and
virtues she overrules and conquers her own sensitive passions, and through which charity she
participates in the wisdom of My Son, in which
she sees and knows, with the eye of her intellect,
My Truth and the deceptions of spiritual self-
love, that is, the imperfect love of her own
consolations, as has been said, and she knows
also the malice and deceit of the devil, which
he practises on those souls who are bound by
that imperfect love. She therefore arises, with
hatred of that imperfection and with love of
perfection, and, through this charity, which is

of the Holy Spirit, she participates in His will, fortifying her own to be willing to suffer pain, and, coming out of the house through My Name, she brings forth the virtues on her neighbour. Not that by coming out to bring forth the virtues, I mean that she issues out of the House of Self-Knowledge, but that, in the time of the neighbour's necessity she loses that fear of being deprived of her own consolations, and so issues forth to give birth to those virtues which she has conceived through affection of love. The souls, who have thus come forth, have reached the fourth state, that is, from the third state, which is a perfect state, in which they taste charity and give birth to it on their neighbours, they have arrived at the fourth state, which is one of perfect union with Me. The two last-mentioned states are united, that is to say, one cannot be without the other, for there cannot be love of Me, without love of the neighbour, nor love of the neighbour without love of Me."

How they who are imperfect desire to follow the Father alone, but they who are perfect desire to follow the Son. And of a vision, which this holy soul had, concerning diverse baptisms, and of many other beautiful and useful things.

" As I have told thee, these latter have issued forth from the house, which is a sign that they have arisen from imperfection and arrived at perfection. Open the eye of thy intellect and see

them running by the Bridge of the doctrine of
Christ crucified, which was their rule, way, and
doctrine. They place none other before the eye
of their intellect than Christ crucified, not the
Father, as they do who are in imperfect love and
do not wish to suffer pain, but only to have the
delight which they find in Me. But they, as if
drunken with love and burning with it, have
gathered together and ascended the three steps,
which I figured to thee as the three powers of
the soul, and also the three actual steps, figured
to thee as in the Body of My only Son, Christ
crucified, by which steps the soul, as I told thee,
ascended, first climbing to the Feet, with the
feet of the soul's affection, from thence arriving
at the Side, where she found the secret of the
Heart and knew the baptism of water, which has
virtue through the Blood, and where I dispose
the soul to receive grace, uniting and kneading
her together in the Blood. Where did the soul
know of this her dignity, in being kneaded and
united with the Blood of the Lamb, receiving the
grace in Holy Baptism, in virtue of the Blood?
In the Side, where she knew the fire of divine
Charity, and so, if thou remember well, My Truth
manifested to thee, when thou askedst, saying:
' *Sweet and Immaculate Lamb, Thou wert dead when
Thy side was opened. Why then didst Thou want to
be struck and have Thy heart divided?* ' And He
replied to thee, telling thee that there was occasion enough for it; but the principal part of
what He said I will tell thee. He said: Because

My desire towards the human generation was
ended, and I had finished the actual work of
bearing pain and torment, and yet I had not
been able to show, by finite things, because My
love was infinite, how much more love I had,
I wished thee to see the secret of the Heart,
showing it to thee open, so that thou mightest
see how much more I loved than I could show
thee by finite pain. I poured from it Blood and
Water, to show thee the baptism of water, which
is received in virtue of the Blood. I also showed
the baptism of love in two ways, first in those
who are baptized in their blood, shed for Me,
which has virtue through My Blood, even if
they have not been able to have Holy Baptism,
and also in those who are baptized in fire, not
being able to have Holy Baptism, but desiring it with the affection of love. There is no
baptism of fire without the Blood, because the
Blood is steeped in and kneaded with the fire
of Divine charity, because, through love was It
shed. There is yet another way by which the
soul receives the baptism of Blood, speaking, as
it were, under a figure, and this way the Divine
charity provided, knowing the infirmity and
fragility of man, through which he offends, not
that he is obliged, through his fragility and
infirmity, to commit sin unless he wish to do
so; but, falling, as he will, into the guilt of
mortal sin, by which he loses the grace which
he drew from Holy Baptism in virtue of the
Blood, it was necessary to leave a continual

baptism of Blood.   This the Divine charity provided in the Sacrament of Holy Confession, the soul receiving the Baptism of Blood, with contrition of heart, confessing, when able, to My ministers, who hold the keys of the Blood, sprinkling It, in absolution, upon the face of the soul.   But, if the soul be unable to confess, contrition of heart is sufficient for this baptism, the hand of My clemency giving you the fruit of this precious Blood.   But if you are able to confess, I wish you to do so, and if you are able to, and do not, you will be deprived of the fruit of the Blood.   It is true that, in the last extremity, a man, desiring to confess and not being able to, will receive the fruit of this baptism, of which I have been speaking.   But let no one be so mad as so to arrange his deeds, that, in the hope of receiving it, he puts off confessing until the last extremity of death, when he may not be able to do so.   In which case, it is not at all certain that I shall not say to him, in My Divine Justice : ' *Thou didst not remember Me in the time of thy life, when thou couldest, now will I not remember thee in thy death.*'

"Thou seest then that these Baptisms, which you should all receive until the last moment, are continual, and though My works, that is the pains of the Cross were finite, the fruit of them which you receive in Baptism, through Me, are infinite.   This is in virtue of the infinite Divine nature, united with the finite human nature, which human nature endures pain in Me, the Word, clothed with your humanity. But because the one nature is steeped in and united with the other, the Eternal Deity drew to Himself the pain, which I suffered with so much fire and love. And therefore can this operation be called infinite, not that My pain, neither the actuality of the body be infinite, nor the pain of the desire that I had to complete your redemption, because it was terminated and finished on the Cross, when the Soul was separated from the Body; but the fruit, which came out of the pain and desire for your salvation, is infinite, and therefore you receive it infinitely. Had it not been infinite, the whole human generation could not have been restored to grace, neither the past, the present, nor the future. This I manifested in the opening of My Side, where is found the secret of the Heart, showing that I loved more than I could show, with finite pain. I showed to thee that My love was infinite. How? By the Baptism of Blood, united with the fire of My charity, and by the general baptism, given to Christians, and to whomsoever will receive it, and by the baptism of water, united with the Blood and the fire, wherein the soul is steeped. And, in order to show this, it was necessary for the Blood to come out of My Side. Now I have shown thee (said My Truth to thee) what thou askedst of Me."

How worldly people render glory and praise to GOD,
whether they will or no.

"And so perfect is her vision that she sees
the glory and praise of My Name, not so much
in the angelic nature as in the human, for, whether
worldly people will or no, they render glory and
praise to My Name, not that they do so in the
way they should, loving Me above everything,
but that My mercy shines in them, in that, in
the abundance of My charity, I give them time,
and do not order the earth to open and swallow
them up on account of their sins. I even wait
for them, and command the earth to give them
of her fruits, the sun to give them light and
warmth, and the sky to move above them. And
in all things created and made for them, I use
My charity and mercy, withdrawing neither on
account of their sins. I even give equally to
the sinner and the righteous man, and often more
to the sinner than to the righteous man, because
the righteous man is able to endure privation,
and I take from him the goods of the world
that he may the more abundantly enjoy the goods
of heaven. So that in worldly men My mercy
and charity shine, and they render praise and
glory to My Name, even when they persecute
My servants; for they prove in them the virtues
of patience and charity, causing them to suffer
humbly and offer to Me their persecutions and
injuries, thus turning them into My praise and
glory.

"So that, whether they will or no, worldly people render to My Name praise and glory, even when they intend to do Me infamy and wrong."

How even the devils render glory and praise to GOD.

"Sinners, such as those of whom I have just spoken, are placed in this life in order to augment virtues in My servants, as the devils are in Hell as My justiciars and augmenters of My Glory; that is, My instruments of justice towards the damned, and the augmenters of My Glory in My creatures, who are wayfarers and pilgrims on their journey to reach Me, their End.   They augment in them the virtues in diverse ways, exercising them with many temptations and vexations, causing them to injure one another and take one another's property, and not for the motive of making them receive injury or be deprived of their property, but only to deprive them of charity.   But in thinking to deprive My servants, they fortify them, proving in them the virtues of patience, fortitude, and perseverance. Thus they render praise and glory to My Name, and My Truth is fulfilled in them, which Truth created them for the praise and glory of Me, Eternal Father, and that they might participate in My beauty.   But, rebelling against Me in their pride, they fell and lost their vision of Me, wherefore they rendered not to Me glory through the affection of love, and I, Eternal Truth, have placed them as instruments to exercise My servants in virtue in this life and as justiciars to those who go, for their sins, to the pains of Purgatory. So thou seest that My Truth is fulfilled in them, that is, that they render Me glory, not as citizens of life eternal, of which they are deprived by their sins, but as My justiciars, manifesting justice upon the damned, and upon those in Purgatory."

How the soul, after she has passed through this life, sees fully the praise and glory of My Name in everything, and, though, in her the pain of desire is ended, the desire is not.

"Thus in all things created, in all rational creatures, and in the devils is seen the glory and praise of My Name. Who can see it? The soul who is denuded of the body and has reached Me, her End, sees it clearly, and, in seeing, knows the truth. Seeing Me, the Eternal Father, she loves, and loving, she is satisfied. Satisfied, she knows the Truth, and her will is stayed in My Will, bound and made stable, so that in nothing can it suffer pain, because it has that which it desired to have, before the soul saw Me, namely, the glory and praise of My Name. She now, in truth, sees it completely in My saints, in the blessed spirits, and in all creatures and things, even in the devils, as I told thee. And although she also sees the injury done to Me, which before

M

caused her sorrow, it no longer now can give her pain, but only compassion, because she loves without pain, and prays to Me continually with affection of love, that I will have mercy on the world. Pain in her is ended, but not love, as the tortured desire, which My Word, the Son, had borne from the beginning when I sent Him into the world, terminated on the Cross in His painful death, but His love—no. For had the affection of My charity, which I showed you by means of Him, been terminated and ended then, you would not be, because by love you are made, and had My love been drawn back, that is, had I not loved your being, you could not be, but My love created you, and My love possesses you, because I am one thing with My Truth, and He, the Word Incarnate with Me. Thou seest then, that the saints and every soul in Eternal Life have desire for the salvation of souls without pain, because pain ended in their death, but not so the affection of love.

"Thus, as if drunk with the Blood of the Immaculate Lamb, and clothed in the love of the neighbour, they pass through the Narrow Gate, bathed in the Blood of Christ crucified, and they find themselves in Me, the Sea Pacific, raised from imperfection, far from satiety, and arrived at perfection, satisfied by every good."

*How after Saint Paul was drawn to the glory of the
blessed, he desired to be loosened from the body,
as they do, who have reached the aforesaid third
and fourth states.*

"Paul, then, had seen and tasted this good,
when I drew him up into the third heaven, that
is into the height of the Trinity, where he tasted
and knew My Truth, receiving fully the Holy
Spirit, and learning the doctrine of My Truth,
the Word Incarnate. The soul of Paul was
clothed, through feeling and union, in Me,
Eternal Father, like the blessed ones in Eternal
Life, except that his soul was not separated from
his body, except through this feeling and union.
But it being pleasing to My Goodness to make
of him a vessel of election in the abyss of Me,
Eternal Trinity, I dispossessed him of Myself,
because on Me can no pain fall, and I wished him
to suffer for My name ; therefore I placed before
him, as an object for the eyes of his intellect,
Christ crucified, clothing him with the garment
of His doctrine, binding and fettering him with
the clemency of the Holy Spirit and inflaming
him with the fire of charity. He became a
vessel, disposed and reformed by My Goodness,
and, on being struck, made no resistance, but
said : '*My Lord, what dost Thou wish me to do ?
Show me that which it is Thy pleasure for me to do,
and I will do it.*' Which I answered when I
placed before him Christ crucified, clothing him
with the doctrine of My charity. I illuminated

him perfectly with the light of true contrition, by which he extirpated his defects, and founded him in My charity."

How the soul who finds herself in the unitive state desires infinitely to leave the barren earthly state and unite herself to GOD.

"And when I depart from the soul in the aforesaid way that the body may return a little to its corporal sentiment, the soul, on account of the union which she had made with Me, is impatient in her life, being deprived of union with Me, and the conversation of the Immortals, who render glory to Me, and finding herself, amid the conversation of mortals, and seeing them so miserably offending Me. This vision of My offence is the torture which such souls always have, and which, with the desire to see Me, renders their life insupportable to them. Nevertheless, as their will is not their own, but becomes one with Mine, they cannot desire other than what I desire, and though they desire to come and be with Me, they are contented to remain, if I desire them to remain, with their pain, for the greater praise and glory of My Name and the salvation of souls. So that in nothing are they in discord with My Will; but they run their course with ecstatic desire, clothed in Christ crucified, and keeping by the ∣Bridge of His doctrine, glorying in His shame and pains. Inasmuch as they appear to be suffering they are

rejoicing, because the enduring of many tribulations is to them a relief in the desire which they
have for death, for oftentimes the desire and the
will to suffer pain mitigates the pain caused them
by their desire to quit the body. These not only
endure with patience, as I told thee they did,
who are in the third state, but they glory,
through My Name, in bearing much tribulation.
In bearing tribulation they find pleasure, and not
having it they suffer pain, fearing that I reward
not their well-doing or that the sacrifice of their
desires is not pleasing to Me ; but when I permit
to them many tribulations they rejoice, seeing
themselves clothed with the suffering and shame
of Christ crucified. Wherefore were it possible
for them to have virtue without toil they would
not want it. They would rather delight in the
Cross, with Christ, acquiring it with pain, than
in any other way obtain Eternal Life. Why?
Because they are inflamed and steeped in the
Blood, where they find the blaze of My charity,
which charity is a fire proceeding from Me,
ravishing their heart and mind and making their
sacrifices acceptable. Wherefore, the eye of the
intellect is lifted up and gazes into My Deity,
when the affection behind the intellect is
nourished and united with Me. This is a sight
which I grant to the soul, infused with grace,
who, in truth, loves and serves Me."

*How they, who are arrived at the aforesaid unitive
    state, have the eye of their intellect illuminated
    by supernatural light infused by grace. And
    how it is better to go for counsel for the salvation
    of the soul, to a humble and holy conscience than
    to a proud lettered man.*

"With this light that is given to the eye of
the intellect, Thomas Aquinas saw Me, wherefore
he acquired the light of much science; also
Augustine, Jerome, and the doctors, and my
saints. They were illuminated by My Truth to
know and understand My Truth in darkness.
By My Truth I mean the Holy Scripture, which
seemed dark because it was not understood; not
through any defect of the Scriptures, but of them
who heard them, and did not understand them.
Wherefore I sent this light to illuminate the
blind and coarse understanding, uplifting the
eye of the intellect to know the Truth. And
I, Fire, Acceptor of sacrifices, ravishing away
from them their darkness, give the light; not a
natural light, but a supernatural, so that, though
in darkness, they know the Truth. Wherefore
that, which at first appeared to be dark, now
appears with the most perfect light, to the gross
or subtle mind; and every one receives according as he is capable or disposed to know Me,
for I do not despise dispositions. So thou seest
that the eye of the intellect has received supernatural light, infused by grace, by which the
doctors and saints knew light in darkness, and of

darkness made light. The intellect was, before
the Scriptures were formed, wherefore, from the
intellect came science, because in seeing they
discerned. It was thus that the holy prophets
and fathers understood, who prophesied of the
coming and death of My Son, and the Apostles,
after the coming of the Holy Spirit, which gave
them that supernatural light. The evangelists,
doctors, professors, virgins, and martyrs were all
likewise illuminated by the aforesaid perfect
light. And every one has had the illumination
of this light according as he needed it for his
salvation or that of others, or for the exposition
of the Scriptures. The doctors of the holy
science had it, expounding the doctrine of My
Truth, the preaching of the Apostles, and the
Gospels of the Evangelists. The martyrs had
it, declaring in their blood the Most Holy Faith,
the fruit and the treasure of the Blood of the
Lamb. The virgins had it in the affection of
charity and purity. To the obedient ones is
declared, by it, the obedience of the Word,
showing them the perfection of obedience, which
shines in my Truth, who for the obedience that
I imposed upon Him, ran to the opprobrious
death of the Cross. This light is to be seen in
the Old and New Testament; in the Old, by it,
were seen by the eye of the intellect, and known
the prophecies of the holy prophets. In the
New Testament of the evangelical life, how is
the Gospel declared to the faithful? By this
same light. And because the New Testament

proceeded from the same light, the new law did not break the old law; rather are the two laws bound together, the imperfection of the old law, founded in fear alone, being taken from it, by the coming of the Word of My only-begotten Son, with the law of Love, completing the old law by giving it love, and replacing the fear of penalty by holy fear. And, therefore, said My Truth to the disciples, to show that He was not a breaker of laws: '*I came not to dissolve the law, but to fulfil it.*' It is almost as if My Truth would say to them—The Law is now imperfect, but with My Blood I will make it perfect, and I will fill it up with what it lacks, taking away the fear of penalty, and founding it in love and holy fear. How was this declared to be the Truth? By this same supernatural light, which was and is given by grace to all, who will receive it? Every light that comes from Holy Scripture comes and came from this supernatural light. Ignorant and proud men of science were blind notwithstanding this light, because their pride and the cloud of self-love had covered up and put out the light. Wherefore they understood the Holy Scripture rather literally than with understanding, and taste only the letter of it, still desiring many other books; and they get not to the marrow of it, because they have deprived themselves of the light, with which is found and expounded the Scripture; and they are annoyed and murmur, because they find much in it that appears to them gross and idiotic.

And, nevertheless, they appear to be much illuminated in their knowledge of Scripture, as if they had studied it for long; and this is not remarkable, because they have of course the natural light from whence proceeds science. But because they have lost the supernatural light, infused by grace, they neither see nor know My Goodness, nor the grace of My servants. Wherefore, I say to thee, that it is much better to go for counsel for the salvation of the soul, to a holy and upright conscience, than to a proud lettered man, learned in much science, because such a one can only offer what he has himself, and, because of his darkness, it may appear to thee, that, from what he says, the Scriptures offer darkness. The contrary wilt thou find with My servants, because they offer the light that is in them, with hunger and desire for the soul's salvation. This I have told thee, my sweetest daughter, that thou mightest know the perfection of this unitive state, when the eye of the intellect is ravished by the fire of My charity, in which charity it receives the supernatural light. With this light the souls in the unitive state love Me, because love follows the intellect, and the more it knows the more can it love. Thus the one feeds the other, and, with this light, they both arrive at the Eternal Vision of Me, where they see and taste Me, in Truth, the soul being separated from the body, as I told thee when I spoke to thee of the blissfulness that the soul received in Me. This state is most excellent, when the soul, being yet in the mortal body, tastes bliss with the immortals, and oft-times she arrives at so great a union that she scarcely knows whether she be in the body or out of it; and tastes the earnest-money of Eternal Life, both because she is united with Me, and because her will is dead in Christ, by which death her union was made with Me, and in no other way could she perfectly have done so. There-fore do they taste life eternal, deprived of the hell of their own will, which gives to man the earnest-money of damnation, if he yield to it."

*How this devout soul seeks knowledge from God
concerning the state and fruit of tears.*

Then this soul, yearning with very great desire, and rising as one intoxicated both by the union which she had had with God, and by what she had heard and tasted of the Supreme and Sweet Truth, yearned with grief over the ignorance of creatures, in that they did not know their Bene-factor, or the affection of the love of God. And nevertheless she had joy from the hope of the promise that the Truth of God had made to her, teaching her the way she was to direct her will (and the other servants of God as well as herself) in order that He should do mercy to the world. And, lifting up the eye of her intellect upon the sweet Truth, to whom she remained united, wish-ing to know somewhat of the aforesaid states of the soul of which God had spoken to her, and seeing that the soul passes through these states with tears, she wished to learn from the Truth concerning the different kinds of tears, and how they came to be, and whence they proceeded, and the fruit that resulted from weeping. Wishing then to know this from the Sweet, Supreme and First Truth, as to the manner of being and reason of the aforesaid tears, and inasmuch as the truth cannot be learnt from any other than from the Truth Himself, and nothing can be learnt in the Truth but what is seen by the eye of the intellect, she made her request of the Truth. For it is necessary for him who is lifted with desire to learn the Truth with the light of faith.

Wherefore, knowing that she had not forgotten the teaching which the Truth, that is, God, had given her, that in no other way could she learn about the different states and fruits of tears, she rose out of herself, exceeding every limit of her nature with the greatness of her desire. And, with the light of a lively faith, she opened the eye of her intellect upon the Eternal Truth, in whom she saw and knew the Truth, in the matter of her request, for God Himself manifested it to her, and condescending in His benignity to her burning desire, fulfilled her petition.

How there are five kinds of tears.

Then said the Supreme and Sweet Truth of God, "Oh, beloved and dearest daughter, thou beggest knowledge of the reasons and fruits of tears, and I have not despised thy desire, Open well the eye of thy intellect and I will show thee, among the aforesaid states of the soul, of which I have told thee, concerning the imperfect tears caused by fear; but first rather of the tears of wicked men of the world. These are the tears of damnation. The former are those of fear, and belong to men who abandon sin from fear of punishment, and weep for fear. The third are the tears of those who, having abandoned sin, are beginning to serve and taste Me, and weep for very sweetness; but since their love is imperfect, so also is their weeping, as I have told thee. The fourth are the tears of those who have arrived at the perfect love of their neighbour, loving Me without any regard whatsoever for themselves. These weep and their weeping is perfect. The fifth are joined to the fourth and are tears of sweetness let fall with great peace, as I will explain to thee. I will tell thee also of the tears of fire, without bodily tears of the eyes, which satisfy those who often would desire to weep and cannot. And I wish thee to know that all these various graces may exist in one soul, who, rising from fear and imperfect love, reaches perfect love in the unitive state. Now I will begin to tell thee of these tears in the following way."

*Of the difference of these tears, arising from the
explanation of the aforesaid state of the soul.*

"I wish thee to know that every tear proceeds
from the heart, for there is no member of the
body that will satisfy the heart so much as the
eye. If the heart is in pain the eye manifests it.
And if the pain be sensual the eye drops hearty
tears which engender death, because proceeding
from the heart, they are caused by a disordinate
love distinct from the love of Me; for such love,
being disordinate and an offence to Me, receives
the meed of mortal pain and tears. It is true
that their guilt and grief are more or less heavy,
according to the measure of their disordinate
love. And these form that first class, who have
the tears of death, of whom I have spoken to
thee, and will speak again. Now, begin to
consider the tears which give the commencement of life, the tears, that is, of those who,
knowing their guilt, set to weeping for fear
of the penalty they have incurred.

"These are both hearty and sensual tears,
because the soul, not having yet arrived at
perfect hatred of its guilt on account of the
offence thereby done to Me, abandons it with
a hearty grief for the penalty which follows
the sin committed, while the eye weeps in
order to satisfy the grief of the heart.

"But the soul, exercising herself in virtue,
begins to lose her fear, knowing that fear alone
is not sufficient to give her eternal life, as I

have already told thee when speaking of the
second stage of the soul. And so she proceeds, with love, to know herself and My goodness in her, and begins to take hope in My
mercy in which her heart feels joy. Sorrow
for her grief, mingled with the joy of her hope
in My mercy, causes her eye to weep, which
tears issue from the very fountain of her heart.

"But, inasmuch as she has not yet arrived at
great perfection, she often drops sensual tears,
and if thou askest Me why, I reply : Because
the root of self-love is not sensual love, for that
has already been removed, as has been said, but
it is a spiritual love with which the soul desires
spiritual consolations or loves some creature
spiritually. (I have spoken to thee at length
regarding the imperfections of such souls.)
Wherefore, when such a soul is deprived of
the thing she loves, that is, internal or external
consolation, the internal being the consolation
received from Me, the external being that which
she had from the creature, and when temptations and the persecutions of men come on her,
her heart is full of grief. And, as soon as the
eye feels the grief and suffering of the heart, she
begins to weep with a tender and compassionate
sorrow, pitying herself with the spiritual compassion of self-love ; for her self-will is not yet
crushed and destroyed in everything, and in this
way she lets fall sensual tears—tears, that is,
of spiritual passion. But, growing, and exercising herself in the light of self-knowledge,

she conceives displeasure at herself and finally perfect self-hatred. From this she draws true knowledge of My goodness with a fire of love, and she begins to unite herself to Me, and to conform her will to Mine and so to feel joy and compassion. Joy in herself through the affection of love, and compassion for her neighbour, as I told thee in speaking of the third stage. Immediately her eye, wishing to satisfy the heart, cries with hearty love for Me and for her neighbour, grieving solely for My offence and her neighbour's loss, and not for any penalty or loss due to herself; for she does not think of herself, but only of rendering glory and praise to My Name, and, in an ecstasy of desire, she joyfully takes the food prepared for her on the table of the Holy Cross, thus conforming herself to the humble, patient, and immaculate Lamb, My only-begotten Son, of whom I made a Bridge, as I have said. Having thus sweetly travelled by that Bridge, following the doctrine of My sweet Truth, enduring with true and sweet patience every pain and trouble which I have permitted to be inflicted upon her for her salvation, having manfully received them all, not choosing them according to her own tastes, but accepting them according to Mine, and not only, as I said, enduring them with patience, but sustaining them with joy, she counts it glory to be persecuted for My Name's sake in whatever she may have to suffer. Then the soul arrives at such delight and tranquillity of mind that no tongue can tell it.

Having crossed the river by means of the Eternal Word, that is, by the doctrine of My only-begotten Son, and, having fixed the eye of her intellect on Me, the Sweet Supreme Truth, having seen the Truth, knows it; and knowing it, loves it. Drawing her affection after her intellect, she tastes My Eternal Deity, and she knows and sees the Divine nature united to your humanity.

"Then she reposes in Me, the Sea Pacific, and her heart is united to Me in love, as I told thee when speaking of the fourth and unitive state. When she thus feels Me, the Eternal Deity, her eyes let fall tears of sweetness, tears indeed of milk, nourishing the soul in true patience; an odoriferous ointment are these tears, shedding odours of great sweetness.

"Oh, best beloved daughter, how glorious is that soul who has indeed been able to pass from the stormy ocean to Me, the Sea Pacific, and in that Sea, which is Myself, the Supreme and Eternal Deity, to fill the pitcher of her heart. And her eye, the conduit of her heart, endeavours to satisfy her heart-pangs, and so sheds tears. This is the last stage in which the soul is blessed and sorrowful.

"Blessed she is through the union which she feels herself to have with Me, tasting the divine love; sorrowful through the offences which she sees done to My goodness and greatness, for she has seen and tasted the bitterness of this in her self-knowledge, by which self-knowledge, together with her knowledge of Me, she arrived at the final stage. Yet this sorrow is no impediment to the unitive state, which produces tears of great sweetness through self-knowledge, gained in love of the neighbour, in which exercise the soul discovers the plaint of My divine mercy, and grief at the offences caused to her neighbour, weeping with those who weep, and rejoicing with those who rejoice—that is, who live in My love. Over these the soul rejoices, seeing glory and praise rendered Me by My servants, so that the third kind of grief does not prevent the fourth, that is, the final grief belonging to the unitive state ; they rather give savour to each other, for, had not this last grief (in which the soul finds such union with Me), developed from the grief belonging to the third state of neighbourly love, it would not be perfect. Therefore it is necessary that the one should flavour the other, else the soul would come to a state of presumption, induced by the subtle breeze of love of her own reputation, and would fall at once, vomited from the heights to the depths. Therefore it is necessary to bear with others and practise continually love to one's neighbour, together with true knowledge of oneself.

"In this way will she feel the fire of My love in herself, because love of her neighbour is developed out of love of Me—that is, out of that learning which the soul obtained by knowing herself and My goodness in her. When, therefore, she sees herself to be ineffably loved by Me, she loves every rational creature with the

N

self-same love with which she sees herself to
be loved. And, for this reason, the soul that
knows Me immediately expands to the love of
her neighbour, because she sees that I love that
neighbour ineffably, and so, herself, loves the
object which she sees Me to have loved still
more. She further knows that she can be of
no use to Me and can in no way repay Me that
pure love with which she feels herself to be loved
by Me, and therefore endeavours to repay it
through the medium which I have given her,
namely, her neighbour, who is the medium
through which you can all serve Me. For, as
I have said to thee, you can perform all virtues
by means of your neighbour, I having given
you all creatures, in general and in particular,
according to the diverse graces each has received
from Me, to be ministered unto by you; you
should therefore love them with the same pure
love with which I have loved you. That pure
love cannot be returned directly to Me, because
I have loved you without being Myself loved,
and without any consideration of Myself whatsoever, for I loved you without being loved by
you—before you existed; it was, indeed, love
that moved Me to create you to My own image
and similitude. This love you cannot repay to
Me, but you can pay it to My rational creature,
loving your neighbour without being loved by
him and without consideration of your own
advantage, whether spiritual or temporal, but
loving him solely for the praise and glory

of My Name, because he has been loved by Me.

"Thus will you fulfil the commandment of the law, to love Me above everything, and your neighbour as yourselves.

"True indeed is it that this height cannot be reached without passing through the second stage, namely the second stage of union which becomes the third (and final) stage. Nor can it be preserved when it has been reached if the soul abandon the affection from which it has been developed, the affection to which the second class of tears belongs. It is therefore impossible to fulfil the law given by Me, the Eternal God, without fulfilling that of your neighbour, for these two laws are the feet of your affection by which the precepts and counsels are observed, which were given you, as I have told thee, by My Truth, Christ crucified. These two states united nourish your soul in virtue, making her to grow in the perfection of virtue and in the unitive state. Not that the other state is changed because this further state has been reached, for this further state does but increase the riches of grace in new and various gifts and admirable elevations of the mind, in the knowledge of the truth, as I said to thee, which, though it is mortal, appears immortal because the soul's perception of her own sensuality is mortified and her will is dead through the union which she has attained with Me.

"Oh, how sweet is the taste of this union to

the soul, for, in tasting it, she sees My secrets! Wherefore she often receives the spirit of prophecy, knowing the things of the future. This is the effect of My Goodness, but the humble soul should despise such things, not indeed in so far as they are given her by My love, but in so far as she desires them by reason of her appetite for consolation, considering herself unworthy of peace and quiet of mind, in order to nourish virtue within her soul. In such a case let her not remain in the second stage, but return to the valley of self-knowledge. I give her this light, My grace permitting, so that she may ever grow in virtue. For the soul is never so perfect in this life that she cannot attain to a higher perfection of love. My only-begotten Son, your Captain, was the only One who could increase in no perfection, because He was one thing with Me, and I with Him, wherefore His soul was blessed through union with the Divine nature. But do ye, His pilgrim-members, be ever ready to grow in greater perfection, not indeed to another stage, for as I have said, ye have now reached the last, but to that further grade of perfection in the last stage, which may please you by means of My Grace."

*How the four stages of the soul, to which belong the
five aforesaid states of tears, produce tears of
infinite value : and how God wishes to be served
as the Infinite, and not as anything finite.*

" These five states are like five principal canals
which are filled with abundant tears of infinite
value, all of which give life if they are disciplined
in virtue, as I have said to thee. Thou askest
how their value can be infinite. I do not say
that in this life your tears can become infinite,
but I call them infinite, on account of the infinite
desire of your soul from which they proceed. I
have already told thee how tears come from the
heart, and how the heart distributes them to the
eye, having gathered them in its own fiery desire.
As, when green wood is on the fire, the moisture
it contains groans on account of the heat, because
the wood is green, so does the heart, made green
again by the renovation of grace drawn into itself
among its self-love which dries up the soul, so
that fiery desire and tears are united. And inasmuch as desire is never ended, it is never satisfied
in this life, but the more the soul loves the less
she seems to herself to love. Thus is holy desire,
which is founded in love, exercised, and with this
desire the eye weeps. But when the soul is
separated from the body and has reached Me,
her End, she does not on that account abandon
desire, so as to no longer yearn for Me or love
her neighbour, for love has entered into her like
a woman bearing the fruits of all other virtues.

It is true that suffering is over and ended, as I have said to thee, for the soul that desires Me possesses Me in very truth, without any fear of ever losing that which she has so long desired; but, in this way, hunger is kept up, because those who are hungry are satisfied, and as soon as they are satisfied hunger again; in this way their satiety is without disgust, and their hunger without suffering, for, in Me, no perfection is wanting.

"Thus is your desire infinite, otherwise it would be worth nothing, nor would any virtue of yours have any life if you served Me with anything finite. For I, who am the Infinite God, wish to be served by you with infinite service, and the only infinite thing you possess is the affection and desire of your souls. In this sense I said that there were tears of infinite value, and this is true as regards their mode, of which I have spoken, namely, of the infinite desire which is united to the tears. When the soul leaves the body the tears remain behind, but the affection of love has drawn to itself the fruit of the tears, and consumed it, as happens in the case of the water in your furnace. The water has not really been taken out of the furnace, but the heat of the fire has consumed it and drawn it into itself. Thus the soul, having arrived at tasting the fire of My divine charity, and having passed from this life in a state of love towards Me and her neighbour, having further possessed that unitive love which caused her tears to fall, does not cease to offer Me her blessed desires, tearful indeed, though without pain or physical weeping, for physical tears have evaporated in the furnace, becoming tears of fire of the Holy Spirit. Thou seest then how tears are infinite, how, as regards the tears shed in this life only, no tongue can tell what different sorrows may cause them. I have now told thee the difference between four of these states of tears."

Of the fruit of worldly men's tears.

"It remains for Me to tell thee of the fruit produced by tears shed with desire, and received into the soul. But first will I speak to thee of that first class of men whom I mentioned at the beginning of this My discourse ; those, that is, who live miserably in the world, making a god of created things and of their own sensuality, from which comes damage to their body and soul. I said to thee that every tear proceeded from the heart, and this is the truth, for the heart grieves in proportion to the love it feels. So worldly men weep when their heart feels pain, that is, when they are deprived of something which they loved.

"But many and diverse are their complainings. Dost thou know how many? There are as many as there exist different loves. And inasmuch as the root of self-love is corrupt, everything that grows from it is corrupt also. Self-love is a tree on which grow nothing but fruits of death, putrid flowers, stained leaves, branches bowed down, and

struck by various winds. This is the tree of the
soul. For ye are all trees of love, and without
love ye cannot live, for ye have been made by
Me for love. The soul who lives virtuously,
places the root of her tree in the valley of true
humility; but those who live thus miserably are
planted on the mountain of pride, whence it
follows that since the root of the tree is badly
planted, the tree can bear no fruits of life but
only of death. Their fruits are their actions,
which are all poisoned by many and diverse kinds
of sin, and if they should produce some good
fruit among their actions, even it will be spoilt
by the foulness of its root, for no good actions
done by a soul in mortal sin are of value for
eternal life, for they are not done in grace. Let
not, however, such a soul abandon on this
account its good works, for every good deed
is rewarded, and every evil deed punished. A
good action performed out of a state of grace
is not sufficient to merit eternal life, as has been
said, but My Justice, My Divine Goodness,
grants an incomplete reward, imperfect as the
action which obtains it. Often such a man is
rewarded in temporal matters; sometimes I give
him more time in which to repent, as I have
already said to thee in another place. This also
will I sometimes do, I grant him the life of
grace by means of My servants who are pleasing
and acceptable to Me. I acted in this way with
My glorious apostle Paul, who abandoned his
infidelity, and the persecutions he directed against

the Christians, at the prayer of St. Stephen.   See
truly, therefore, that, in whatever state a man
may be, he should never stop doing good.

"I said to thee that the flowers of this tree
were putrid, and so in truth they are. Its flowers
are the stinking thoughts of the heart, displeasing
to Me, and full of hatred and unkindness towards
their neighbour.   So if a man be a thief, he robs
Me of honour, and takes it himself.   This flower
stinks less than that of false judgment, which is
of two kinds.   The first with regard to Me, by
which men judge My secret judgments, gauging
falsely all My mysteries, that is, judging that
which I did in love, to have been done in hatred ;
that which I did in truth to have been done in
falsehood ; that which I give them for life, to
have been given them for death.   They condemn
and judge everything according to their weak
intellect ; for they have blinded the eye of their
intellect with sensual self-love, and hidden the
pupil of the most holy Faith, which they will not
allow to see or know the Truth.   The second
kind of false judgment is directed against a man's
neighbour, from which often come many evils,
because the wretched man wishes to set himself
up as the judge of the affections and heart of
other rational creatures, when he does not yet
know himself.   And, for an action which he may
see, or for a word he may hear, he will judge the
affection of the heart.   My servants always judge
well, because they are founded on Me, the Supreme
Good ; but such as these always judge badly, for

they are founded on evil. Such critics as these cause hatreds, murders, unhappinesses of all kinds to their neighbours, and remove themselves far away from the love of My servants' virtue.

"Truly these fruits follow the leaves, which are the words which issue from their mouth in insult to Me and the Blood of My only-begotten Son, and in hatred to their neighbours. And they think of nothing else but cursing and condemning My works, and blaspheming and saying evil of every rational creature, according as their judgment may suggest to them. The unfortunate creatures do not remember that the tongue is made only to give honour to Me, and to confess sins, and to be used in love of virtue, and for the salvation of the neighbour. These are the stained leaves of that most miserable fault, because the heart from which they proceeded was not clean, but all spotted with duplicity and misery. How much danger, apart from the spiritual privation of grace to the soul, of temporal loss may not occur! For ye have all heard and seen how, through words alone, have come revolutions of states, and destructions of cities, and many homicides and other evils, a word having entered the heart of the listener, and having passed through a space not large enough for a knife.

"I say that this tree has seven branches drooping to the earth, on which grow the flowers and leaves in the way I have told you. These branches are the seven mortal sins which are full of many and diverse wickednesses, contained in the roots and trunk of self-love and of pride, which first made both branches and flowers of many thoughts, the leaves of words, and the fruits of wicked deeds. They stand drooping to the earth because the branches of mortal sin can turn no other way than to the earth, the fragile disordinate substance of the world. Do not marvel, they can turn no way but that in which they can be fed by the earth; for their hunger is insatiable, and the earth is unable to satisfy them. They are insatiable and unbearable to themselves, and it is conformable to their state that they should always be unquiet, longing and desiring that thing which they have to satiety. This is the reason why such satiety cannot content them, because they (who are infinite in their being) are always desiring something finite; because their being will never end, though their life to grace ends when they commit mortal sin.

"Man is placed above all creatures, and not beneath them, and he cannot be satisfied or content except in something greater than himself. Greater than himself there is nothing but Myself, the Eternal God. Therefore I alone can satisfy him, and, because he is deprived of this satisfaction by his guilt, he remains in continual torment and pain. Weeping follows pain, and when he begins to weep the wind strikes the tree of self-love, which he has made the principle of all his being."

How this devout soul, thanking God for His explana-
tion of the above-mentioned states of tears, makes
three petitions.

Then this soul, eager with the greatness of her
desire, through the sweetness of the explanation
and satisfaction which she had received from the
Truth, concerning the state of tears, said as one
enamoured—"Thanks, thanks be to Thee, Supreme and Eternal Father, Satisfier of holy desires,
and Lover of our Salvation, who, through Thy
Love, didst give us Love Himself, in the time
of our warfare with Thee, in the person of Thy
only-begotten Son.   By this abyss of Thy fiery
Love, I beg of Thee grace and mercy that I may
come to Thee truly in the light, and not flee far
in darkness away from Thy doctrine, of which
Thou hast clearly demonstrated to me the truth,
so that, by the light thereof, I perceive two other
points, concerning which I fear that they are, or
may become, stumbling-blocks to me.   I beg,
Eternal Father, that, before I leave the subject
of these states of tears, Thou wouldst explain
these points also to me.   The first is—when
a person desirous of serving Thee, comes to me,
or to some other servant of Thine to ask for
counsel, how should I teach him?   I know,
Sweet and Eternal God, that Thou didst reply
above to this question—'I am He who takes
delight in few words and many deeds.'   Nevertheless, if it please Thy Goodness to grant me
a few more words on the subject, it will cause

me the greatest pleasure. And also, if on some
occasion, when I am praying for Thy creatures,
and in particular for Thy servants, and I seem
to see the subjects of my prayer, in one I find
(in the course of my prayer) a well-disposed mind,
a soul rejoicing in Thee; and in another, as it
might seem to me, a mind full of darkness;
have I the right, O Eternal Father, to judge the
one soul to be in light, and the other in darkness? Or, supposing I should see that the one
lives in great penance, and the other does not,
should I be right to judge that he who does the
greater penance has the higher perfection? I
pray Thee, so that I may not be deceived through
my limited vision, that Thou wouldst declare to
me in detail, what Thou hast already said in
general on this matter. The second request I
have to make is, that Thou wilt explain further
to me about the sign which Thou didst say the
soul received on being visited by Thee—the sign
which revealed Thy Presence. If I remember
well, oh, Eternal Truth, Thou didst say that
the soul remained in joy and courageous virtue.
I would fain know whether this joy can consist
with the delusion of the passion of spiritual self-
love; for if it were so, I would humbly confine
myself to the sign of virtue. These are the
things which I beg Thee to tell me, so that I
may serve Thee and my neighbour in truth, and
not fall into false judgment concerning Thy
creatures and servants. For it seems to me
that the habit of judging keeps the soul far

from Thee, so I do not wish to fall into this
snare."

*How the light of reason is necessary to every soul that
    wishes to serve God in truth ; and first of the
    light of reason in general.*

Then the Eternal God, delighting in the
thirst and hunger of that soul, and in the purity
of her heart, and the desire with which she longed
to serve Him, turned the eye of His benignity
and mercy upon her, saying—"Oh, best-beloved,
dearest and sweetest daughter, my spouse ! rise
out of thyself, and open the eye of thy intellect
to see Me, the Infinite Goodness, and the ineffable love which I have towards thee and My
other servants.   And open the ear of the desire
which thou feelest towards Me, and remember,
that if thou dost not see, thou canst not hear,
that is to say, that the soul that does not see into
My Truth with the eye of her intellect, cannot
hear or know My Truth, wherefore in order that
thou mayest the better know it, rise above the
feelings of thy senses.

"And I, who take delight in thy request, will
satisfy thy demand.   Not that thou canst increase My delight, for I am the cause of thee and
of thy increase ; not those of Mine.   Yet the
very pleasure that I take in the work of My own
hands causes Me delight."

Then that soul obeyed and rose out of herself,
in order to learn the true solution of her diffi-

culty. And the Eternal God said to her, "In order that thou mayest the better understand what I shall say to thee, I shall revert to the beginning of thy request concerning the three lights which issue from Me, the True Light. The first is a general light dwelling in those who live in ordinary charity. (I shall repeat to thee here many things concerning these lights, which I have already told thee, in spite of My having done so, in order that thy creeping intelligence may better understand that which thou wishest to know.) The other two lights dwell in those who, having abandoned the world, desire perfection. Besides this I will explain to thee thy request, telling thee in great detail that which I have already pointed out to thee in general. Thou knowest, as I have told thee, that, without the light, no one can walk in the truth, that is, without the light of reason, which light of reason you draw from Me the True Light, by means of the eye of thy intellect and the light of faith which I have given you in holy baptism, though you may have lost it by your own defects. For, in baptism, and through the mediation of the Blood of My only-begotten Son, you have received the form of faith; which faith you exercise in virtue by the light of reason, which gives you life and causes you to walk in the path of truth, and, by its means, to arrive at Me, the True Light, for, without it, you would plunge into darkness.

"It is necessary for you to have two lights

derived from this primary light, and to these two I will also add a third. The first lightens you all to know the transitory nature of the things of the world, all of which pass like the wind. But this you cannot know thoroughly, unless you first recognise your own fragility, how strong is your inclination, through the law of perversity with which your members are bound, to rebel against Me, your Creator (not that by this law any man can be constrained to commit any, even the smallest sin, against his will, but that this law of perversity fights lustily against the spirit). I did not impose this law upon you, in order that My rational creature should be conquered by it, but in order that he should prove and increase the virtue of his soul, because virtue cannot be proved, except by its contrary. Sensuality is contrary to the spirit, and yet, by means of sensuality, the soul is able to prove the love which she has for Me, her Creator. How does she prove it? When, with anger and displeasure, she rises against herself. This law has also been imposed in order to preserve the soul in true humility. Wherefore thou seest that, while I created the soul to Mine own image and similitude, placing her in such dignity and beauty, I caused her to be accompanied by the vilest of all things, imposing on her the law of perversity, imprisoning her in a body, formed of the vilest substance of the earth, so that, seeing in what her true beauty consisted, she should not raise her head in pride against Me. Wherefore, to one who possesses this light, the fragility of his body is a cause of humiliation to the soul, and is in no way matter for pride, but rather for true and perfect humility. So that this law does not constrain you to any sin by its strivings, but supplies a reason to make you know yourselves and the instability of the world. This should be seen by the eye of the intellect, with light of the holy faith, of which I said to thee that it was the pupil of the eye. This is that light which is necessary in general to every rational creature, whatever may be his condition, who wishes to participate in the life of grace, in the fruit of the Blood of the immaculate Lamb. This is the ordinary light, that is, the light which all persons must possess, as has been said, for, without it, the soul would be in a state of damnation. And, for this reason, because the soul, being without the light, is not in a state of grace, inasmuch as, not having the light, she does not know the evil of her sin or its cause, and therefore cannot avoid or hate it.

"And similarly if the soul know not good, and the reason of good, that is to say virtue, she cannot love or desire either Me, who am the Essential Good, or virtue, which I have given you as an instrument and means for you to receive My grace, and Myself the True Good. See then how necessary is this light, for your sins consist in nothing else than in loving that which I hate, and in hating that which I love. I love virtue and hate vice ; he who loves vice and hates virtue offends Me, and is deprived of My grace. Such a one walks as if blind, for he knows not the cause of vice, that is, his sensual self-love, nor does he hate himself on account of it; he is ignorant of vice and of the evil which follows it: he is ignorant of virtue and of Me, who am the cause of his obtaining life-giving virtue; he is ignorant of his own dignity, which he should maintain by advancing to grace, by means of virtue. See, therefore, how his ignorance is the cause of all his evil, and how thou also needest this light, as has been said."

Of those who have placed their desire rather in the mortification of the body than in the destruction of their own will; and of the second light, more perfect than the former general one.

"When the soul has arrived at the attainment of the general light, of which I have spoken, she should not remain contented, because, as long as you are pilgrims in this life, you are capable of growth, and he who does not go forward, by that very fact, is turning back. She should either grow in the general light, which she has acquired through My Grace, or anxiously strive to attain to the second and perfect light, leaving the imperfect and reaching the perfect. For, if the soul truly have light, she will wish to arrive at perfection. In this second perfect light are to be found two kinds of perfection; for they may be called perfect who have abandoned the general

way of living of the world. One perfection is
that of those who give themselves up wholly
to the castigation of the body, doing great and
severe penance. These, in order that their
sensuality may not rebel against their reason,
have placed their desire rather in the mortification
of the body than in the destruction of their self-
will, as I have explained to thee in another place.
These feed their souls at the table of penance,
and are good and perfect, if their penance be
illuminated by discretion, and founded on Me,
if, that is to say, they act with true knowledge
of themselves and of Me, with great humility, and
wholly conformed to the judgment of My Will,
and not to that of the will of man. But, if they
were not thus clothed with My Will, in true
humility, they would often offend against their
own perfection, esteeming themselves the judges
of those who do not walk in the same path.
Knowest thou why this would happen to them?
Because they have placed all their labour and
desire in the mortification of the body, rather
than in the destruction of their own will. Such
as these wish always to choose their own times,
and places, and consolations, after their own
fashion, and also the persecutions of the world
and of the Devil, as I have narrated to thee in
speaking of the second state of perfection.

" They say, cheating themselves with the
delusion of their own self-will, which I have
already called their spiritual self-will, ' I wish
to have that consolation, and not these battles,

or these temptations of the Devil, not, indeed, for my own pleasure, but in order to please God the more, and in order to retain Him the more in my soul through grace; because it seems to me that I should possess Him more, and serve Him better in that way than in this.' And this is the way the soul often falls into trouble, and becomes tedious and insupportable to herself; thus injuring her own perfection; yet she does not perceive it, nor that, within her, lurks the stench of pride, and there she lies. Now, if the soul were not in this condition, but were truly humble and not presumptuous, she would be illuminated to see that I, the Primary and Sweet Truth, grant condition, and time, and place, and consolations, and tribulations as they may be needed for your salvation, and to complete the perfection to which I have elected the soul. And she would see that I give everything through love, and that therefore, with love and reverence, should she receive everything, which is what the souls in the second state do, and, by doing so, arrive at the third state. Of whom I will now speak to thee, explaining to thee the nature of these two states which stand in the most perfect light."

*Of the third and most perfect state, and of reason, and
of the works done by the soul who has arrived
at this light. And of a beautiful vision which
this devout soul once received, in which the
method of arriving at perfect purity is fully
treated, and the means to avoid judging our
neighbour is spoken of.*

" Those who belong to the third state, which
immediately follows the last, having arrived at
this glorious light, are perfect in every condition
in which they may be, and receive every event
which I permit to happen to them with due
reverence, as I have mentioned to thee when
speaking of the third and unitive state of the
soul. These deem themselves worthy of the
troubles and stumbling-blocks caused them by
the world, and of the privation of their own
consolation, and indeed of whatever circumstance
happens to them. And inasmuch as they deem
themselves worthy of trouble, so also do they
deem themselves unworthy of the fruit which
they receive after their trouble. They have
known and tasted in the light My Eternal Will,
which wishes naught else but your good, and
gives and permits these troubles in order that
you should be sanctified in Me. Wherefore the
soul having known My Will, clothes herself with
it, and fixes her attention on nothing else except
seeing in what way she can preserve and increase
her perfection to the glory and praise of My
Name, opening the eye of her intellect and

fixing it in the light of faith upon Christ crucified, My only-begotten Son, loving and following His doctrine, which is the rule of the road
for perfect and imperfect alike. And see, how
My Truth, the Lamb, who became enamoured
of her when He saw her, gives the soul the
doctrine of perfection. She knows what this
perfection is, having seen it practised by the
sweet and amorous Word, My only-begotten
Son, who was fed at the table of holy desire,
seeking the honour of Me, the Eternal Father,
and your salvation. And, inflamed with this
desire, He ran, with great eagerness, to the
shameful death of the Cross, and accomplished
the obedience which was imposed on Him by
Me, His Father, not shunning labours or insults
or withdrawing on account of your ingratitude
or ignorance of so great a benefit, or because of
the persecutions of the Jews, or on account of
the insults, derision, grumbling, and shouting of
the people. But all this He passed through like
the true Captain and Knight that He was, whom
I had placed on the battle-field to deliver you
from the hands of the Devil, so that you might
be free, and drawn out of the most terrible
slavery in which you could ever be, and also to
teach you His road, His doctrine, and His rule,
so that you might open the Door of Me, Eternal
Life, with the key of His precious Blood, shed
with such fire of love, with such hatred of your
sins. It was as if the sweet and amorous Word,
My Son, should have said to you: 'Behold, I

have made the road, and opened the door with
My Blood.' Do not you then be negligent to
follow, laying yourselves down to rest in self-
love and ignorance of the road, presuming to
choose to serve Me in your own way, instead of
in the way which I have made straight for you
by means of My Truth, the Incarnate Word,
and built up with His Blood. Rise up then,
promptly, and follow Him, for no one can reach
Me, the Father, if not by Him; He is the Way
and the Door by which you must enter into Me,
the Sea Pacific.

"When therefore the soul has arrived at
seeing, knowing, and tasting, in its full sweetness, this light, she runs, as one enamoured and
inflamed with love, to the table of holy desire;
she does not see herself in herself, seeking her
own consolation either spiritual or temporal, but,
like one who has placed his all in this light and
knowledge, and has destroyed his own will, she
shuns no labour from whatever source it comes,
but rather enduring the troubles, the insults, the
temptations of the Devil, and the murmurings of
men, eats at the table of the most holy Cross, the
food of the honour of Me, the Eternal God, and
of the salvation of souls; seeking no reward,
either from Me or from creatures, because she is
stripped of mercenary love, that is of love for
Me based on interested motives, and is clothed
in perfect light, loving Me in perfect purity,
with no other regard than for the praise and
glory of My Name, serving neither Me for her

own delight, nor her neighbour for her own profit, but purely through love alone. Such as these have lost themselves, and have stripped themselves of the Old Man, that is of their own sensuality, and, having clothed themselves with the New Man, the sweet Christ Jesus, My Truth, follow Him manfully. These are they who sit at the table of holy desire, having been more anxious to slay their own will than to slay and mortify their own body. They have indeed mortified their body, though not as an end in itself, but as a means which helps them to stay their own will, as I said to thee when explaining that sentence that I wished few words and many deeds, and so ought you to do. Their principal desire should be to slay their own will, so that it may not seek or wish anything else than to follow My sweet Truth, Christ crucified, seeking the honour and glory of My Name and the salvation of souls. Those who are in this sweet light know it, and remain constantly in peace and quiet, and no one scandalises them, for they have cut away that thing by which stumbling-blocks are caused, namely their own will. And all the persecutions, with which the world and the Devil can attack them, slide under their feet, standing, as they do, in the waters of many tribulations and temptations, and do not hurt them, for they remain attached to Me by the umbilical cord of fiery desire. Such a man rejoices in everything, nor does he make himself judge of My servants, or of any rational creature, but rejoices in every condition and in every manner of holiness which he sees, saying: 'Thanks be to Thee, Eternal Father, who hast in Thy House many mansions.' And he rejoices more in the different ways of holiness which he sees, than if he were to see all travelling by one road, because, in this way, he perceives the greatness of My Goodness become more manifest, and thus, rejoicing draws from all the fragrance of the rose. And not only in the case of good, but even when he sees something evidently sinful, he does not fall into judgment, but rather into true and holy compassion, interceding with Me for sinners and saying, with perfect humility: 'To-day it is thy turn, and to-morrow it will be mine unless the Divine Grace preserve me.'

"Enamour thyself, dearest daughter, of this sweet and excellent state, and gaze at those who run in this glorious light and holiness, for they have holy minds, and eat at the table of holy desire, and, with the light, have arrived at feeding on the food of souls, that is, the honour of Me, the Eternal Father, being clothed with burning love in the sweet garment of My Lamb, My only-begotten Son, namely His doctrine. These do not lose their time in passing false judgments, either on My servants or the servants of the world, and they are never scandalised by any murmurings of men, either for their own sake or that of others. That is to say, in their own case they are content to endure anything for My Name's sake; and when an injury is done to some one else, they endure it with compassion of this injured neighbour, and without murmuring against him who caused the injury, or him who received it, because their love is not disordinate, but has been ordered in Me, the Eternal God.

"And, since their love is so ordered, these souls, my dearest daughter, never take offence from those they love, nor from any rational creature, their will being dead and not alive, wherefore they never assume the right to judge the will of men, but only the will of My Clemency. These observe the doctrine which, as thou knowest, was given thee by My Truth at the beginning of thy life, when thou wast thinking in what way thou couldst arrive at perfect purity, and wast praying to Me with a great desire of doing so. Thou knowest what was replied to thee, while thou wast asleep, concerning this holy desire, and that the words resounded not only in thy mind, but also in thine ear. So much so, that, if thou rememberest truly, thou didst return to thy waking body, when My Truth said, 'Wilt thou arrive at perfect purity, and be freed from stumbling-blocks, so that thy mind may not be scandalised by anything?' Unite thyself always to Me by the affection of love, for I am the Supreme and Eternal Purity. I am that Fire which purifies the soul, and the closer the soul is to Me, the purer she becomes, and the further she is from Me, the more does her purity leave her; which is the reason why men of the world fall into such iniquities, for they are separated from Me, while the soul, who, without any medium, unites herself directly to Me, participates in My Purity. Another thing is necessary for thee to arrive at this union and purity, namely, that thou shouldest never judge the will of man in anything that thou mayest see done or said by any creature whatsoever, either to thyself or to others. My will alone shouldst thou consider, both in them and in thyself. And, if thou shouldest see evident sins or defects, draw out of those thorns the rose, that is to say, offer them to Me, with holy compassion. In the case of injuries done to thyself, judge that My will permits this in order to prove virtue in thyself, and in My other servants, esteeming that he who acts thus does so as the instrument of My will; perceiving, moreover, that such apparent sinners may frequently have a good intention, for no one can judge the secrets of the heart of man. That which thou dost not see thou shouldst not judge in thy mind, even though it may externally be open mortal sin, seeing nothing in others, but My will, not in order to judge, but, as has been said, with holy compassion. In this way thou wilt arrive at perfect purity, because acting thus, thy mind will not be scandalised, either in Me or in thy neighbour. Otherwise thou fallest into contempt of thy neighbour, if thou judgest his evil will towards thee, instead of My will acting in him. Such contempt and scandal separates the soul from Me, and prevents perfection, and, in some cases, deprives a man of grace, more or less according to the gravity of his contempt, and the hatred which his judgment has conceived against his neighbour.

"A different reward is received by the soul who perceives only My will, which, as has been said, wishes nothing else but your good; so that everything which I give or permit to happen to you, I give so that you may arrive at the end for which I created you. And because the soul remains always in the love of her neighbour, she remains always in Mine, and thus remains united to Me. Wherefore, in order to arrive at purity, thou must entreat Me to do three things — to grant thee to be united to Me by the affection of love, retaining in thy memory the benefits thou hast received from Me; and with the eye of thy intellect to see the affection of My love, with which I love you inestimably; and in the will of others to discern My will only, and not their evil will, for I am their Judge, not thou, and, in doing this, thou wilt arrive at all perfection.

"This was the doctrine given to thee by My Truth, if thou rememberest well. Now I tell thee, dearest daughter, that such as these, who have learnt this doctrine, taste the earnest of eternal life in this life; and, if thou hast well retained this doctrine, thou wilt not fall into the snares of the Devil, because thou wilt recognise them in the case about which thou hast asked Me.

"But, nevertheless, in order to satisfy thy

desire more clearly, I will tell thee and show thee how men should never discern by judgment, but with holy compassion."

In what way they, who stand in the above-mentioned third most perfect light, receive the earnest of eternal life in this life.

" Why did I say to thee that they received the earnest of eternal life? I say that they receive the earnest-money, but not the full payment, because they wait to receive it in Me, the Eternal Life, where they have life without death, and satiety without disgust, and hunger without pain, for from that divine hunger pain is far away, and though they have what they desire, disgust is far from satiety, for I am the flawless Food of Life. It is true that, in this life, they receive the earnest, and taste it in this way, namely that the soul begins to hunger for the honour of the Eternal God, and for the food of the salvation of other souls, and being hungry, she eats, that is to say, nourishes herself with love of her neighbour, which causes her hunger and desire, for the love of the neighbour is a food which never satiates him who feeds on it, the eater being insatiable and always remains hungry. So this earnest-money is a commencement of a guarantee which is given to man, in virtue of which he expects one day to receive his payment, not through the perfection of the earnest-money in itself, but through faith, through the certitude which he has of reaching the completion of his being and receiving his payment. Wherefore this enamoured soul, clothed in My Truth, having already received in this life the earnest of My love, and of her neighbour's, is not yet perfect, but expects perfection in immortal life. I say that this earnest is not perfect, because the soul who tastes it has not, as yet, the perfection which would prevent her feeling pain in herself, or in others. In herself, through the offence done to Me by the law of perversity which is bound in her members and struggles against the spirit, and in others by the offence of her neighbour. She has indeed, in a sense, a perfect grace, but not that perfection of My saints, who have arrived at Me, Eternal Life, for, as has been said, their desires are without suffering, and yours are not. These servants of Mine, as I have said to thee in another place, who nourish themselves at this table of holy desire, are blessed and full of grief, even as My only-begotten Son was, on the wood of the holy Cross, because, while His flesh was in grief and torment, His soul was blessed through its union with the divine nature. In like manner these are blessed by the union of their holy desire towards Me, clothed, as has been said, in My sweet Will, and they are full of grief through compassion for their neighbour, and because they afflict their own self-love, depriving it of sensual delights and consolations."

*How this soul, rendering thanks to God, humiliates
herself; then she prays for the whole world and
particularly for the mystical body of the holy
Church, and for her spiritual children, and for
the two fathers of her soul; and, after these
things, she asks to hear something about the
defects of the ministers of the holy Church.*

Then that soul, as if, in truth, inebriated,
seemed beside herself, as if the feelings of the
body were alienated through the union of love
which she had made with her Creator, and as
if, in elevation of mind, she had gazed into
the eternal truth with the eye of her intellect,
and, having recognised the truth, had become
enamoured of it, and said, "Oh! Supreme and
Eternal Goodness of God, who am I, miserable
one, that Thou, Supreme and Eternal Father,
hast manifested to me Thy Truth, and the hidden
deceits of the Devil, and the deceitfulness of
personal feeling, so that I, and others in this
life of pilgrimage, may know how to avoid
being deceived by the Devil or ourselves! What
moved thee to do it? Love, because Thou
lovedst me, without my having loved Thee.
Oh, Fire of Love! Thanks, thanks be to
Thee, Eternal Father! I am imperfect and
full of darkness, and Thou, Perfection and
Light, hast shown to me perfection, and the
resplendent way of the doctrine of Thy only-
begotten Son. I was dead, and Thou hast
brought me to life. I was sick, and Thou

hast given me medicine, and not only the medicine of the Blood which Thou gavest for the diseased human race in the person of Thy Son, but also a medicine against a secret infirmity that I knew not of, in this precept that, in no way, can I judge any rational creature, and particularly Thy servants, upon whom ofttimes I, as one blind and sick with this infirmity, passed judgment under the pretext of Thy honour and the salvation of souls. Wherefore, I thank Thee, Supreme and Eternal Good, that, in the manifesting of Thy truth and the deceitfulness of the Devil, and our own passions, Thou hast made me know my infirmity. Wherefore I beseech Thee, through grace and mercy, that, from to-day henceforward, I may never again wander from the path of Thy doctrine, given by Thy goodness to me and to whoever wishes to follow it, because without Thee is nothing done. To Thee, then, Eternal Father, do I have recourse and flee, and I do not beseech Thee for myself alone, Father, but for the whole world, and particularly for the mystical body of the holy Church, that this truth given to me, miserable one, by Thee, Eternal Truth, may shine in Thy ministers; and also I beseech Thee especially for all those whom Thou hast given me, and whom Thou hast made one thing with me, and whom I love with a particular love, because they will be my refreshment to the glory and praise of Thy Name, when I see them running on this sweet and straight road, pure, and dead to their own will and opinion, and without any passing judgment on their neighbour, or causing him any scandal or murmuring. And I pray Thee, Sweetest Love, that not one of them may be taken from me by the hand of the infernal Devil, so that at last they may arrive at Thee, their End, Eternal Father.

"Also I make another petition to Thee for my two fathers, the supports whom Thou hast placed on the earth to guard and instruct me, miserable infirm one, from the beginning of my conversion until now, that Thou unite them, and of two bodies make one soul, and that they attend to nothing else than to complete in themselves, and in the mysteries that Thou hast placed in their hands, the glory and praise of Thy Name, and the salvation of souls, and that I, an unworthy and miserable slave, and no daughter, may behave to them with due reverence and holy fear, for love of Thee, in a way that will be to Thine honour, and their peace and quiet, and to the edification of the neighbour. I now know for certain, Eternal Truth, that Thou wilt not despise the desire of the petitions that I have made to Thee, because I know, from seeing what it has pleased Thee to manifest, and still more from proof, that Thou art the Acceptor of holy desires. I, Thy unworthy servant, will strive, according as Thou wilt give me grace, to observe Thy commandments and Thy doctrine. Now, O Eternal Father, I remember a word which thou didst say to me in speaking of the ministers of the holy Church, to the effect that

P

Thou wouldst speak to me more distinctly, in some other place, of the sins which they commit to-day; wherefore if it should please Thy goodness to tell me aught of this matter, I will gladly hear it, so as to have material for increasing my grief, compassion, and anxious desire for their salvation; for I remember that Thou didst say, that, on account of the endurance and tears, the grief, and sweat and prayers of Thy servants, Thou wouldst reform the holy Church, and comfort her with good and holy pastors. I ask Thee this in order that these sentiments may increase in me."

How God renders this soul attentive to prayer, replying to one of the above-mentioned petitions.

Then the Eternal God, turning the eye of His mercy upon this soul, not despising her desire, but granting her requests, proceeded to satisfy the last petition, which she had made concerning His promise, saying, "Oh! best beloved and dearest daughter, I will fulfil thy desire in this request, in order that, on thy side, thou mayest not sin through ignorance or negligence; for a fault of thine would be more serious and worthy of graver reproof now than before, because thou hast learnt more of My truth; wherefore apply thyself attentively to pray for all rational creatures, for the mystical body of the holy Church, and for those friends whom I have given thee, whom thou lovest with particular love, and be

careful not to be negligent in giving them the
benefit of thy prayers, and the example of thy
life, and the teaching of thy words, reproving
vice and encouraging virtue according to thy
power.

"Concerning the supports which I have given
thee, of whom thou didst speak to Me, know
that thou art, in truth, a means by which they
may each receive, according to their needs and
fitness.   And as I, thy Creator, grant thee the
opportunity, for without Me thou canst do
nothing, I will fulfil thy desires, but do not
thou fail, or they either, in your hope in Me.
My Providence will never fail you, and every
man, if he be humble, shall receive that which
he is fit to receive ; and every minister, that
which I have given him to administer, each in
his own way, according to what he has received
and will receive from My goodness."

*Of the dignity of the priest ; and of the Sacrament of
the Body of Christ ; and of worthy and unworthy communicants.*

"Now I will reply to that which thou didst
ask Me concerning the ministers of the holy
Church, and, in order that thou mayest the
better understand the truth, open the eye of
thy intellect, and look at their excellence and
the dignity in which I have placed them.   And,
since one thing is better known by means of
contrast with its contrary, I will show thee the

dignity of those who use virtuously the treasure
I have placed in their hands; and, in this way,
thou wilt the better see the misery of those who
to-day are suckled at the breast of My Spouse."
Then this soul obediently contemplated the truth,
in which she saw virtue resplendent in those
who truly taste it.   Then said the Eternal God :
" I will first, dearest daughter, speak to thee of
the dignity of priests, having placed them where
they are through My Goodness, over and above
the general love which I have had to My creatures, creating you in My image and similitude
and re-creating you all to the life of grace in
the Blood of My only-begotten Son, whence you
have arrived at such excellence, through the
union which I made of My Deity with human
nature; so that in this you have greater dignity
and excellence than the angels, for I took your
human nature and not that of the angels.
Wherefore, as I have said to you, I, God, have
become man, and man has become God by the
union of My Divine Nature with your human
nature.   This greatness is given in general to
all rational creatures, but, among these I have
especially chosen My ministers for the sake of
your salvation, so that, through them, the Blood
of the humble and immaculate Lamb, My only-
begotten Son, may be administered to you.   To
them have I given the Sun to administer, giving
them the light of science and the heat of Divine
Love, united together in the colour of the Body
and Blood of My Son, whose Body is a Sun,

because He is one thing with Me, the True Sun, in such a way that He cannot be separated or divided from Me, as in the case of the natural sun, in which heat and light cannot be separated, so perfect is their union; for, the sun, never leaving its orbit, lights the whole world and warms whoever wishes to be warmed by it, and is not defiled by any impurity on which it shines, for its light and heat and colour are united.

"So this Word, My Son, with His most sweet Blood, is one Sun, all God and all man, because He is one thing with Me and I with Him. My power is not separated from His wisdom, nor the fiery heat of the Holy Spirit from Me, the Father, or from Him, the Son; for He is one thing with us, the Holy Spirit proceeding from the Father and the Son, and We together forming one and the same Sun; that is to say, I, the Eternal God, am that Sun whence have proceeded the Son and the Holy Spirit. To the Holy Spirit is attributed fire and to the Son wisdom, by which wisdom My ministers receive the light of grace, so that they may administer this light to others, with gratitude for the benefits received from Me, the Eternal Father, following the doctrine of the Eternal Wisdom, My only-begotten Son. This is that Light, which has the colour of your humanity, colour and light being closely united. Thus was the light of My Divinity united to the colour of your humanity, which colour shone brightly when it became perfect through its union with the Divine nature, and, by this means of the Incarnate Word mixed with the Light of My Divine nature and the fiery heat of the Holy Spirit, have ye received the Light. Whom have I entrusted with its administration?

"My ministers in the mystical body of the holy Church, so that you may have life, receiving His Body in food and His Blood in drink. I have said to thee that this Body is, as it were, a Sun. Wherefore, you cannot receive the Body without the Blood, or the Blood or the Body without the Soul of the Incarnate Word; nor the Soul, nor the Body, without the Divinity of Me, the Eternal God, because none of these can be separated from each other, as I said to thee in another place that the Divine nature never left the human nature, either by death or from any other cause. So that you receive the whole Divine Essence in that most Sweet Sacrament concealed under the whiteness of the bread; for as the sun cannot be divided into light, heat, and colour, the whole of God and the whole of man cannot be separated under the white mantle of the host; for even if the host should be divided into a million particles (if it were possible) in each particle should I be present, whole God and whole Man. When you break a mirror the reflection to be seen in it is not broken; similarly, when the host is divided God and man are not divided, but remain in each particle. Nor is the Sacrament diminished in itself, except as far as may be in the following example.

"If thou hast a light, and the whole world should come to thee in order to take light from it—the light itself does not diminish—and yet each person has it all. It is true that every one participates more or less in this light, according to the substance into which each one receives the fire. I will develop this metaphor further that thou mayest the better understand Me. Suppose that there are many who bring their candles, one weighing an ounce, others two or six ounces, or a pound, or even more, and light them in the flame, in each candle, whether large or small, is the whole light, that is to say, the heat, the colour, and the flame; nevertheless thou wouldst judge that he whose candle weighs an ounce has less of the light than he whose candle weighs a pound. Now the same thing happens to those who receive this Sacrament. Each one carries his own candle, that is the holy desire, with which he receives this Sacrament, which of itself is without light, and lights it by receiving this Sacrament. I say without light, because of yourselves you can do nothing, though I have given you the material, with which you can receive this light and feed it. The material is love, for through love I created you, and without love you cannot live.

"Your being, given to you through love, has received the right disposition in holy baptism, which you receive in virtue of the Blood of the Word, for, in no other way, could you participate in this light; you would be like a candle with no wick inside it, which cannot burn or receive light, if you have not received in your souls the wick which catches this Divine Flame, that is to say, the Holy Faith, which you receive, by grace, in baptism, united with the disposition of your soul created by Me, so fitted for love, that, without love, which is her very food, she cannot live. Where does the soul united in this way obtain light? At the fire of My Divine love, loving and fearing Me, and following the Doctrine of My Truth. It is true that the soul becomes more or less lighted according to the material which it brings to the fire; for although you all have one and the same material, in that you are all created to My image and similitude, and, being Christians, possess the light of holy baptism, each of you may grow in love and virtue by the help of My grace, as may please you. Not that you change the form of what I have given you, but that you increase your strength in love, and your free-will, by using it while you have time, for when time is past you can no longer do so. So that you can increase in love, as has been said, coming with love to receive this Sweet and Glorious Light, which I have given you as Food for your service, through My ministers, and you receive this Light according to the love and fiery desire with which you approach It.

"The Light Itself you receive entire, as I have said (in the example of those, who in spite of the difference in weight of their candles, all

receive the entire light), and not divided, because
It cannot be divided, as has been said, either on
account of any imperfection of yours who receive, or of the minister; but you personally
participate in this light, that is in the grace
which you receive in this Sacrament, according
to the holy desire with which you dispose yourselves to receive it. He who should go to this
sweet Sacrament in the guilt of mortal sin, will
receive no grace therefrom, though he actually
receive the whole of God and the whole of Man.
Dost thou know the condition of the soul who
receives unworthily? She is like a candle on
which water has fallen, which can do nothing
but crackle when brought near the flame, for
no sooner has the fire touched it, than it is
extinguished, and nothing remains but smoke;
so this soul has cast the water of guilt within her
mind upon the candle which she received in holy
baptism, which has drenched the wick of the
grace of baptism, and, not having heated it at
the fire of true contrition and confession, goes
to the table of the altar to receive this Light
with her body, and not with her mind, wherefore
the Light, since the soul is not disposed as she
should be for so great a mystery, does not remain
by grace in that soul, but leaves her, and, in the
soul, remains only greater confusion, for her light
is extinguished and her sin increased by her darkness. Of the Sacrament she feels nothing but the
crackling of a remorseful conscience, not through
the defect of the Light Itself, for that can receive

no hurt, but on account of the water that was in the soul, which impeded her proper disposition so that she could not receive the Light. See, therefore, that in no way can this Light, united with its heat and its colour, be divided, either by the scanty desire of the soul when she receives the Sacrament, or by any defect which may be in the soul, or by any defect of him who administers it, as I told thee of the sun which is not defiled by shining on anything foul, so the sweet Light of this Sacrament cannot be defiled, divided, or diminished in any way, nor can it be detached from its orbit.

" If all the world should receive in communion the Light and Heat of this Sun, the Word, My only-begotten Son, would not be separated from Me—the True Sun, His Eternal Father—because in His mystical Body, the holy Church, He is administered to whoever will receive Him. He remains wholly with Me, and yet you have Him, whole God and whole man, as I told thee, in the metaphor of the light, that, if all the world came to take light from it, each would have it entire, and yet it would remain whole."

How the bodily sentiments are all deceived in the afore-said Sacrament, but not those of the soul, therefore it is, with the latter, that one must see, taste, and touch It ; and of a beautiful vision this soul had upon this subject.

" Oh, dearest daughter, open well the eye of thy intellect and gaze into the abyss of My love, for there is no rational creature whose heart would not melt for love in contemplating and considering, among the other benefits she receives from Me, the special Gift that she receives in the Sacrament.

"And with what eye, dearest daughter, shouldest thou and others look at this mystery, and how shouldest thou touch it? Not only with the bodily sight and touch, because in this Sacrament all bodily perceptions fail.

"The eye can only see, and the hand can only touch, the white substance of the bread, and the taste can only taste the savour of the bread, so that the grosser bodily sentiments are deceived; but the soul cannot be deceived in her sentiments unless she wish to be—that is, unless she let the light of the most holy faith be taken away from her by infidelity.

"How is this Sacrament to be truly tasted, seen, and touched? With the sentiment of the soul. With what eye is It to be seen? With the eye of the intellect if within it is the pupil of the most holy faith. This eye sees in that whiteness whole God and whole man, the Divine nature united with the human nature, the Body, the Soul, and the Blood of Christ, the Soul united to the Body, the Body and the Soul united with My Divine nature, not detached from Me, as I revealed to thee, if thou remember well, almost in the beginning of thy life; and not so much at first through the eye of thy intellect as through thy bodily eye, although the light being so great thy bodily eyes lost their vision, and only the sight of the eye of thy intellect remained. I showed it to thee for thine enlightenment in the battle that the Devil had been waging against thee in this Sacrament; and to make thee increase in love in the light of the most holy faith.

"Thou knowest that thou wentest one morning to church at sunrise to hear Mass, having beforehand been tormented by the Devil, and thou placedst thyself upright at the Altar of the Crucifix, while the priest went to the Altar of Mary; thou stoodst there to consider thy sin, fearing to have offended Me through the vexation which the Devil had been causing thee, and to consider My love, which had made thee worthy to hear Mass, seeing that thou did'st deem thyself unworthy to enter into My holy temple. When the minister came to consecrate, thou raisedst thine eyes above his head while he was saying the words of consecration, and I manifested Myself to thee, and thou didst see issue from My breast a light, like a ray from the sun, which proceeds from the circle of the sun without being separated from it, out of the midst of which light came a dove and hovered over the host, in virtue of the words which the minister was saying. But sight remained alone in the eye of thy intellect, because thy bodily sight was not strong enough to stand the light, and in that place thou didst see and taste the Abyss of the Trinity, whole God and whole man concealed and veiled in that whiteness that thou sawedst in the

bread; and thou perceivedst that the seeing of
the Light and the presence of the Word, which
thou sawedst intellectually in the whiteness of
the bread, did not prevent thee seeing at the
same time the actual whiteness of the bread, the
one vision did not prevent the other vision, that
is to say, the sight of the God-Man revealed in
the bread did not prevent the sight of the bread,
for neither its whiteness, nor its touch, nor its
savour were taken away.   This was shown thee
by My goodness, as I have said to thee.   The
eye of the intellect had the true vision, using
the pupil of the holy faith, for this eye should
be thy principal means of vision, inasmuch as
it cannot be deceived; wherefore, with it thou
shouldest look on this Sacrament.   How dost
thou touch It?   By the hand of love.   With
this hand alone canst thou touch that which the
eye of the intellect has recognised in this Sacrament.   The soul touches Me with the hand of
love, as if to certify to herself that which she
has seen and known through faith.   How dost
thou taste It?   With the palate of holy desire.
The corporal palate tastes only the savour of the
bread; but the palate of the soul, which is holy
desire, tastes God and Man.   See, therefore, that
the perceptions of the body are deluded, but
not those of the soul, for she is illuminated and
assured in her own perceptions, for she touches
with the hand of love that which the eye of her
intellect has seen with the pupil of holy faith;
and with her palate—that is, with fiery desire—

she tastes My Burning Charity, My Ineffable
Love, with which I have made her worthy to
receive the tremendous mystery of this Sacrament
and the Grace which is contained therein.   See,
therefore, that thou shouldst receive and look on
this Sacrament, not only with bodily perceptions,
but rather with thy spiritual perceptions, disposing
thy soul in the way that has been said, to receive,
and taste, and see this Sacrament."

*Of the excellent state of the soul who receives the
sacrament in grace.*

"See, dearest daughter, in what an excellent
state is the soul who receives, as she should, this
Bread of Life, this Food of the Angels.   By
receiving this Sacrament she dwells in Me and I
in her, as the fish in the sea, and the sea in the
fish—thus do I dwell in the soul, and the soul
in Me—the Sea Pacific.   In that soul grace
dwells, for, since she has received this Bread of
Life in a state of grace, My grace remains in
her, after the accidents of bread have been consumed.   I leave you the imprint of grace, as
does a seal, which, when lifted from the hot wax
upon which it has been impressed, leaves behind
its imprint, so the virtue of this Sacrament remains in the soul, that is to say, the heat of My
Divine charity, and the clemency of the Holy
Spirit.   There also remains to you the wisdom
of My only-begotten Son, by which the eye of
your intellect has been illuminated to see and to

know the doctrine of My Truth, and, together with this wisdom, you participate in My strength and power, which strengthen the soul against her sensual self-love, against the Devil, and against the world. Thou seest then that the imprint remains, when the seal has been taken away, that is, when the material accidents of the bread, having been consumed, this True Sun has returned to Its Centre, not that it was ever really separated from It, but constantly united to Me. The Abyss of My loving desire for your salvation has given you, through My dispensation and Divine Providence, coming to the help of your needs, the sweet Truth as Food in this life, where you are pilgrims and travellers, so that you may have refreshment, and not forget the benefit of the Blood. See then how straitly you are constrained and obliged to render Me love, because I love you so much, and, being the Supreme and Eternal Goodness, deserve your love."

How the things which have been said about the excellence of this Sacrament, have been said that we might know better the dignity of priests ; and how God demands in them greater purity than in other creatures.

"I have told thee all this, dearest daughter, that thou mayest the better recognise the dignity to which I have called My ministers, so that thy grief at their miseries may be more intense. If they themselves considered their own dignity they would not be in the darkness of mortal sin, or defile the face of their soul. They would not only see their offences against Me, but also, that, if they gave their bodies to be burned, they would not repay the tremendous grace and favour which they have received, inasmuch as no greater dignity exists in this life. They are My anointed ones, and I call them My Christs, because I have given them the office of administering Me to you, and have placed them like fragrant flowers in the mystical body of the holy Church. The angel himself has no such dignity, for I have given it to those men whom I have chosen for My ministers, and whom I have appointed as earthly angels in this life. In all souls I demand purity and charity, that they should love Me and their neighbour, helping him by the ministration of prayer, as I said to thee in another place. But far more do I demand purity in My ministers, and love towards Me, and towards their fellow-creatures, administering to them the Body and Blood of My only-begotten Son, with the fire of charity, and a hunger for the salvation of souls, for the glory and honour of My Name. Even as these ministers require cleanness in the chalice in which this Sacrifice is made, even so do I require the purity and cleanness of their heart and soul and mind. And I wish their body to be preserved, as the instrument of the soul in perfect charity; and I do not wish them to feed upon and wallow in the mire of filth, or to be inflated by pride, seeking great prelacies, or to be cruel to themselves or to their fellow-creatures, because they cannot use cruelty to themselves without being cruel to their fellow-creatures; for, if by sin they are cruel to themselves, they are cruel to the souls of their neighbours, in that they do not give them an example of life, nor care to draw them out of the hands of the Devil, nor to administer to them the Body and Blood of My only-begotten Son, and Me the True Light, as I told thee, and the other Sacraments of the holy Church. So that, in being cruel to themselves, they are cruel to others."

Of the excellence, virtues, and holy works of virtuous and holy ministers; and how such are like the sun.

"I will now speak to thee, in order to give a little refreshment to thy soul, and to mitigate thy grief at the darkness of these miserable subjects, of the holy life of some of My ministers, of whom I have spoken to thee, who are like the sun, for the odour of their virtues mitigates the stench of the vices of the others, and the light thereof shines in their darkness. And, by means of this light, wilt thou the better be able to understand the darkness and sins of My unworthy ministers. Open then the eye of thy intellect and gaze at the Sun of Justice, and thou wilt see those glorious ministers, who, through ministering the Sun, have become like to It, as I told thee of Peter, the prince of the Apostles, who

received the keys of the kingdom of Heaven. I
say the same of these others, who have administered, in the garden of the holy Church, the
Light, that is to say, the Body and the Blood
of My only-begotten Son, who is Himself the
undivided Sun, as has been said, and all the
Sacraments of the holy Church, which all give
life in virtue of the Blood. Each one, placed
in a different rank, has administered, according
to his state, the grace of the Holy Spirit. With
what have they administered it? With the light
of grace, which they have drawn from this True
Light. With light alone? No; because the
light cannot be separated from the warmth and
colour of grace, wherefore a man must either
have the light, warmth, and colour of grace, or
none at all. A man in mortal sin is deprived
of the life of grace, and he who is in grace has
illuminated the eye of his intellect to know Me,
who gave him both grace and the virtue which
preserves it, and, in that light, he knows the
misery and the reason of sin, that is to say, his
own self-love, on which account he hates it, and
thereby receives the warmth of Divine love into
his affection, which follows his intellect, and he
receives the colour of this glorious Light, following the doctrine of My sweet Truth, by which
his memory is filled with the benefit of the
Blood. Thou seest, therefore, that no one can
receive the light without receiving the warmth
and the colour, for they are united together and
are one thing; wherefore he cannot, as I have said

to thee, have one power of his soul so ordered
as to receive Me, the True Sun, unless all three
powers of his soul are brought together and
ordered in My Name. For, as soon as the eye
of the intellect lifts itself with the pupil of faith
above sensual vision in the contemplation of Me,
affection follows it, loving that which the intellect
sees and knows, and the memory is filled with
that which the affection loves; and, as soon as
these powers are thus disposed, the soul participates in Me, the Sun who illuminates her with
My power, and with the wisdom of My only-
begotten Son, and the fiery clemency of the
Holy Spirit. See, then, that these have taken
on them the condition of the Sun, for, having
clothed themselves, and filled the power of their
soul with Me, the true Sun, they become like
Me. The Sun illuminates them and causes the
earth of their souls to germinate with Its heat.
Thus do My sweet ministers, elected and anointed
and placed in the mystical body of the holy
Church, in order to administer Me, the Sun,
that is to say, the Body and Blood of My only-
begotten Son, together with the other Sacraments,
which draw their life from this Blood ; this they
do in two ways, actually, in administering the
Sacraments, and spiritually, by shedding forth in
the mystical body of the holy Church, the light
of supernatural science, together with the colour
of an honourable and holy life, following the
doctrine of My Truth, which they administer in
the ardent love with which they cause barren souls

to bear fruit, illuminating them with the light
of their science, and driving away the darkness
of their mortal sin and infidelity, by the example
of their holy and regular life, and reforming the
lives of those who live in disorder and darkness
of sin, and in coldness, through the privation of
charity.   So thou seest that they are the Sun,
because they have taken the condition of the
Sun from Me, the True Sun, because, through
affection of love, they are one thing with Me,
and I with them, as I narrated to thee in another
place, and each one has given light in the holy
Church, according to the position to which I
have elected him : Peter with preaching and doctrine, and in the end with blood ; Gregory with
science, and holy scripture, and with the mirror
of his life ; Sylvester, against the infidels, and
with disputation and proving of the most holy
faith, which he made in word and in deed,
receiving virtue from Me.   If thou turnest to
Augustine, and to the glorious Thomas and
Jerome, and the others, thou wilt see how much
light they have thrown over this spouse, extirpating error, like lamps placed upon the can-
delabra, with true and perfect humility.   And,
as if famished for such food, they feed upon My
honour, and the salvation of souls, upon the
table of the most holy Cross.   The martyrs,
indeed, with blood, which blood cast up sweet
perfume before My countenance ; and, with the
perfume of blood, and of the virtues, and with
the light of science, they brought forth fruit in

this spouse and extended the faith, and, by their
means, the light of the most holy faith was
rekindled in the darkened. And prelates, placed
in the position of the prelacy of Christ on earth,
offered Me the sacrifice of justice with holy and
upright lives. The pearl of justice, with true
humility, and most ardent love, shone in them,
and in their subjects, with the light of discretion. In them, principally because they justly
paid Me My due, in rendering glory and praise
to My Name, and, to their own sensuality, hatred
and displeasure, despising vice and embracing
virtue, with love of Me and of their neighbour.
With humility they trampled on pride, and, with
purity of heart and of body, came, like angels,
to the table of the altar, and, with sincerity of
mind, celebrated, burning in the furnace of love.
And, because they first had done justice to themselves, they therefore did justice to those under
them, wishing to see them live virtuously, and
correcting them without any servile fear, because
they were not thinking of themselves, but solely
of My honour and the salvation of souls, like
good shepherds, followers of the Good Shepherd,
My Truth, whom I gave you to lead your
sheep, having willed that He should give His
life for you. These have followed His footsteps, and therefore did they correct them, and
did not let their members become putrid for
want of correcting, but they charitably corrected
them with the unction of benignity, and with
the sharpness of fire, cauterising the wound of

sin with reproof and penance, little or much, according to the graveness of the fault. And, in order to correct it and to speak the truth, they did not even fear death. They were true gardeners who, with care and holy tears, took away the thorns of mortal sins, and planted plants odoriferous of virtue. Wherefore, those under them lived in holy, true fear, and grew up like sweet smelling flowers in the mystic body of the holy Church (because they were not deprived of correction, and so were not guilty of sin), for My gardeners corrected them without any servile fear, being free from it, and without any sin, for they balanced exactly the scales of holy justice, reproving humbly and without human respect. And this justice was and is that pearl which shines in them, and which gave peace and light in the minds of the people and caused holy fear to be with them, and unity of hearts. And I would that thou know that, more darkness and division have come into the world amongst seculars and religious and the clergy and pastors of the holy Church, through the lack of the light of justice, and the advent of the darkness of injustice, than from any other causes.

"Neither the civil law, nor the divine law, can be kept in any degree without holy justice, because he who is not corrected, and does not correct others, becomes like a limb which putrefies, and corrupts the whole body, because the bad physician, when it had already begun to corrupt, placed ointment immediately upon it,

without having first burnt the wound. So, were
the prelate, or any other lord having subjects,
on seeing one putrefying from the corruption of
mortal sin, to apply to him the ointment of soft
words of encouragement alone, without reproof,
he would never cure him, but the putrefaction
would rather spread to the other members, who,
with him, form one body under the same pastor.
But if he were a physician, good and true to
those souls, as were those glorious pastors of
old, he would not give salving ointment without
the fire of reproof. And, were the member still
to remain obstinate in his evil doing, he would
cut him off from the congregation in order that
he corrupt not the other members with the
putrefaction of mortal sin. But they act not
so to-day, but, in cases of evil doing, they even
pretend not to see. And knowest thou wherefore? The root of self-love is alive in them,
wherefore they bear perverted and servile fear.
Because they fear to lose their position or their
temporal goods, or their prelacy, they do not
correct, but act like blind ones, in that they see
not the real way by which their position is to be
kept. If they would only see that it is by holy
justice they would be able to maintain it; but
they do not, because they are deprived of light.
But, thinking to preserve their position with
injustice, they do not reprove the faults of those
under them; and they are deluded by their own
sensitive self-love, or by their desire for lordship
and prelacy, and they correct not the faults they

should correct in others, because the same or greater ones are their own. They feel themselves comprehended in the guilt, and they therefore lose all ardour and security, and, fettered by servile fear, they make believe not to see. And, moreover, if they do see they do not correct, but allow themselves to be bound over with flattering words and with many presents, and they themselves find the excuse for the guilty ones not to be punished. In such as these are fulfilled the words spoken by My Truth, saying : ' *These are blind and leaders of the blind, and if the blind lead the blind, they both fall into the ditch.*' My sweet ministers, of whom I spoke to thee, who have the properties and condition of the sun, did not, and do not (if there be any now) act so. And they are truly suns, as I have told thee, because in them is no darkness of sin, or of ignorance, because they follow the doctrine of My Truth. They are not tepid, because they burn in the furnace of My love, and because they are despisers of the grandeurs, positions, and delights of the world. They fear not to correct, for he who does not desire lordship or prelacy will not fear to lose it, and will reprove manfully, and he whose conscience does not reprove him of guilt, does not fear.

" And therefore this pearl of justice was not dimmed in My anointed ones, My Christs (of whom I have narrated to thee), but was resplendent in them, wherefore they embraced voluntary poverty, and sought out vileness with profound humility, and cared not for scorn or villainies, or the detractions of men, or insult, or opprobrium, or pain, or torment.

"They were cursed, and they blessed, and, with true patience, they bore themselves like terrestrial angels, not by nature, but by their ministry, and the supernatural grace given to them, of administering the Body and Blood of My only-begotten Son.   And they are truly angels.   Because, as the angel, which I give thee to be thy guardian, ministers to thee holy and good inspirations, so were these ministers angels, and were given by My goodness to be guardians, and therefore had they their eye continually over those under them, like real guardian angels, inspiring in their hearts holy and good thoughts, and offering up for them before Me, sweet and amorous desires with continual prayer, and the doctrine of words, and with example of life.   So thou seest that they are angels, placed by My burning love, like lanterns in the mystic body of the holy Church, to be your guardians, so that ye blind ones may have guides to direct you into the way of truth, giving you good inspirations, with prayers and example of life, and doctrine as I said.   With how much humility did they govern those under them, and converse with them !   With how much hope and lively faith, and therefore with liberality, did they distribute to the poor the substance of the holy Church, not fearing, or caring if for them and their subjects temporal substance diminished. And they scarcely observed that which they were really bound to do, that is, to distribute the temporal substance to their own necessity being the poor in the Church. They saved nothing, and after their death there remained no money at all, and there were some even who, for the sake of the poor, left the Church in debt. This was because through the largeness of their charity, and of the hope that they had placed in My Providence, they were without servile fear that aught should diminish to them, either spiritual or temporal.

"The sign that a creature hopes in Me and not in himself, is that he does not fear with a servile fear. They who hope in themselves are the ones who fear, and are afraid of their own shadow, and doubt lest the sky and earth fade away before them. With such fears as these, and a perverted hope in their own small knowledge, they spend so much miserable solicitude in acquiring and preserving temporal things, that they turn their back on the spiritual, caring not for them. But they, miserable, faithless, proud ones consider not that I alone am He who provides all things necessary for the soul and the body, and that with the same measure that My creatures hope in Me, will My providence be measured to them. The miserable presumptuous ones do not regard the fact that I am He who is, and they are they who are not, and that they have received their being, and every other additional grace, from My Good-

ness. And therefore his labour may be reputed
to be in vain, who watches the city if it be not
guarded by Me. All his labour will be vain, if
he thinks by his labour or solicitude to keep it,
because I alone keep it. It is true that I desire
you to use your being, and exercise the graces
which I have bestowed upon you, in virtue using
the free-will which I have given you, with the
light of reason, because though I created you
without your help I will not save you without
it. I loved you before you were, and those My
beloved ones saw and knew this, and therefore
they loved Me ineffably, and through their love
hoped so greatly in Me that they feared nothing.
Sylvester feared not when he stood before the
Emperor Constantine disputing with those twelve
Jews before the whole crowd, but with lively
faith he believed that I being for him, no one
could be against him ; and in the same way the
others all lost their every fear, because they were
not alone but were accompanied, because being
in the enjoyment of love, they were in Me, and
from Me they acquired the light of the wisdom
of My only-begotten Son, and from Me they
received the faculty to be strong and powerful
against the princes and tyrants of the world, and
from Me they had the fire of the Holy Spirit,
sharing the clemency and burning love of that
Spirit.

"This love was and is the companion of
whosoever desires it, with the light of faith,
with hope, with fortitude, true patience and

long perseverance even until death. So thou seest that because they were not alone but were accompanied they feared nothing. He only who feels himself to be alone, and hopes in himself, deprived of the affection of love, fears, and is afraid of every little thing, because he alone is without Me who give supreme security to the soul who possesses Me through the affection of love. And of this did those glorious ones, My beloved, have full experience, for nothing could injure their souls; but they on the contrary could injure men and the devils, who ofttimes remained bound by the virtue and power that I had given My servants over them. This was because I responded to the love, faith, and hope they had placed in Me. Thy tongue would not be sufficient to relate their virtues, neither the eye of thy intellect to see the fruit which they receive in everlasting life, and that all will receive who follow in their footsteps. They are like precious stones, and as such do they stand in My presence, because I have received their labour and poverty and the light which they shed with the odour of virtues in the mystic body of the holy Church. And in the life eternal I have placed them in the greatest dignity, and they receive blessing and glory in My sight, because they gave the example of an honourable and holy life, and with light administered the Light of the Body and Blood of My only-begotten Son, and all the Sacraments. And these My anointed ones and ministers are

peculiarly beloved by Me, on account of the
dignity which I placed in them, and because this
Treasure which I placed in their hands they did
not hide through negligence and ignorance, but
rather recognised it to be from Me, and exercised it with care and profound humility with
true and real virtues; and because I, for the
salvation of souls, having placed them in so
much excellency they never rested like good
shepherds from putting the sheep into the fold
of the holy Church, and even out of love and
hunger for souls they gave themselves to die, to
get them out of the hands of the devil. They
made themselves infirm with those who were
infirm, so that they might not be overcome with
despair, and to give them more courage in ex-
posing their infirmity, they would ofttimes lend
countenance to their infirmity and say, ' I, too,
am infirm with thee.' They wept with those
who wept, and rejoiced with those who rejoiced;
and thus sweetly they knew to give every one
his nourishment, preserving the good and rejoicing in their virtues, not being gnawed by
envy, but expanded with the broadness of love
for their neighbours, and those under them.
They drew the imperfect ones out of imperfection, themselves becoming imperfect and infirm
with them, as I told thee, with true and holy
compassion, and correcting them and giving
them penance for the sins they committed—
they through love endured their penance together with them. For through love, they who

gave the penance, bore more pain than they who received it; and there were even those who actually performed the penance, and especially when they had seen that it had appeared particularly difficult to the penitent. Wherefore by that act the difficulty became changed into sweetness.

"Oh! My beloved ones, they made themselves subjects, being prelates, they made themselves servants, being lords, they made themselves infirm, being whole, and without infirmity and the leprosy of mortal sin, being strong they made themselves weak, with the foolish and simple they showed themselves simple, and with the small insignificant. And so with love they knew how to be all things to all men, and to give to each one his nourishment. What caused them to do thus? The hunger and desire for My honour and the salvation of souls which they had conceived in Me. They ran to feed on it at the table of the holy Cross, not fleeing from or refusing any labour, but with zeal for souls and for the good of the holy Church and the spread of the faith, they put themselves in the midst of the thorns of tribulation, and exposed themselves to every peril with true patience, offering incense odoriferous with anxious desires, and humble and continual prayers. With tears and sweat they anointed the wounds of their neighbour, that is the wounds of the guilt of mortal sin, which latter were perfectly cured, the ointment so made, being received in humility."

*A brief repetition of the preceding chapter; and of
the reverence which should be paid to priests,
whether they are good or bad.*

"I have shown thee, dearest daughter, a sample
of the excellence of good priests (for what I have
shown thee is only a sample of what that excellence really is), and I have told thee of the dignity
in which I have placed them, having elected them
for My ministers, on account of which dignity
and authority I do not wish them to be punished
by the hand of seculars on account of any personal
defect, for those who punish them offend Me
miserably.   But I wish seculars to hold them in
due reverence, not for their own sakes, as I have
said, but for Mine, by reason of the authority
which I have given them.   Wherefore this reverence should never diminish in the case of
priests whose virtue grows weak, any more than
in the case of those virtuous ones of whose goodness I have spoken to thee; for all alike have
been appointed ministers of the Sun—that is of
the Body and Blood of My Son, and of the other
Sacraments.

"This dignity belongs to good and bad alike—
all have the Sun to administer, as has been said,
and perfect priests are themselves in a condition
of light, that is to say, they illuminate and warm
their neighbours through their love.   And with
this heat they cause virtues to spring up and
bear fruit in the souls of their subjects.   I have
appointed them to be in very truth your guardian

angels to protect you; to inspire your hearts with good thoughts by their holy prayers, and to teach you My doctrine reflected in the mirror of their life, and to serve you by administering to you the holy Sacraments, thus serving you, watching over you, and inspiring you with good and holy thoughts as does an angel.

"See, then, that besides the dignity to which I have appointed them, how worthy they are of being loved; when they also possess the adornment of virtue, as did those of whom I spoke to thee, which are all bound and obliged to possess, and in what great reverence you should hold them, for they are My beloved children and shine each as a sun in the mystical body of the holy Church by their virtues, for every virtuous man is worthy of love, and these all the more by reason of the ministry which I have placed in their hands. You should love them therefore by reason of the virtue and dignity of the Sacrament, and by reason of that very virtue and dignity you should hate the defects of those who live miserably in sin, but not on that account appoint yourselves their judges, which I forbid, because they are My Christs, and you ought to love and reverence the authority which I have given them. You know well that if a filthy and badly dressed person brought you a great treasure from which you obtained life, you would not hate the bearer, however ragged and filthy he might be, through love of the treasure and of the lord who sent it to you. His state would indeed displease you, and you would be anxious through love of his master that he should be cleansed from his foulness and properly clothed. This, then, is your duty according to the demands of charity, and thus I wish you to act with regard to such badly ordered priests, who themselves filthy and clothed in garments ragged with vice through their separation from My love, bring you great Treasures—that is to say, the Sacraments of the holy Church—from which you obtain the life of grace, receiving Them worthily (in spite of the great defects there may be in them) through love of Me, the Eternal God, who send them to you, and through love of that life of grace which you receive from the great treasure, by which they administer to you the whole of God and the whole of Man, that is to say, the Body and Blood of My Son united to My Divine nature. Their sins indeed should displease you, and you should hate them, and strive with love and holy prayer to re-clothe them, washing away their foulness with your tears—that is to say, that you should offer them before Me with tears and great desire, that I may re-clothe them in My goodness, with the garment of charity. Know well that I wish to do them grace, if only they will dispose themselves to receive it, and you to pray for it ; for it is not according to My will that they should administer to you the Sun being themselves in darkness, not that they should be stripped of the garment of virtue, foully living in dishonour ;

on the contrary I have given them to you, and
appointed them to be earthly angels and suns,
as I have said. It not being My will that they
should be in this state, ye should pray for them,
and not judge them, leaving their judgment to
Me. And I, moved by your prayers, will do
them mercy if they will only receive it, but if
they do not correct their life, their dignity will
be the cause of their ruin. For if they do not
accept the breadth of My mercy, I, the Supreme
Judge, shall terribly condemn them at their last
extremity, and they will be sent to the eternal
fire."

*Of the difference between the death of a just man
and that of a sinner, and first of the death
of the just man.*

"Having told thee how the world and the
devils accuse these wretches, which is indeed the
truth, I wish to speak to thee in more detail on
this point (so that thou mayest have greater compassion on these poor wretches), telling thee how
different are the struggles of the soul of a just
man to those of a sinner, and how different are
their deaths, and how the peace of the just man's
death is greater or less according to the perfection of his soul. For I wish thee to know that
all the sufferings which rational creatures endure
depend on their will, because if their will were
in accordance with mine they would endure no
suffering, not that they would have no labours

on that account, but because labours cause no suffering to a will which gladly endures them, seeing that they are ordained by My will. Such men as these wage war with the world, the Devil, and their own sensuality through holy hatred of themselves. Wherefore when they come to the point of death, they die peacefully, because they have vanquished their enemies during their life. The world cannot accuse such a man, because he saw through its deceptions and therefore renounced it with all its delights. His sensual fragility and his body do not accuse him, because he bound sensuality like a slave with the rein of reason, macerating his flesh with penance, with watchings, and humble and continual prayer. The will of his senses he slew with hatred and dislike of vice, and with love of virtue. He has entirely lost all tenderness for his body, which tenderness and love between the soul and the body makes death seem difficult, and on account of it man naturally fears death ; but since the virtue of a just and perfect man transcends nature, extinguishing his natural fear and overcoming it with holy hatred of himself and desire of arriving at his last end, his natural tenderness cannot make war on him, and his conscience remains in peace ; for during his life his conscience kept a good guard, warning him when enemies were coming to attack the city of his soul, like a watch-dog which stands at the door, and when it sees enemies warns the guards by its barking, for in this way the dog of conscience warns the sentry of reason, and the reason

together with the free-will know by the light of
the intellect whether the stranger be friend or
enemy. To a friend, that is to say, to virtue
and holy thoughts, he gave his delighted love,
receiving and using these with great solicitude;
to an enemy, that is to say, to vice and wicked
thoughts, he gave hatred and displeasure. And
with the knife of hatred of self, and love of Me,
and with the light of reason, and the hand of
free-will he struck his enemies; so that at the
point of death his conscience, having been a
faithful guardian, does not gnaw but remains
in peace.

"It is true that a just soul, through humility,
and because at the moment of death she realises
better the value of time and of the jewels of
virtue, reproves herself, seeming to herself to
have used her time but little; but this is not
an afflictive pain, but rather profitable, for the
soul recollected in herself, is caused by it to
throw herself before the Blood of the humble
and immaculate Lamb My Son. The just man
does not turn his head to admire his past virtues,
because he neither can nor will hope in his own
virtues, but only in the Blood in which he has
found mercy; and as he lived in the memory
of that Blood, so in death he is inebriated and
drowned in the same. How is it that the devils
cannot reprove him of sin? Because during his life
he conquered their malice with wisdom, yet they
come round him to see if they can acquire anything, and appear in horrible shapes in order to

frighten him with hideous aspect, and many diverse phantasms, but the poison of sin not being in his soul, their aspect causes him no terror or fear, as it would do to another who had lived wickedly in the world. Wherefore the devils, seeing that the soul has entered into the Blood with ardent love, cannot endure the sight, but stand afar off shooting their arrows. But their war and their shouts cannot hurt that soul, who already is beginning to taste eternal life, as I said to thee in another place, for with the eye of the intellect illuminated by the pupil of the holy faith, she sees Me, the Infinite and Eternal Good, whom she hopes to obtain by grace, not as her due, but by virtue of Jesus Christ My Son.

"Wherefore opening the arms of hope and seizing Him with the hands of love, she seems to enter into His possession before she actually does so, in the way which I have narrated to thee in another place. Passing suddenly, drowned in the Blood, by the narrow door of the Word she reaches Me, the Sea Pacific. For sea and door are united together. I and the Truth, My only-begotten Son being one and the same thing. What joy such a soul receives who sees herself so sweetly arrived at this pass, for in Truth she tastes the happiness of the angelic nature! This joy is received by all those who pass in this sweet manner, but to a far greater extent by My ministers, of whom I spoke to thee, who have lived like angels, for in this life have they lived with greater knowledge, and with greater

hunger for the salvation of souls. I do not speak
only of the light of virtue which all can have in
general, but of the supernatural light which these
men possessed over and above the light of virtuous
living, the light, that is, of holy science, by which
science they knew more of My Truth, and he
who knows more loves Me more, and he who
loves Me more receives more. Your reward is
measured according to the measure of your love,
and if thou shouldest ask Me, whether one who
has no science can attain to this love, I should
reply, yes it is possible that he may attain to it,
but an individual case does not make a general
law and I always discourse to thee in general.

"They also receive greater dignity on account
of their priesthood, because they have personally
received the office of eating souls in My honour.
For just as every one has the office of remaining
in charity with his neighbour, to them is given
the office of administering the Blood, and of
governing souls.

"Wherefore if they do this solicitously and
with love of virtue they receive, as has been
said, more than others. Oh! how happy are
their souls when they come to the extremity of
death! For they have been the defenders and
preachers of the faith to their neighbour. This
faith they have incarnated in their very marrow,
and with it they see their place of repose in Me.
The hope with which they have lived, confiding
in My providence and losing all trust in themselves, in that they did not hope in their own

knowledge, and having lost hope in themselves, placed no inordinate love in any fellow-creature or in any created thing ; having lived in voluntary poverty, causes them now with great delight to lift their confidence towards Me. Their heart, which was a vessel of love, inscribed by their ardent charity with My name, they showed forth with the example of their good and holy life and by the doctrine of their words to their neighbour. This heart then arises and seizes Me, who am its End, with ineffable love, restoring to Me the pearl of justice which it always carried before it, doing justice to all, and discreetly rendering to each his due.   Wherefore this man renders to Me justice with true humility, and renders glory and praise to My Name, because he refers to Me the grace of having been able to run his course with a pure and holy conscience, and with himself he is indignant, deeming himself unworthy of receiving such grace.

"His conscience gives good testimony of him to Me, and I justly give him the crown of justice, adorned with the pearls of the virtues—that is, of the fruit which love has drawn from the virtues.   Oh, earthly angel ! happy thou art in that thou hast not been ungrateful for the benefits received from Me, and hast not been negligent or ignorant, but hast solicitously opened thine eye by the true light, and kept it on thy subjects, and hast faithfully and manfully followed the doctrine of the Good Shepherd, sweet Christ Jesus, My only-begotten Son, wherefore thou art really now passing through Him, the Door, bathed and drowned in His blood, with thy troop of lambs of whom thou hast brought many by thy holy doctrine and example to eternal life, and hast left many behind thee in a state of grace.

"Oh, dearest daughter! to such as these the vision of the devils can do no harm, because of the vision which they have of Me, which they see by faith and hold by love; the darkness and the terrible aspect of the demons do not give them trouble or any fear, because in them is not the poison of sin. There is no servile fear in them, but holy fear. Wherefore they do not fear the demon's deception, because with supernatural light and with the light of Holy Scripture they know them, so that they do not cause them darkness or disquietude. So thus they gloriously pass, bathed in the blood, with hunger for the salvation of souls, all on fire with love for the neighbour, having passed through the door of the word and entered into Me; and by My goodness each one is arranged in his place, and to each one is measured of the affection of love according as he has measured to Me."

Of the death of sinners, and of their pains in the hour of death.

"Not so excellent, dearest daughter, is the end of these other poor wretches who are in great misery as I have related to thee. How terrible and dark is their death! Because in the moment

of death, as I told thee, the Devil accuses them
with great terror and darkness, showing his face,
which thou knowest is so horrible that the creature would rather choose any pain that can be
suffered in this world than see it; and so greatly
does he freshen the sting of conscience that it
gnaws him horribly.   The disordinate delights
and sensuality of which he made lords over his
reason, accuse him miserably, because then he
knows the truth of that which at first he knew
not, and his error brings him to great confusion.

"In his life he lived unfaithfully to Me—
self-love having veiled the pupil of the most
holy faith—wherefore the Devil torments him
with infidelity in order to bring him to despair.
Oh! how hard for them is this battle, because
it finds them disarmed, without the armour of
affection and charity; because, as members of
the Devil, they have been deprived of it all.
Wherefore they have not the supernatural light,
neither the light of science, because they did not
understand it, the horns of their pride not letting
them understand the sweetness of its marrow.
Wherefore now in the great battle they know
not what to do.   They are not nourished in
hope, because they have not hoped in Me, neither
in the Blood of which I made them ministers,
but in themselves alone, and in the dignities
and delights of the world.   And the incarnate
wretch did not see that all was counted to him
with interest, and that as a debtor he would
have to render an account to Me; now he finds

himself denuded and without any virtue, and on whichever side he turns he hears nothing but reproaches with great confusion. His injustice which he practised in his life accuses him to his conscience, wherefore he dares not ask other than justice.

"And I tell thee that so great is that shame and confusion that unless in their life they have taken the habit of hoping in My mercy, that is, have taken the milk of mercy (although on account of their sins this is great presumption, for you cannot truly say that he who strikes Me with the arm of My mercy has a hope in mercy, but rather has presumption), there is not one who would not despair, and with despair they would arrive with the Devil in eternal damnation.

"But arriving at the extremity of death, and recognising his sin, his conscience unloaded by holy confession, and presumption taken away, so that he offends no more, there remains mercy, and with this mercy he can, if he will, take hold on hope. This is the effect of Mercy to cause them to hope therein during their life, although I do not grant them this, so that they should offend Me by means of My mercy, but rather that they should dilate themselves in charity, and in the consideration of My goodness. But they act in a contrary way, because they offend Me in the hope which they have in My mercy. And nevertheless, I keep them in this hope so that at the last moment they may have something which they may lay hold of, and by so doing not faint away with the condemnation which they receive, and thus arrive at despair; for this final sin of despair is much more displeasing to Me and injures them much more than all the other sins which they have committed. And this is the reason why this sin is more dangerous to them and displeasing to Me, because they commit other sins through some delight of their own sensuality, and they sometimes grieve for them, and if they grieve in the right way their grief will procure them mercy. But it is no fragility of your nature which moves you to despair, for there is no pleasure and nothing but intolerable suffering in it. One who despairs despises My mercy, making his sin to be greater than mercy and goodness. Wherefore, if a man fall into this sin, he does not repent, and does not truly grieve for his offence against Me as he should, grieving indeed for his own loss, but not for the offence done to Me, and therefore he receives eternal damnation. See, therefore, that this sin alone leads him to hell, where he is punished for this and all the other sins which he has committed; whereas had he grieved and repented for the offence done to Me, and hoped in My mercy, he would have found mercy, for, as I have said to thee, My mercy is greater without any comparison than all the sins which any creature can commit; wherefore it greatly displeases Me that they should consider their sins to be greater.

" Despair is that sin which is pardoned neither

here nor hereafter, and it is because despair displeases Me so much that I wish them to hope
in My mercy at the point of death, even if their
life have been disordered and wicked. This is
why during their life I use this sweet trick with
them, making them hope greatly in My mercy,
for when, having fed themselves with this hope,
they arrive at death, they are not so inclined to
abandon it, on account of the severe condemnation they receive, as if they had not so nourished
themselves.

"All this is given them by the fire and abyss
of My inestimable love, but because they have
used it in the darkness of self-love, from which
has proceeded their every sin, they have not
known it in truth, but in so far as they have
turned their affections towards the sweetness of
My mercy they have thought of it with great
presumption. And this is another cause of
reproof which their conscience gives them in
the likeness of the Devil, reproving them in that
they should have used the time and the breadth
of My mercy in which they hoped, in charity
and love of virtue, and that time which I gave
them through love should have been spent in
holiness, whereas with all their time and great
hope of My mercy they did nothing but offend Me
miserably. Oh! blinder than the blind! Thou
hast hidden thy pearl and thy talent which I
placed in thy hands in order that thou mightest
gain more with it, but thou in thy presumption
wouldst not do My will, rather thou didst hide

it under the ground of disordinate self-love, which now renders thee the fruit of death.

"Thy miseries are not hid from thee now, for the worm of conscience sleeps no longer, but is gnawing thee, the devils shout and render to thee the reward which they are accustomed to give their servants, that is to say, confusion and condemnation; they wish to bring thee to despair, so that at the moment of death thou mayest not escape from their hands, and therefore they try to confuse thee, so that afterwards when thou art with them they may render to thee of the part which is theirs. Oh, wretch! the dignity in which I placed thee, thou now seest shining as it really is, and thou knowest to thy shame that thou hast held and used in such guilty darkness the substance of the holy Church, that thou seest thyself to be a thief, a debtor, who ought to pay his debt to the poor and the holy Church. Then thy conscience represents to thee that thou hast spent the money on public harlots, and hast brought up thy children and enriched thy relations, and hast thrown it away on gluttony and on many silver vessels and other adornments for thy house. Whereas thou shouldst have lived in voluntary poverty.

"Thy conscience represents to thee the divine office which thou didst neglect, by which thou didst fall into the guilt of mortal sin, and how even when thou didst recite it with thy mouth thy heart was far from Me. Conscience also shows thee thy subjects, that is to say, the love and hunger which thou shouldest have felt towards nourishing them in virtue, giving them the example of thy life and striking them with the hand of mercy and the rod of justice, and because thou didst the contrary thy conscience and the horrible likeness of the Devil reproves thee.

"And if as a prelate thou hast given prelacies or any charge of souls unjustly to one of thy subjects, that is, that thou hast not considered to whom and how thou wert giving it, the Devil puts this also before thy conscience, because thou oughtest to have given it, not on account of pleasant words, nor in order to please creatures, nor for the sake of gifts, but solely with regard to virtue, My honour and the salvation of souls. And since thou hast not done so thou art reproved, and for thy greater pain and confusion thou hast before thy conscience and the light of thine intellect that which thou hast done and ought not to have done, and that which thou oughtest to have done and hast not done.

"I wish thee to know, dearest daughter, that whiteness is better seen when placed on a black ground, and blackness on a white, than when they are separated. So it happens to these wretches, to these in particular and to all others in general, for at death when the soul begins to see its woes, and the just man his beatitude, his evil life is represented to a wicked man, and there is no reason that any one should remind him of the sins that he has committed, for his conscience

places them before him, together with the virtues
which he ought to have practised. Why the
virtues ? For his greater shame. For vice being
placed on a ground of virtue is known better on
account of the virtue, and the better he knows
his sin, the greater his shame, and by comparison
with his sin he knows better the perfection of
virtue, wherefore he grieves the more, for he
sees that his own life was devoid of any ; and I
wish thee to know that in this knowledge which
dying sinners have of virtue and vice they see
only too clearly the good which follows the
virtue of a just man, and the pain that comes
on him who has lain in the darkness of mortal
sin. I do not give him this knowledge so that
he may despair, but so that he may come to a
perfect self-knowledge and shame for his sins,
with hope, so that with that pain and knowledge
he may pay for his sins, and appease My anger,
humbly begging My mercy. The virtuous
woman increases thereby in joy and in knowledge of My love, for he attributes the grace of
having followed virtue in the doctrine of My
truth to Me and not to himself, wherefore he
exalts in Me, with this truly illuminated knowledge, and tastes and receives the sweet end of
his being in the way which I have related to
thee in another place. So that the one, that is
to say, the just man, who has lived in ardent
charity, exults in joy, while the wicked man is
darkened and confounded in sorrow.

" To the just man the appearance and vision

of the Devil causes no harm or fear, for fear and harm can only be caused to him by sin; but those who have passed their lives lasciviously and in many sins, receive both harm and fear from the appearance of the devils, not indeed the harm of despair if they do not wish it, but the suffering of condemnation, of the refreshing of the worm of conscience, and of fear and terror at their horrible aspect. See now, dearest daughter, how different are the sufferings and the battle of death to a just man and to a sinner, and how different is their end.

"I have shown to the eye of thy intellect a very small part of what happens, and so small is what I have shown thee with regard to what it really is, to the suffering, that is, of the one, and the happiness of the other, that it is but a trifle. See how great is the blindness of man, and in particular of these ministers, for the more they have received of Me, and the more they are enlightened by the Holy Scripture, the greater are their obligations and more intolerable confusion do they receive for not fulfilling them; the more they knew of Holy Scripture during their life, the better do they know at their death the great sins they have committed, and their torments are greater than those of others, just as good men are placed in a higher degree of excellence.   Theirs is the fate of the false Christian, who is placed in Hell in greater torment than a pagan, because he had the light of faith and renounced it, while the pagan never had it.

" So these wretches will be punished more than other Christians for the same sin, on account of the ministry which I entrusted to them, appointing them to administer the sun of the holy Sacrament, and because they had the light of science, in order to discern the truth both for themselves and others had they wished to; wherefore they justly receive the greater pains. But the wretches do not know this, for did they consider their state at all, they would not come to such misery, but would be that which they ought to be and are not. For the whole world has thus become corrupt, they being much more guilty than seculars, according to their state; for with their stench they defile the face of their soul, and corrupt their subjects, and suck the blood from My spouse, that is, the holy Church, wherefore through these sins they make her grow pale, because they divert to themselves the love and charity which they should have to this divine spouse, and think of nothing but stripping her for their own advantage, seizing prelacies, and great properties, when they ought to be seeking souls. Wherefore through their evil life, seculars become irreverent and disobedient to the holy Church, not that they ought on that account to do so, or that their sins are excused through the sins of My ministers."

How this devout soul, praising and thanking GOD,
made a prayer for the Holy Church.

Then this soul, as if inebriated, tormented, and
on fire with love, her heart wounded with great
bitterness, turned herself to the Supreme and
Eternal Goodness, saying: "Oh! Eternal God!
oh! Light above every other light, from whom
issues all light! Oh! Fire above every fire,
because Thou art the only Fire who burnest
without consuming, and consumest all sin and
self-love found in the soul, not afflicting her,
but fattening her with insatiable love, and though
the soul is filled she is not sated, but ever desires
Thee, and the more of Thee she has, the more
she seeks—and the more she desires, the more
she finds and tastes of Thee — Supreme and
Eternal Fire, Abyss of Charity. Oh! Supreme
and Eternal Good, who has moved Thee, Infinite
God, to illuminate me, Thy finite creature, with
the light of Thy Truth? Thou, the same Fire
of Love art the cause, because it is always love
which constrained and constrains Thee to create
us in Thine image and similitude, and to do us
mercy, giving immeasurable and infinite graces
to Thy rational creatures. Oh! Goodness above
all goodness! Thou alone art He who is
Supremely Good, and nevertheless Thou gavest
the Word, Thy only-begotten Son, to converse
with us filthy ones and filled with darkness.
What was the cause of this? Love. Because
Thou lovedst us before we were. Oh! Good!

oh! Eternal Greatness! Thou madest Thyself low and small to make man great. On whichever side I turn I find nothing but the abyss and fire of Thy charity. And can a wretch like me pay back to Thee the graces and the burning charity that Thou hast shown and showest with so much burning love in particular to me beyond common charity, and the love that Thou showest to all Thy creatures? No, but Thou alone, most sweet and amorous Father, art He who will be thankful and grateful for me, that is, that the affection of Thy charity itself will render Thee thanks, because I am she who is not, and if I spoke as being anything of myself, I should be lying by my own head, and should be a lying daughter of the Devil, who is the father of lies, because Thou alone art He who is. And my being and every further grace that Thou hast bestowed upon me, I have from Thee, who givest them to me through love, and not as my due.

"Oh! sweetest Father, when the human race lay sick through the sin of Adam, Thou didst send it a Physician, the sweet and amorous Word —Thy Son; and now, when I was lying infirm with the sickness of negligence and much ignorance, Thou, most soothing and sweet Physician, Eternal God, hast given a soothing, sweet, and bitter medicine, that I may be cured and rise from my infirmity. Thou hast soothed me because with Thy love and gentleness Thou hast manifested Thyself to me, Sweet above all sweetness, and hast illuminated the eye of my intellect with the light of most holy faith, with which light, according as it has pleased Thee to manifest it to me, I have known the excellence of grace which Thou hast given to the human race, administering to it the entire God-Man in the mystic body of the holy Church. And I have known the dignity of Thy ministers whom Thou hast appointed to administer Thee to us. I desired that Thou wouldest fulfil the promise that Thou madest to me, and Thou gavest much more, more even than I knew how to ask for. Wherefore I know in truth that the heart of man knows not how to ask or desire as much as Thou canst give, and thus I see that Thou art He who is the Supreme and Eternal Good, and that we are they who are not. And because Thou art infinite, and we are finite, Thou givest that which Thy rational creature cannot desire enough; for she cannot desire it in itself, nor in the way in which Thou canst and wilt satisfy the soul, filling her with things for which she does not ask Thee. Moreover, I have received light from Thy Greatness and Charity, through the love which Thou hast for the whole human race, and in particular for Thy anointed ones, who ought to be earthly angels in this life. Thou hast shown me the virtue and beatitude of these Thy anointed ones who have lived like burning lamps, shining with the Pearl of Justice in the holy Church. And by comparison with these I have better understood the sins of those who live wretchedly. Wherefore I have conceived a very great sorrow at Thy offence and the harm done to the whole world, for they do harm to the world, being mirrors of sin when they ought to be mirrors of virtue. And because Thou hast manifested and grieved over their iniquities to me—a wretch who am the cause and instrument of many sins—I am plunged in intolerable grief.

"Thou, oh! inestimable love, hast manifested this to me, giving me a sweet and bitter medicine that I might wholly arise out of the infirmity of my ignorance and negligence, and have recourse to Thee with anxious and solicitous desire, knowing myself and Thy goodness and the offences which are committed against Thee by all sorts of people, so that I might shed a river of tears, drawn from the knowledge of Thy infinite goodness, over my wretched self and over those who are dead in that they live miserably. Wherefore I do not wish, oh! Eternal Father, ineffable Fire of Love, that my heart should ever grow weary, or my eyes fail through tears, in desiring Thy honour and the salvation of souls, but I beg of Thee, by Thy grace, that they may be as two streams of water issuing from Thee, the Sea Pacific. Thanks, thanks to Thee, oh! Father, for having granted me that which I asked Thee and that which I neither knew nor asked, for by thus giving me matter for grief Thou hast invited me to offer before Thee sweet, loving, and yearning desires, with humble and continual prayer. Now I beg of Thee that Thou wilt do mercy to the world and to the holy Church. I pray Thee to fulfil that which Thou didst cause me to ask Thee. Alas! what a wretched and sorrowful soul is mine, the cause of all these evils. Do not put off any longer Thy merciful designs towards the world, but descend and fulfil the desire of Thy servants.

"Ah me! Thou causest them to cry in order to hear their voices! Thy truth told us to cry out, and we should be answered; to knock, and it would be opened to us; to beg, and it would be given to us. Oh! Eternal Father, Thy servants do cry out to Thy mercy; do Thou then reply.

"I know well that mercy is Thine own attribute, wherefore Thou canst not destroy it or refuse it to him who asks for it. Thy servants knock at the door of Thy truth, because in the truth of Thy only-begotten Son they know the ineffable love which Thou hast for man, wherefore the fire of Thy love ought not and cannot refrain from opening to him who knocks with perseverance. Wherefore open, unlock, and break the hardened hearts of Thy creatures, not for their sakes who do not knock, but on account of Thy infinite goodness, and through love of Thy servants who knock at Thee for their sakes. Grant the prayer of those, Eternal Father who, as Thou seest, stand at the door of Thy truth and pray. For what do they pray? For with the Blood of this door—Thy truth—hast

Thou washed our iniquities and destroyed the stain of Adam's sin. The Blood is ours, for Thou hast made it our bath, wherefore Thou canst not deny it to any one who truly asks for it. Give, then, the fruit of Thy Blood to Thy creatures. Place in the balance the price of the blood of Thy Son, so that the infernal devils may not carry off Thy lambs. Thou art the Good Shepherd who, to fulfil Thy obedience, laid down His life for Thy lambs, and made for us a bath of His Blood.

"That Blood is what Thy hungry servants beg of Thee at this door, begging Thee through it to do mercy to the world, and to cause Thy holy Church to bloom with the fragrant flowers of good and holy pastors, who by their sweet odour shall extinguish the stench of the putrid flowers of sin. Thou hast said, Eternal Father, that through the love which Thou hast for Thy rational creatures, and the prayers and the many virtues and labours of Thy servants, Thou wouldest do mercy to the world, and reform the Church, and thus give us refreshment; wherefore do not delay, but turn the eye of Thy mercy towards us, for Thou must first reply to us before we can cry out with the voice of Thy mercy. Open the door of Thy inestimable love which Thou hast given us through the door of Thy Word. I know indeed that Thou openest before even we can knock, for it is with the affection of love which Thou hast given to Thy servants, that they knock and cry to Thee, seeking Thy honour and the salvation of souls. Give them then the bread of life, that is to say, the fruit of the Blood of Thy only-begotten Son, which they ask of Thee for the praise and glory of My name and the salvation of souls. For more glory and praise will be Thine in saving so many creatures, than in leaving them obstinate in their hardness of heart. To Thee, Eternal Father, everything is possible, and even though Thou hast created us without our own help, Thou wilt not save us without it. I beg of Thee to force their wills, and dispose them to wish for that for which they do not wish; and this I ask Thee through Thy infinite mercy. Thou hast created us from nothing, now, therefore, that we are in existence, do mercy to us, and remake the vessels which Thou hast created to Thy image and likeness. Re-create them to Grace in Thy mercy and the Blood of Thy Son sweet Christ Jesus."

A TREATISE OF OBEDIENCE

Here begins the treatise of obedience, and first of where obedience may be found, and what it is that destroys it, and what is the sign of a man's possessing it, and what accompanies and nourishes obedience.

THE Supreme and Eternal Father, kindly turning the eye of His mercy and clemency towards her, replied : " Thy holy desire and righteous request, oh ! dearest daughter, have a right to be heard, and inasmuch as I am the Supreme Truth, I will keep My word, fulfilling the promise which I made to thee, and satisfying thy desire. And if thou ask Me where obedience is to be found, and what is the cause of its loss, and the sign of its possession, I reply that thou wilt find it in its completeness in the sweet and amorous Word, My only-begotten Son. So prompt in Him was this virtue, that, in order to fulfil it, He hastened to the shameful death of the Cross. What destroys obedience ? Look at the first man and thou wilt see the cause which destroyed the obedience imposed on him by Me, the Eternal Father. It was pride, which was pro-duced by self-love, and desire to please his companion. This was the cause that deprived him of the perfection of obedience, giving him instead disobedience, depriving him of the life of grace, and slaying his innocence, wherefore he fell into impurity and great misery, and not only he, but the whole human race, as I said to thee. The sign that thou hast this virtue is patience, and impatience the sign that you have it not, and thou wilt find that this is indeed so, when I speak to thee further concerning this virtue. But observe that obedience may be kept in two ways, of which one is more perfect than the other, not that they are on that account separated, but united as I explained to thee of the precepts and counsels. The one way is the most perfect, the other is also good and perfect; for no one at all can reach eternal life if he be not obedient, for the door was unlocked by the key of obedience, which had been fastened by the disobedience of Adam. I, then, being constrained by My infinite goodness, since I saw that man whom I so much loved, did not return to Me, his End, took the keys of obedience and placed them in the hands of My sweet and amorous Word—the Truth—and He becoming the porter of that door, opened it, and no one can enter except by means of that door and that Porter. Wherefore He said in the Holy Gospel that '*no one could come to Me, the Father, if not by Him.*' When He returned to Me, rising to Heaven from the conversation of men at the Ascension, He left you this sweet key of obedience; for as thou knowest He left His vicar,

the Christ, on earth, whom you are all obliged
to obey until death, and whoever is outside His
obedience is in a state of damnation, as I have
already told thee in another place.   Now I wish
thee to see and know this most excellent virtue
in that humble and immaculate Lamb, and the
source whence it proceeds.   What caused the
great obedience of the Word?   The love which
He had for My honour and your salvation.
Whence proceeded this love?   From the clear
vision with which His soul saw the divine essence
and the eternal Trinity, thus always looking on
Me, the eternal God.   His fidelity obtained this
vision most perfectly for Him, which vision you
imperfectly enjoy by the light of holy faith.
He was faithful to Me, His eternal Father, and
therefore hastened as one enamoured along the
road of obedience, lit up with the light of glory.
And inasmuch as love cannot be alone, but is
accompanied by all the true and royal virtues,
because all the virtues draw their life from love,
He possessed them all, but in a different way
from that in which you do.   Among the others
he possessed patience, which is the marrow of
obedience, and a demonstrative sign, whether a
soul be in a state of grace and truly love or not.
Wherefore charity, the mother of patience, has
given her as a sister to obedience, and so closely
united them together that one cannot be lost
without the other.   Either thou hast them both
or thou hast neither.   This virtue has a nurse
who feeds her, that is, true humility; therefore

a soul is obedient in proportion to her humility, and humble in proportion to her obedience. This humility is the foster-mother and nurse of charity, and with the same milk she feeds the virtue of obedience. Her raiment given her by this nurse is self-contempt, and insult, desire to displease herself, and to please Me. Where does she find this? In sweet Christ Jesus, My only-begotten Son. For who abased Himself more than He did! He was sated with insults, jibes, and mockings. He caused pain to Himself in His bodily life, in order to please Me. And who was more patient than He? for His cry was never heard in murmuring, but He patiently embraced His injuries like one enamoured, fulfilling the obedience imposed on Him by Me, His Eternal Father. Wherefore in Him thou wilt find obedience perfectly accomplished. He left you this rule and this doctrine, which gives you life, for it is the straight way, having first observed them Himself. He is the way, wherefore He said, ' *He was the Way, the Truth, and the Life.*' For he who travels by that way, travels in the light, and being enlightened cannot stumble, or be caused to fall, without perceiving it. For He has cast from Himself the darkness of self-love, by which he fell into disobedience; for as I spoke to thee of a companion virtue proceeding from obedience and humility, so I tell you that disobedience comes from pride, which issues from self-love depriving the soul of humility. The sister given by self-love to disobedience is impatience, and pride, her foster-mother, feeds her with the darkness of infidelity, so she hastens along the way of darkness, which leads her to eternal death. All this you should read in that glorious book, where you find described this and every other virtue."

How obedience is the key with which Heaven is opened, and how the soul should fasten it by means of a cord to her girdle, and of the excellences of obedience.

"Now that I have shown thee where obedience is to be found, and whence she comes, and who is her companion, and who her foster-mother, I will continue to speak of the obedient and of the disobedient together, and of obedience in general, which is the obedience of the precepts; and in particular, which is that of the counsels. The whole of your faith is founded upon obedience, for by it you prove your fidelity. You are all in general by My truth to obey the command-ments of the law, the chief of which is to love Me above everything, and your neighbour as yourself, and the commandments are so bound up together, that you cannot observe or trans-gress one without observing or transgressing all. He who observes this principal commandment observes all the others; he is faithful to Me and his neighbour, for he loves Me and My creature, and is therefore obedient, becoming subject to the commandments of the law, and to creatures

for My sake, and with humble patience he endures every labour, and even his neighbour's
detraction of him. This obedience is of such
excellence that ye all derive grace from it, just
as from disobedience you all derive death.
Wherefore it is not enough that it should be
only in word, and not practised by you. I have
already told you that this word is the key which
opens heaven, which key My Son placed in the
hands of His vicar. This vicar placed it in the
hands of every one who receives holy baptism,
promising therein to renounce the world and all
its pomps and delights, and to obey. So that
each man has in his own person that very same
key which the Word had, and if a man does not
unlock in the light of faith, and with the hand
of love the gate of heaven by means of this key,
he never will enter there, in spite of its having
been opened by the Word; for though I created
you without yourselves, I will not save you
without yourselves. Wherefore you must take
the key in your hand and walk by the doctrine
of My Word, and not remain seated, that is to
say, placing your love in finite things, as do
foolish men who follow the first man, their first
father, following his example, and casting the
key of obedience into the mud of impurity,
breaking it with the hammer of pride, rusting
it with self-love. It would have been entirely
destroyed had not My only-begotten Son, the
Word, come and taken this key of obedience in
His hands and purified it in the fire of divine

love, having drawn it out of the mud, and
cleansed it with His blood, and straightened it
with the knife of justice, and hammered your
iniquities into shape on the anvil of His own
body.   So perfectly did He repair it that no
matter how much a man may have spoilt his
key by his free-will, by the self-same free-will,
assisted by My grace, he can repair it with the
same instruments that were used by My Word.
Oh! blinder than the blind, for, having spoilt
the key of obedience, thou dost not think of
mending it!   Dost thou think, forsooth, that the
disobedience which closed the door of Heaven
will open it? that the pride which fell can rise?
Dost thou think to be admitted to the marriage
feast in foul and disordered garments?   Dost
thou think that sitting down and binding thyself with the chain of mortal sin, thou canst
walk? or that without a key thou canst open
the door?   Do not imagine that thou canst, for
it is a fantastical delusion; thou must be firm,
thou must leave mortal sin by a holy confession,
contrition of heart, satisfaction, and purpose of
amendment.   Then thou wilt throw off that
hideous and defiled garment and, clothed in the
shining nuptial robe, will hasten, the key of
obedience in thy hand, to open the door.   But
bind this key with the cord of self-contempt,
and hatred of thyself and of the world, and
fasten it to the love of pleasing Me, Thy creator,
of which thou shouldest make a girdle to thyself to bind thy loins with it, for fear thou lose

it. Know, My daughter, there are many who take up this key of obedience, having seen by the light of faith that in no other way can they escape eternal damnation; but they hold it in their hand without wearing this girdle, or fastening the key to it with the cord of self-contempt, that is to say that they are not perfectly clothed with My pleasure, but still seek to please themselves; they do not wear the cord of self-contempt, for they do not desire to be despised, but rather take delight in the praise of men. Such as these are apt to lose their key; for if they suffer a little extra fatigue, or mental or corporal tribulation, and if, as often happens, the hand of holy desire loosens its grasp, they will lose it. They can indeed find it again if they wish to while they live, but if they do not wish they will never find it, and what will prove to them, that they have lost it? Impatience, for patience was united to obedience, and their impatience proves that obedience does not dwell in their soul. Oh! how sweet and glorious is this virtue, which contains all the rest, for she is conceived and born of charity, on her is founded the rock of the holy faith. She is a queen whose consort will feel no trouble, but only peace and quiet; the waves of the stormy sea cannot hurt her, nor can any tempest reach the interior of the soul in whom she dwells. Such a one feels no hatred when injured, because he wishes to obey the precept of forgiveness, he suffers not when his appetites are not satisfied, because obedience

has ordered him to desire Me alone, who can
and will satisfy all his desires, if he strip himself
of worldly riches. And so in all things which
would be too long to relate, he who has chosen
as spouse Queen Obedience, the appointed key
of heaven, finds peace and quiet. Oh! blessed
obedience! thou voyagest without fatigue, and
reachest without danger the port of salvation,
thou art conformed to My only-begotten Son,
the Word, thou boardest the ship of the holy
cross, forcing thyself to endure, so as not to
transgress the obedience of the Word, nor
abandon His doctrine, of which thou makest
a table when thou eatest the food of souls,
dwelling in the love of thy neighbour, being
anointed with true humility, which saves thee
from coveting, contrary to My will, his possessions, thou walkest erect, without bending, for
thy heart is sincere and not false, loving generously and truly My creatures, thou art a sunrise drawing after thee the light of divine grace,
thou art a sun which makes the earth, that is to
say, the organs of the soul, to germinate with
the heat of charity, all of which as well as those
of the body produce life-giving fruit for thyself
and thy neighbour. Thou art even cheerful, for
thy face is never wrinkled with impatience, but
smooth and pleasant with the happiness of
patience, and even in its fortitude thou art great
by thy long endurance, so long that it reaches
from earth to heaven and unlocks the celestial
door. Thou art a hidden pearl, trampled by the

world, abasing thyself, submitting to all creatures. Yet thy kingdom is so great that no one
can rule thee, for thou hast come out of the
mortal servitude of thy own sensuality, which
destroyed thy dignity, and having slain this
enemy with hatred and dislike of thy own pleasure hast re-obtained thy liberty."

*Here both the misery of the disobedient and the
excellence of the obedient are spoken of.*

"All this, dearest daughter, has been done by
My goodness and providence as I have told thee,
for by My providence the Word repaired the
key of obedience, but worldly men devoid of
every virtue do the contrary, they, like un-
bridled horses, without the bit of obedience, go
from bad to worse, from sin to sin, from misery
to misery, from darkness to darkness, from
death to death, until they finally reach the edge
of the ditch of death, gnawed by the worm of
their conscience, and though it is true that they
can obey the precepts of the law if they will,
and have the time repenting of their disobedience, it is very hard for them to do so, on
account of their long habit of sin. Therefore
let no man trust to this, putting off his finding
of the key of obedience to the moment of his
death, for although every one may and should
hope as long as he has life, he should not put
such trust in this hope as to delay repentance.
What is the reason of all this, and of such

blindness that prevents them recognising this
treasure? The cloud of self-love and wretched
pride, through which they abandoned obedience,
and fell into disobedience. Being disobedient
they are impatient, as has been said, and in their
impatience endure intolerable pain, for it has
seduced them from the way of Truth, leading
them along a way of lies, making them slaves
and friends of the devils with whom, unless
indeed they amend themselves with patience,
they will go to the eternal torments. Contrariwise, My beloved sons, obedient and observers
of the law rejoice and exult in My eternal vision
with the Immaculate and humble Lamb, the
Maker, Fulfiller, and Giver of this law of
obedience. Observing this law in this life they
taste peace without any disturbance, they receive
and clothe themselves in the most perfect peace,
for there they possess every good without any
evil, safety without any fear, riches without any
poverty, satiety without disgust, hunger without
pain, light without darkness, one supreme infinite
good, shared by all those who taste it truly.
What has placed them in so blessed a state?
The blood of the Lamb, by virtue of which the
key of obedience has lost its rust, so that, by
the virtue of the blood, it has been able to
unlock the door. Oh! fools and madmen,
delay no longer to come out of the mud of impurity, for you seem like pigs to wallow in the
mire of your own lust. Abandon the injustice,
murders, hatreds, rancours, detractions, mur-

murings, false judgments, and cruelty, with which you use your neighbours, your thefts and treacheries, and the disordinate pleasures and delights of the world; cut off the horns of pride, by which amputation you will extinguish the hatred which is in your heart against your neighbours. Compare the injuries which you do to Me and to your neighbour with those done to you, and you will see that those done to you are but trifles. You will see that remaining in hatred you injure Me by transgressing My precept, and you also injure the object of your hate, for you deprive him of your love, whereas you have been commanded to love Me above everything, and your neighbour as yourself. No gloss has been put upon these words as if it should have been said, if your neighbour injures you do not love him; but they are to be taken naturally and simply, as they were said to you by My Truth, who Himself literally observed this rule. Literally also should you observe it, and if you do not you will injure your own soul, depriving it of the life of grace. Take, oh! take, then, the key of obedience with the light of faith, walk no longer in such darkness or cold, but observe obedience in the fire of love, so that ye may taste eternal life together with the other observers of the law."

Of those who have such love for obedience that they
do not remain content with the general obedience
of precepts, but take on themselves a particular
obedience.

"There are some, My dearest daughter, in
whom the sweet and amorous fire of love towards obedience burns so high (which fire of love
cannot exist without hatred of self-love, so that
when the fire increases so does this self-hatred),
that they are not content to observe the precepts
of the Law with a general obedience as you are
all obliged to do if you will have life and not
death, but take upon themselves a particular
obedience, following the greatest perfection, so
that they become observers of the counsels both
in deed and in thought. Such as these wish to
bind themselves more tightly through self-hatred,
and in order to restrain in everything their own
will. They either place themselves under the
yoke of obedience in holy religion, or, without
entering religion, they bind themselves to some
creature, submitting their will to his, so as more
expeditiously to unlock the door of Heaven.
These are they, as I have told thee, who have
chosen the most perfect obedience. I have already
spoken to thee of obedience in general, and as I
know it to be thy will that I should speak to thee
of this particular and most perfect obedience, I
will now relate to thee somewhat of this second
kind, which is not divided from the first, but is
more perfect, for, as I have already told thee,

these two kinds of obedience are so closely united together that they cannot be separated. I have told thee where general obedience is to be found and whence it proceeds, and the cause of its loss. Now I will speak to thee of this particular obedience, not altering, however, the fundamental principle of the virtue."

How a soul advances from general to particular obedience; and of the excellence of the religious orders.

"The soul who with love has submitted to the yoke of obedience, to the Commandments, following the doctrine of My truth virtuously exercising herself, as has been said, in this general kind of obedience will advance to the second kind by means of the same light which brought her to the first, for by the light of the most holy faith she would have learnt, in the blood of the humble Lamb, My truth — the ineffable love which I have for her, and her own fragility, which cannot respond to Me with due perfection. So she wanders, seeking by that light in what place and in what way she can pay her debt, trampling on her own fragility, and restraining her own will. Enlightened in her search by faith, she finds the place—namely, holy religion—which has been founded by the Holy Spirit, appointed as the ship to receive souls who wish to hasten to perfection, and to bring them to the port of salvation. The Captain of this ship is the Holy

Spirit, who never fails in Himself through the defects of any of His religious subjects who may transgress the rule of the order. The ship itself cannot be damaged, but only the offender. It is true that the mistake of the steersman may send her down into the billows, and these are wicked pastors and prelates appointed by the Master of the ship. The ship herself is so delightful that thy tongue could not narrate it. I say, then, that the soul, on fire with desire and a holy self-hatred, having found her place by the light of faith, enters there as one dead, if she is truly obedient; that is to say, if she have perfectly observed general obedience. And even if she should be imperfect when she enters, it does not follow that she cannot attain perfection. On the contrary, she attains it by exercising herself in the virtue of obedience; indeed, most of those who enter are imperfect. There are some who enter already in perfection, others in the childhood of virtue, others through fear, others through penance, others through allurements, everything depends on whether after they have entered they exercise themselves in virtue, and persevere till death, for no true judgment can be made on a person's entrance into religion, but only on their perseverance, for many have appeared to be perfect who have afterwards turned back, or remained in the order with much imperfection, so that, as I have said, the act of entrance into this ship ordained by Me, who call men in different ways, does not supply

material for a real judgment, but only the love
of those who persevere therein with true obedience. This ship is rich, so that there is no need
for the subject to think about his necessities
either temporal or spiritual, for if he is truly
obedient, and observes his order, he will be provided for by his Master, who is the Holy Spirit,
as I told thee when I spoke to thee of My providence, saying that though thy servants might
be poor, they were never beggars. No more
are these, for they find everything they need,
and those who observe this order find this to
be indeed true. Wherefore, see that in the
days when the religious orders lived virtuously,
blossoming with true poverty and fraternal
charity, their temporal substance never failed
them, but they had more than their needs demanded. But because the stench of self-love
has entered and caused each to keep his private
possessions and to fail in obedience, their temporal substance has failed, and the more they
possess to the greater destitution do they come.
It is just that even in the smallest matters they
should experience the fruit of disobedience, for
had they been obedient and observed the vow
of poverty, each would not have taken his own,
and lived privately. See the riches of these holy
rules, so thoughtfully and luminously appointed
by those who were temples of the Holy Spirit.
See with what judgment Benedict ordered his
ship; see with what perfection and order of
poverty Francis ordered his ship, decked with

the pearls of virtue, steering it in the way of
lofty perfection, being the first to give his order
for spouse, true and holy poverty, whom he had
chosen for himself, embracing self-contempt and
self-hatred, not desiring to please any creature
but only thy will; desiring rather to be thought
vile by the world, macerating his body and slaying
his will, clothing himself in insults, sufferings,
and jibes, for love of the humble Lamb, with
whom he was fastened and nailed to the cross
by love, so that by a singular grace there appeared
in his body the very wounds of thy Truth, showing
in the vessel of his body that which was in the
love of his soul, so he prepared the way.

"But thou wilt say, 'Are not all the other
religious orders equally founded on this point?'
Yes, but though they are all founded on it, in
no other is this the principal foundation; as with
the virtues, though all the virtues draw their life
from charity, nevertheless, as I explained to thee
in another place, one virtue belongs especially
to one man, and another to another, and yet
they all remain in charity, so with the principal
foundation of the religious orders.   Poverty
belonged especially to My poor man Francis,
who placed the principal foundation of his order
in love for this poverty, and made it very strict
for those who were perfect, for the few and the
good, not for the majority.   I say few because
they are not many who choose this perfection,
though now through their sins they are multi-
plied in numbers and deficient in virtue, not

through defect of the ship, but through disobedient subjects and wicked rulers. Now look
at the ship of thy father Dominic, My beloved
son: he ordered it most perfectly, wishing that
his sons should apply themselves only to My
honour and the salvation of souls, with the light
of science, which light he laid as his principal
foundation, not, however, on that account, being
deprived of true and voluntary poverty, but
having it also. And as a sign that he had it
truly, and that the contrary displeased him, he
left as an heirloom to his sons his curse and
Mine, if they should hold any possessions, either
privately or in community, as a sign that he had
chosen for his spouse Queen Poverty. But for
his more immediate and personal object he took
the light of science in order to extirpate the
errors which had arisen in his time, thus taking
on him the office of My only-begotten Son, the
Word. Rightly he appeared as an apostle in the
world, and sowed the seed of My Word with
much truth and light, dissipating darkness and
giving light. He was a light which I gave the
world by means of Mary, placed in the mystical
body of the Holy Church as an extirpator of
heresies. Why do I say by means of Mary?
Because Mary gave him his habit—this office
was committed to her by My goodness. At
what table does he feed his sons with the light
of science? At the table of the cross, which is
the table of holy desire, when souls are eaten for
My honour. Dominic does not wish his sons

to apply themselves to anything, but remaining
at this table, there to seek with the light of
science, the glory and praise of My name alone,
and the salvation of souls. And in order that
they might do nothing else, he chose poverty for
them, so that they might not have the care of
temporal things. It is true that some failed in
faith, fearing that they would not be provided
for, but he never. Being clothed in faith, and
hoping with firm confidence in My providence,
He wishes his sons to observe obedience and do
their duty, and since impure living obscures the
eye of the intellect, and not only the eye of the
intellect, but also of the body, he does not wish
them to obscure their physical light with which
they may more perfectly obtain the light of
science ; wherefore he imposed on them the third
vow of continence, and wishes that all should
observe it, with true and perfect obedience,
although to-day it is badly observed. They also
prevent the light of science with the darkness of
pride, not that this light can be darkened in
itself, but only in their souls, for there, where
pride is, can be no obedience. I have already
told thee that a man's humility is in proportion
to his obedience, and his obedience to his humility,
and similarly, when he transgresses the vow of
obedience, it rarely happens that he does not
also transgress the vow of continence, either in
thought or deed ; so that he has rigged his ship
with the three ropes of obedience, continence,
and true poverty ; he made it a royal ship, not

obliging his subjects under pain of mortal sin, and illuminated by Me the true light, he provided for those who should be less perfect, for though all who observe the order are perfect in kind, yet one possesses a higher degree of perfection than another, yet all perfect or imperfect live well in this ship. He allied himself with My truth, showing that he did *not desire the death of a sinner, but rather that he should be converted and live.* Wherefore his religion is a delightful garden, broad and joyous and fragrant, but the wretches who do not observe the order, but transgress its vows, have turned it into a desert and defiled it with their scanty virtue and light of science, though they are nourished at its breast. I do not say that the order itself is in this condition, for it still possesses every delight, but in the beginning its subjects were not as they are now, but blooming flowers, and men of great perfection. Each seemed to be another St. Paul, their eyes so illuminated that the darkness of error was dissipated by their glance. Look at My glorious Thomas, who gazed with the gentle eye of his intellect at My Truth, whereby he acquired supernatural light and science infused by grace, for he obtained it rather by means of prayer than by human study. He was a brilliant light, illuminating his order and the mystical body of the Holy Church, dissipating the clouds of heresy. Look at My Peter, virgin and martyr, who by his blood gave light among the darkness of many heresies, and

the heretics hated him so that at last they took
his life; yet while he lived he applied himself
to nothing but prayer, preaching, and disputation
with heretics, hearing confessions, announcing the
truth, and spreading the faith without any fear,
to such an extent that he not only confessed it
in his life but even at the moment of his death,
for when he was at the last extremity, having
neither voice nor ink left, having received his
death-blow, he dipped his finger in his blood,
and this glorious martyr, having not paper on
which to write, leaned over, confessing the faith,
and wrote the Credo on the ground. His heart
burnt in the furnace of My charity, so that he
never slackened his pace nor turned his head
back, though he knew that he was to die, for I
had revealed to him his death, but like a true
knight he fearlessly came forth on to the battle-
field; and I could tell thee the same of many
others, who though they did not actually experience martyrdom, were martyrs in will like
Dominic; great labourers were these sent by
My Father to labour in His vineyard to extirpate
the thorns of vice, planting the virtues in their
stead. Of a truth Dominic and Francis were two
columns of the holy Church. Francis with the
poverty which was specially his own, as has been
said, and Dominic with his learning."

*Of the excellence of the obedient, and of the misery of
the disobedient members of the religious orders.*

"Now that places suitable for obedience have
been found, namely, these ships commanded by
the Holy Spirit through the medium of their
superiors, for, as I told thee, the Holy Spirit is
the true Master of these ships, which are built
in the light of the most holy faith by those who
have the light to know that My clemency, the
Holy Spirit, will steer them, and having thus
shown thee the place of obedience and its perfection, I will speak to thee of the obedience and
of the disobedience of those who travel in such
a ship, speaking of all together and not of one
ship—that is, one order—in particular, showing
thee the sin of the disobedient and the virtue of
the obedient, so that a man may better know
the one by contrast with the other, and how
he should walk if he would enter the ship of
a religious order. How should he walk who
wishes to enter this state of perfect and particular obedience? With the light of holy faith,
by which he will know that he must slay his
self-will with the knife of hatred of every sensual
passion, taking the spouse which charity gives
him, together with her sister. The spouse is
true and prompt obedience, and the sister,
patience; and he must also take the nurse of
humility, for without this nurse obedience
would perish of hunger, for obedience soon

dies in a soul deprived of this little virtue of humility.

"Humility is not alone but has the handmaid of contempt of self and of the world, which causes the soul to hold herself vile, and not to desire honour but shame. Thus dead to himself, should he who is old enough enter the ship of a religious order, but however he may enter it (for I have told thee that I call souls in diverse ways), he should acquire and preserve this affection, hurrying generously to seize the key of the obedience of his order, which will open the little door which is in the panel of the door of Heaven. Such as these have undertaken to open the little door, doing without the great key of general obedience, which opens the door of Heaven, as I have said to thee. They have taken a little key, passing through a low and narrow opening in the great door. This small door is part of the great door, as thou mayest see in any real door. They should keep this key when they have got it, and not throw it away. And because the truly obedient have seen with the light of faith that they will never be able to pass through this little door with the load of their riches and the weight of their own will without great fatigue and without losing their life, and that they cannot walk with head erect without breaking their neck, whether they wish to or not, they cast from them the load of their riches, and of their own will observing the vow of voluntary poverty, refusing to possess anything, for they see by the light of faith to what ruin they would come if they transgressed obedience, and the vow of poverty which they promised to keep. The disobedient walk in pride, holding their heads erect, and if sometimes it suits their convenience to obey they do not incline their heads with humility, but proudly do so, because they must, which force breaks the neck of their will, for they fulfil their obedience with hatred of their order and of their superior. Little by little they are ruined on another point, for they transgress the vow of continence, for he who does not constrain his appetite or strip himself of temporal substance makes many relations and finds plenty of friends who love him for their own profit. From these relations they go on to close intimacies, their body they tend luxuriously, for being without either the nurse of humility or her sister, self-contempt, they live in their own pleasure richly and delicately, not like religious but like nobles, without watching or prayer. This and many other things happen to them because they have money to spend, for if they had it not they could not spend it. They fall into mental and physical impurity, for if sometimes from shame or through lack of means they abstain physically, they indulge themselves mentally, for it is impossible for a man with many worldly relations, of delicate habits and disordinate greediness, who watches not nor prays, to preserve his mind pure. Wherefore the perfectly obedient man sees from afar with

the light of holy faith the evil and the loss
which would come to him from temporal
possessions and from walking weighed down by
his own will; he also sees that he is obliged
to pass by this narrow door, and that in such
a state he would die before he would be able
to pass it, having no key of obedience where-
with to open it, for as I said to thee, he is
obliged to pass through it. Wherefore it is
that whether he will or no he should not leave
the ship of the order, but should walk the
narrow path of obedience to his superior.

"Wherefore the perfectly obedient man rises
above himself and his own sensuality, and rising
above his own feelings with living faith, places
self-hatred as servant in the house of his soul
to drive out the enemy of self-love, for he does
not wish that his spouse, Obedience, given him
with the light of faith by her mother, Charity,
should be offended; so he drives out the enemy
and puts in his place the nurse and companions
of his spouse.

"The love of obedience places in the house of
his soul the lovers of his spouse, Obedience, who
are the true and royal virtues, the customs and
observances of his order, so that this sweet spouse
enters his soul with her sister, Patience, and her
nurse, Humility, together with Self-contempt
and Self-hatred, and when she has entered she
possesses peace and quiet, for her enemies have
been exiled. She dwells in the garden of true
continence, with the sun of intellectual light

shining in, the eye of holy faith fixed on the object of My Truth, for her object is My Truth, and the fire of love with which she observes the rules of the order, warms all her servants and companions.

"Who are her enemies who have been expelled? The chief is self-love, producing pride, the enemy of humility and charity. Impatience is the enemy of patience, disobedience of true obedience, infidelity of faith, presumption and self-confidence do not accord with the true hope which the soul should have in Me; injustice cannot be conformed to justice, nor imprudence to prudence, nor intemperance to temperance, nor the transgression of the commandments of the order to perfect observance of them, nor the wicked conversation of those who live in sin to the good conversation of My servants. These are a man's enemies, causing him to leave the good customs and traditions of his order. He has also those other cruel enemies, anger, which wars against his benevolence; cruelty, against his kindness; wrath, against his benignity; hatred of virtue, against the love of virtue; impurity, against chastity; negligence, against solicitude; ignorance, against knowledge; and sloth against watchfulness and continued prayer.

"And since he knew by the light of faith that all these were his enemies who would defile his spouse, holy obedience, he appointed hatred to drive them out, and love to replace them with

her friends.   Wherefore with the knife of hatred
he slew his perverse self-will, who, nourished by
self-love, gave life to all these enemies of true
obedience, and having cut off the source by which
all the others are preserved in life, he remains
free and in peace without any war, for there is
no one to make war on him, for the soul has
cut off from herself that which kept her in
bitterness and in sadness.   What makes war
on obedience ?   Injuries ?   No, for the obedient
man is patient, patience being the sister of
obedience.   The weight of the observances of
the order ?   No, for obedience causes him to
fulfil them.   Does the weight of obedience give
him pain ?   No, for he has trampled on his
own will, and does not care to examine or judge
the will of his superior, for with the light of
faith he sees My will in him, believing truly
that My clemency causes him to command
according to the needs of his subject's salvation.   Is he disgusted and angry at having to
perform the humble duties of the order or to
endure the mockeries, reproofs, jibes, and insults
which are often cast at him, or to be held at
little worth ?   No, for he has conceived love
for self-contempt and self-hatred.   Wherefore
he rejoices with patience, exulting with delight
and joy in the company of his spouse, true
obedience, for the only thing which saddens him
is to see Me, his Creator, offended.   His conversation is with those who truly fear Me, and
if he should converse with those who are sepa-

rated from My Will, it is not in order to conform himself to their sins, but to draw them out
of their misery, for through the brotherly love
which he has in his heart towards them he would
like to give them the good which he possesses,
seeing that more glory and praise would be given
to My name by many observing aright their order
than by him doing so alone. Wherefore he
endeavours to convert religious and seculars by
his words and by prayer, and by every means by
which he can draw them out of the darkness of
mortal sin. Thus the conversations of a truly
obedient man are good and perfect, whether they
be with just men or with sinners, through his
rightly ordered love and the breadth of his charity.
Of his cell he makes a heaven, delighting there
to converse with Me, his supreme and eternal
Father, with the affection of love, flying idleness
with humble and continual prayer, and when,
through the illusion of the Devil, thoughts come
crowding into his cell, he does not sit down on
the bed of negligence embracing idleness, nor
care to examine by reason the thoughts or opinions
of his heart, but he flies sloth, rising above himself and his senses with hatred and true humility,
patiently enduring the weariness which he feels in
his mind, and resisting by watching and humble
prayer, fixing the eye of his intellect on Me, and
seeing with the light of faith that I am his helper,
and both can and will help him, and open to him
the eyes of My kindness, and that it is I who
permit this suffering in order that he may be

more eager to fly himself and come to Me. And
if it should seem to him that on account of his
great weariness and the darkness of his mind,
mental prayer is impossible, he recites vocal
prayers, or busies himself with some corporal
exercises, so that by these means he may avoid
idleness. He looks at Me with the light which
I give him through love, which draws forth true
humility, for he deems himself unworthy of the
peace and quiet of mind of My other servants,
but rather worthy of pain, for he despises himself
in his own mind with hatred and self-reproach,
thinking that he can never endure enough pain,
for neither his hope nor My providence fail him,
but with faith and the key of obedience he passes
over this stormy sea in the ship of his order,
dwelling thus in his cell as has been said, and
avoiding idleness.

"The obedient man wishes to be the first to
enter choir and the last to leave it, and when he
sees a brother more obedient than himself he
regards him in his eagerness with a holy envy,
stealing from him the virtue in which he excels,
not wishing, however, that his brother should
have less thereof, for if he wished this he would
be separated from brotherly love. The obedient
man does not leave the refectory, but visits it
continually and delights at being at table with
the poor. And as a sign that he delights
therein, and so as to have no reason to remain
without, he has abandoned his temporal substance, observing so perfectly the vow of

poverty that he blames himself for considering
even the necessities of his body. His cell is
full of the odour of poverty, and not of clothes;
he has no fear that thieves will come to rob
him, or that rust or moths will corrupt his
garments; and if anything is given to him, he
does not think of laying it by for his own use,
but freely shares it with his brethren, not thinking of the morrow, but rather depriving himself
to-day of what he needs, thinking only of the
kingdom of heaven and how he may best observe
true obedience.

"And in order that he may better keep to the
path of humility, he submits to small and great,
to poor and rich, and becomes the servant of all,
never refusing labour, but serving all with
charity. The obedient man does not wish to
fulfil his obedience in his own way, or to choose
his time or place, but prefers the way of his
order and of his superior. All this the truly
and perfectly obedient man does without pain
and weariness of mind. He passes with this
key in his hand through the narrow door of the
order, easily and without violence, because he
observes the vows of poverty, true obedience,
and continence, having abandoned the heights
of pride, and bowed his head to obedience
through humility. He does not break his neck
through impatience, but is patient with fortitude
and enduring perseverance, the friends of obedience. Thus he passes by the assaults of the
devils, mortifying and macerating his flesh,

stripping it bare of all pleasures and delights and clothing it with the labours of the order in a faith which despises nothing, for as a child who does not remember the blows and injuries inflicted on him by his father, so this child of the spirit does not remember the injuries, pains, or blows inflicted on him by his superior in the order, but calling him humbly, turns to him without anger, hatred, or rancour, but with meekness and benevolence.

"These are those little ones of whom My Truth spoke to the disciples, who were contending among themselves which of them should be the greater, for calling a child, He said : '*Allow the little ones to come to Me, for of such is the kingdom of heaven to be; whoever will not humble himself like this child* (that is, who will not keep this childlike condition), *shall not enter the kingdom of heaven. For he who humbles himself,* dearest daughter, *will be exalted, and he who exalts himself will be humbled,*' which also was said to you by My Truth. Justly, therefore, are these humble little ones, humiliated and subjected through love, with true and holy obedience, who do not kick against the pricks of their order or superior, exalted by Me, the supreme and eternal Father, with the true citizens of the blessed life, when they are rewarded for all their labours, and in this life also do they taste eternal life."

How the truly obedient receive a hundredfold for one,
and also eternal life; and what is meant by this
one, and this hundredfold.

"In them is fulfilled the saying of the sweet
and amorous Word, My only-begotten Son, in
the gospel when He replied to Peter's demand,
'*Master, we have left everything for thy love's sake,*
and have followed Thee, what wilt Thou give us?'
My Truth replied, '*I will give you a hundredfold*
for one, and you shall possess eternal life.' As if
My Truth had wished to say, 'Thou hast done
well, Peter, for in no other way couldest thou
follow Me. And I, in this life, will give thee a
hundredfold for one.' And what is this hundredfold, beloved daughter, besides which the apostle
obtained eternal life? To what did My Truth
refer? To temporal substance?

"Properly speaking, no. Do I not, however,
often cause one who gives alms to multiply in
temporal goods? In return for what do I this?
In return for the gift of his own will. This is
the one for which I repay him a hundredfold.
What is the meaning of the number a hundred?
A hundred is a perfect number, and cannot be
added to except by recommencing from the first.
So charity is the most perfect of all the virtues,
so perfect that no higher virtue can be attained
except by recommencing at the beginning of self-
knowledge, and thus increasing many hundredfold in merit; but you always necessarily arrive

at the number one hundred. This is that
hundredfold which is given to those who have
given Me the unit of their own will, both in
general obedience, and in the particular obedience of the religious life. And in addition to
this hundred you also possess eternal life, for
charity alone enters into eternal life, like a mistress bringing with her the fruit of all the other
virtues, while they remain outside, bringing their
fruit, I say, into Me, the eternal life, in whom
the obedient taste eternal life. It is not by faith
that they taste eternal life, for they experience
in its essence that which they have believed
through faith ; nor by hope, for they possess that
for which they had hoped, and so with all the
other virtues, Queen Charity alone enters and
possesses Me, her possessor. See, therefore, that
these little ones receive a hundredfold for one,
and also eternal life, for here they receive the fire
of divine charity figured by the number of a
hundred (as has been said). And because they
have received this hundredfold from Me, they
possess a wonderful and hearty joy, for there is
no sadness in charity, but the joy of it makes
the heart large and generous, not narrow or
double. A soul wounded by this sweet arrow
does not appear one thing in face and tongue
while her heart is different. She does not serve,
or act towards her neighbour with dissembling
and ambition, because charity is an open book
to be read by all. Wherefore the soul who
possesses charity never falls into trouble, or the

affliction of sadness, or jars with obedience, but remains obedient until death."

Of the perversities, miseries, and labours of the disobedient man; and of the miserable fruits which proceed from disobedience.

"Contrariwise, a wicked disobedient man dwells in the ship of a religious order with so much pain to himself and others, that in this life he tastes the earnest of hell, he remains always in sadness and confusion of mind, tormented by the sting of conscience, with hatred of his order and superior, insupportable to himself. What a terrible thing it is, My daughter, to see one who has once taken the key of obedience of a religious order, living in disobedience, to which he has made himself a slave, for of disobedience he has made his mistress with her companion impatience, nourished by pride, and his own pleasure, which pride (as has been said) issues from self-love. For him everything is the contrary to what it would be for the obedient man. For how can this wretch be in any other state than suffering, for he is deprived of charity, he is obliged by force to incline the neck of his own will, and pride keeps it erect, all his desires are in discord with the will of the order. The order commands obedience, and he loves disobedience; the order commands voluntary poverty, and he avoids it, possessing and acquiring riches; the order commands continence and purity, and

he desires lewdness. By transgressing these three
vows, My daughter, a religious comes to ruin,
and falls into so many miseries, that his aspect
is no longer that of a religious but of an incarnate
devil, as in another place I related to thee at
greater length. I will, however, tell thee something now of their delusion, and of the fruit
which they obtained by disobedience to the
commendation and exhortation of obedience.
This wretched man is deluded by his self-love,
because the eye of his intellect is fixed, with a
dead faith, on pleasing his self-will, and on
things of the world. He left the world in body,
but remained there in his affections, and because
obedience seems wearisome to him he wishes to
disobey in order to avoid weariness ; whereby he
arrives at the greatest weariness of all, for he is
obliged to obey either by force or by love, and
it would have been better and less wearisome to
have obeyed by love than without it. Oh! how
deluded he is, and no one else deceives him but
himself. Wishing to please himself he only gives
himself displeasure, for the actions which he will
have to do, through the obedience imposed on
him, do not please him. He wishes to enjoy
delights and make this life his eternity, but the
order wishes him to be a pilgrim, and continually proves it to him ; for when he is in a
nice pleasant resting place, where he would like
to remain for the pleasures and delights he finds
there, he is transferred elsewhere, and the change
gives him pain, for his will was active against

his obedience, and yet he is obliged to endure
the discipline and labours of the order, and thus
remains in continual torment.   See, therefore,
how he deludes himself; for, wishing to fly pain,
he on the contrary falls into it, for his blindness
does not let him know the road of true obedience,
which is a road of truth founded by the obedient
Lamb, My only-begotten Son, who removed pain
from it, so that he walks by the road of lies,
believing that he will find delight there, but finding on the contrary pain and bitterness.   Who is
his guide?   Self-love, that is his own passion for
disobedience.   Such a man thinks like a fool to
navigate this tempestuous sea, with the strength
of his own arms, trusting in his own miserable
knowledge, and will not navigate it in the arms
of his order, and of his superior.   Such a one
is indeed in the ship of the order in body, and
not in mind; he has quitted it in desire, not
observing the regulations or customs of the order,
nor the three vows which he promised to observe
at the time of his profession; he swims in the
tempestuous sea, tossed to and fro by contrary
winds, fastened only to the ship by his clothes,
wearing the religious habit on his body but not
on his heart.   Such a one is no friar, but a
masquerader, a man only in appearance.   His
life is lower than an animal's, and he does not
see that he labours more swimming with his
arms, than the good religious in the ship, or
that he is in danger of eternal death; for if his
clothes should be suddenly torn from the ship,

which will happen at the moment of death, he
will have no remedy. No, he does not see,
for he has darkened his light with the cloud
of self-love, whence has come his disobedience,
which prevents him seeing his misery, wherefore
he miserably deceives himself. What fruit is
produced by this wretched tree?

"The fruit of death, because the root of his
affection is planted in pride, which he has drawn
from self-love. Wherefore everything that issues
from this root—flowers, leaves, and fruit—is
corrupt, and the three boughs of this tree, which
are obedience, poverty, and continence, which
spring from the foot of the tree; that is, his
affections are corrupted. The leaves produced
by this tree, which are his words, are so corrupt
that they would be out of place in the mouth
of a ribald secular; and if he have to preach
My doctrine, he does so in polished terms, not
simply, as one who should feed souls with the
seed of My Word, but with eloquent language.
Look at the stinking flowers of this tree, which
are his diverse and various thoughts, which he
voluntarily welcomes with delight and pleasure,
not flying the occasions of them, but rather seeking them in order to be able to accomplish a
sinful act, the which is the fruit which kills him,
depriving him of the light of grace, and giving
him eternal death. And what stench comes
from this fruit, sprung from the flowers of the
tree? The stench of disobedience, for, in the
secret of his heart, he wishes to examine and

judge unfaithfully his superior's will; a stench of impurity, for he takes delight in many foul conversations, wretchedly tempting his penitents.

"Wretch that thou art, dost thou not see that under the colour of devotion thou concealest a troop of children? This comes from thy disobedience. Thou hast not chosen the virtues for thy children as does the truly obedient religious; thou strivest to deceive thy superior when thou seest that he denies thee something which thy perverse will desires, using the leaves of smooth or rough words, speaking irreverently and reproving him. Thou canst not endure thy brother, nor even the smallest word and reproof which he may make to thee, but in such a case thou immediately bringest forth the poisoned fruit of anger and hatred against him, judging that to be done to thy hurt which was done for thy good, and thus taking scandal, thy soul and body living in pain. Why has thy brother displeased thee? Because thou livest for thy own sensual pleasure, thou fliest thy cell as if it were a prison, for thou hast abandoned the cell of self-knowledge, and thus fallen into disobedience, wherefore thou canst not remain in thy material cell. Thou wilt not appear in the refectory against thy will whilst thou hast anything to spend; when thou hast nothing left necessity takes thee there.

"Therefore the obedient have done well, who have chosen to observe their vow of poverty, so that they have nothing to spend, and therefore are not led away from the sweet table of the refectory, where obedience nourishes both body and soul in peace and quiet. The obedient religious does not think of laying a table, or of providing food for himself like this wretched man, to whose taste it is painful to eat in the refectory, wherefore he avoids it; he is always the last to enter the choir, and the first to leave it; with his lips he approaches Me, with his heart he is far from Me. He gladly escapes from the chapter-house when he can through fear of penance. When he is obliged to be there, he is covered with shame and confusion for the faults which he felt it no shame to commit. What is the cause of this? Disobedience. He does not watch in prayer, and not only does he omit mental prayer, but even the Divine office to which he is obliged. He has no fraternal charity, because he loves no one but himself, and that not with a reasonable but with a bestial love. So great are the evils which fall on the disobedient; so many are the fruits of sorrow which he produces, that thy tongue could not relate them. Oh! disobedience, which deprives the soul of the light of obedience, destroying peace, and giving war! Disobedience destroys life and gives death, drawing the religious out of the ship of the observance of his order, to drown him in the sea, making him swim in the strength of his own arms, and not repose on those of the order. Disobedience clothes him with every misery, causes him to die of hunger, taking away from him the food of the merit of obedience, it gives him continual bitterness, depriving him of every sweetness and good, causing him to dwell with every evil. In life it gives him the earnest of cruel torments to endure, and if he do not amend before his clothes are loosened from the ship at death, disobedience will lead the soul to eternal damnation, together with the devils who fell from heaven, because they rebelled against Me. In the same way hast thou, oh! disobedient man, having rebelled against obedience and cast from thee the key which would have opened the door of heaven, opened instead the door of hell with the key of disobedience."

How God does not reward merit according to the labour of the obedient, nor according to the length of time which it takes, but according to the love and promptitude of the truly obedient; and of the miracles which God has performed by means of this virtue; and of discretion in obedience, and of the works and reward of the truly obedient man.

" I have appointed you all to labour in the vineyard of obedience in different ways, and every man will receive a price, according to the measure of his love, and not according to the work he does, or the length of time for which he works, that is to say, that he who comes early will not have more than he who comes late, as My Truth told you in the holy gospel by the example of those who were standing idle and were sent by

the lord of the vineyard to labour; for he gave
as much to those who went at dawn, as to those
who went at prime or at tierce, and those who
went at sext, at none, and even at vespers, received
as much as the first: My Truth showing you in
this way that you are rewarded not according to
time or work, but according to the measure of
your love. Many are placed in their childhood
to work in the vineyard; some enter later in life,
and others in old age; sometimes these latter
labour with such fire of love, seeing the shortness of the time, that they rejoin those who
entered in their childhood, because they have
advanced but slowly. By love of obedience, then,
does the soul receive her merit, filling the vessel
of her heart in Me, the Sea Pacific. There are
many whose obedience is so prompt, and has
become, as it were, so incarnate in them, that
not only do they wish to see reason in what is
ordered them by their superior, but they hardly
wait until the word is out of his mouth, for with
the light of faith they understand his intention.
Wherefore the truly obedient man obeys rather
the intention than the word, judging that the will
of his superior is fixed in My will, and that therefore his command comes from My dispensation,
and from My will, wherefore I say to thee that
he rather obeys the intention than the word. He
also obeys the word, having first spiritually obeyed
in affection his superior's will, seeing and judging
it by the light of faith to be Mine. This is well
shown in the lives of the fathers, where you read

of a religious, who at once obeyed in his affection
the command of his superior, commencing to
write the letter o, though he had not space to
finish it ; wherefore to show how pleasing his
prompt obedience was to Me, My clemency gave
him a proof by writing the other half of the letter
in gold. This glorious virtue is so pleasing to
Me, that to no other have I given so many
miraculous signs and testimonies, for it proceeds
from the height of faith.

"In order to show how pleasing it is to Me,
the earth obeys this virtue, the animals obey it
—water grows solid under the feet of the obedient
man. And as for the obedience of the earth,
thou rememberest having read of that disciple
who, being given a dry stick by his abbot, and
being ordered by obedience to plant it in the
earth and water it every day, did not proceed to
ask how could it possibly do any good, but,
without inquiring about possibilities, he fulfilled
his obedience in such virtue of faith that the dry
wood brought forth leaves and fruits, as a sign
that that soul had risen from the dryness of disobedience, and, covered by the green leaves of
virtue, had brought forth the fruit of obedience,
wherefore the fruit of this tree was called by the
holy fathers the fruit of obedience. Thou wilt
also find that animals obey the obedient man ;
for a certain disciple, commanded by obedience,
through his purity and virtue caught a dragon
and brought it to his abbot, but the abbot, like
a true physician of the soul, in order that he

might not be tossed about by the wind of vainglory, and to prove his patience, sent him away
with harsh words, saying: 'Beast that thou art,
thou hast brought along another beast with thyself.' And as to fire, thou hast read in the holy
scripture that many were placed in the fire, rather
than transgress My obedience, and, at My command were not hurt by it. This was the case of
the three children, who remained happily in the
furnace—and of many others of whom I could
tell thee. The water bore up Maurus who had
been sent by obedience to save a drowning disciple; he did not think of himself, but thought
only with the light of faith of how to fulfil the
command of his superior, and so walked upon
the water as if he had been on dry land, and so
saved the disciple. In everything, if thou openest
the eye of the intellect, thou wilt find shown forth
the excellence of this virtue. Everything else
should be abandoned for the sake of obedience.
If thou wert lifted up in such contemplation and
union of mind with Me, that thy body was raised
from the earth, and an obedience were imposed
on thee (speaking generally, and not in a particular case, which cannot give a law), thou
oughtest, if possible, to force thyself to arise,
to fulfil the obedience imposed on thee, though
thou shouldest never leave prayer, except for
necessity, charity, or obedience. I say this in
order that thou mayest see how prompt I wish
the obedience of My servants to be, and how
pleasing it is to Me. Everything that the

obedient man does is a source of merit to him. If he eats, obedience is his food; if he sleeps, his dreams are obedience; if he walks, if he remains still, if he fasts, if he watches—everything that he does is obedience; if he serve his neighbour, it is obedience that he serves. How is he guided in the choir, in the refectory, or his cell? By obedience, with the light of the most holy faith, with which light he has slain and cast from him his humbled self-will, and abandoned himself with self-hatred to the arms of his order and superior. Reposing with obedience in the ship, allowing himself to be guided by his superior, he has navigated the tempestuous sea of this life, with calm and serene mind and tranquillity of heart, because obedience and faith have taken all darkness from him; he remains strong and firm, having lost all weakness and fear, having destroyed his own will, from which comes all feebleness and disordinate fear. And what is the food of this spouse obedience? She eats knowledge of self, and of Me, knowing her own non-existence and sinfulness, and knowing that I am He who is, thus eating and knowing My Truth in the Incarnate Word. What does she drink? The Blood, in which the Word has shown her, My Truth, and the ineffable love which I have for her, and the obedience imposed on Him by Me, His Eternal Father, so she becomes inebriated with the love and obedience of the Word, losing herself and her own opinions and knowledge, and possessing Me by grace, tasting Me by love, with the light of faith in holy obedience.

"The obedient man speaks words of peace all his life, and at his death receives that which was promised him at his death by his superior, that is to say, eternal life, the vision of peace, and of supreme and eternal tranquillity and rest, the inestimable good which no one can value or understand, for, being the infinite good, it cannot be understood by anything smaller than itself, like a vessel, which, dipped into the sea, does not comprehend the whole sea, but only that quantity which it contains. The sea alone contains itself. So I, the Sea Pacific, am He who alone can comprehend and value Myself truly. And in My own estimate and comprehension of Myself I rejoice, and this joy, the good which I have in Myself, I share with you, and with all, according to the measure of each. I do not leave you empty, but fill you, giving you perfect beatitude; each man comprehends and knows My goodness in the measure in which it is given to him. Thus, then, the obedient man, with the light of faith in the truth burning in the furnace of charity, anointed with humility, inebriated with the Blood, in company with his sister patience, and with self-contempt, fortitude, and enduring perseverance, and all the other virtues (that is, with the fruit of the virtues), receives his end from Me, his Creator."

This is a brief repetition of the entire book.

" I have now, oh dearest and best beloved daughter, satisfied from the beginning to the end thy desire concerning obedience.

" If thou rememberest well, thou didst make four petitions of Me with anxious desire, or rather I caused thee to make them in order to increase the fire of My love in thy soul : one for thyself, which I have satisfied, illuminating thee with My Truth, and showing thee how thou mayest know this truth which thou didst desire to know ; explaining to thee how thou mightest come to the knowledge of it through the knowledge of thyself and Me, through the light of faith. The second request thou didst make of Me was that I should do mercy to the world. In the third thou didst pray for the mystical body of the holy Church, that I would remove darkness and persecutions from it, punishing its iniquities at own desire in thy person. As to this I explained that no penalty inflicted in finite time can satisfy for a sin committed against Me, the Infinite Good, unless it is united with the desire of the soul and contrition of the heart. How this is to be done I have explained to thee. I have also told thee that I wish to do mercy to the world, proving to thee that mercy is My special attribute, for through the mercy and the inestimable love which I had for man, I sent to the earth the Word, My only-begotten Son, whom, that thou mightest understand things quite

clearly, I represented to thee under the figure
of a Bridge, reaching from earth to heaven,
through the union of My divinity with your
human nature.

" I also showed thee, to give thee further light
concerning My truth, how this Bridge is built
on three steps; that is, on the three powers of
the soul. These three steps I also represented
to thee, as thou knowest, under figures of thy
body—the feet, the side, and the mouth—by
which I also figured three states of soul—the
imperfect state, the perfect state, and the most
perfect state, in which the soul arrives at the
excellence of unitive love. I have shown thee
clearly in each state the means of cutting away
imperfection and reaching perfection, and how
the soul may know by which road she is walking and of the hidden delusions of the devil and
of spiritual self-love. Speaking of these three
states I have also spoken of the three judgments
which My clemency delivers—one in this life, the
second at death on those who die in mortal sin
without hope, of whom I told thee that they
went under the Bridge by the Devil's road, when
I spoke to thee of their wretchedness. And the
third is that of the last and universal judgment.
And I who told thee somewhat of the suffering
of the damned and the glory of the blessed, when
all shall have reassumed their bodies given by
Me, also promised thee, and now again I repeat
my proisme, that through the long endurance of
My servants I will reform My spouse. Where-

fore I invite thee to endure, Myself lamenting with thee over her iniquities. And I have shown thee the excellence of the ministers I have given her, and the reverence in which I wish seculars to hold them, showing thee the reason why their reverence towards My ministers should not diminish on account of the sins of the latter, and how displeasing to me is such diminution of reverence; and of the virtue of those who live like angels. And while speaking to thee on this subject, I also touched on the excellence of the sacraments. And further wishing thee to know of the states of tears and whence they proceed, I spoke to thee on the subject and told thee that all tears issue from the fountain of the heart, and pointed out their causes to thee in order.

"I told thee not only of the four states of tears, but also of the fifth, which germinates death. I have also answered thy fourth request, that I would provide for the particular case of an individual; I have provided as thou knowest. Further than this, I have explained My providence to thee, in general and in particular, showing thee how everything is made by divine providence, from the first beginning of the world until the end, giving you and permitting everything to happen to you, both tribulations and consolations temporal and spiritual, and every circumstance of your life for your good, in order that you may be sanctified in Me, and My Truth be fulfilled in you, which truth is that I created you in order to possess eternal life, and manifested this with the blood of My only-begotten Son, the Word.

"I have also in My last words fulfilled thy desire and My promise to speak of the perfection of obedience and the imperfection of disobedience; and how obedience can be obtained and how destroyed. I have shown it to thee as a universal key, and so it is. I have also spoken to thee of particular obedience, and of the perfect and imperfect, and of those in religion, and of those in the world, explaining the condition of each distinctly to thee, and of the peace given by obedience, and the war of disobedience, and how the disobedient man is deceived, showing thee how death came into the world by the disobedience of Adam, and how I, the Eternal Father, supreme and eternal Truth, give thee this conclusion of the whole matter, that in the obedience of the only-begotten Word, My Son, you have life, and as from that first old man you contracted the infection of death, so all of you who will take the key of obedience have contracted the infection of the life of the new Man, sweet Jesus, of whom I made a Bridge, the road to Heaven being broken. And now I urge thee and My other servants to grief, for by your grief and humble and continual prayer I will do mercy to the world. Die to the world and hasten along this way of truth, so as not to be taken prisoner if thou goest slowly. I demand this of thee now more than at first, for now I have manifested to thee My Truth. Beware that thou never leave the cell of self-knowledge, but in this cell preserve and spend the treasure which I have given thee, which is a doctrine of truth founded upon the living stone, sweet Christ Jesus, clothed in light which scatters darkness, with which doctrine clothe thyself, My best beloved and sweetest daughter, in the truth."

How this most devout soul, thanking and praising God, makes prayer for the whole world and for the Holy Church, and commending the virtue of faith brings this work to an end.

Then that soul, having seen with the eye of the intellect, and having known by the light of holy faith the truth and excellence of obedience, hearing and tasting it with love and ecstatic desire, gazed upon the divine majesty and gave thanks to Him, saying, "Thanks, thanks to Thee, oh eternal Father, for Thou hast not despised me, the work of Thy hands, nor turned Thy face from me, nor despised my desires, Thou, the Light, hast not regarded my darkness; Thou, true Life, hast not regarded my living death; Thou, the Physician, hast not been repelled by my grave infirmities; Thou, the eternal Purity, hast not considered the many miseries of which I am full; Thou, who art the Infinite, hast overlooked that I am finite; Thou, who art Wisdom, hast overlooked my folly; Thy wisdom, Thy goodness, Thy clemency, Thy infinite good, have overlooked these infinite evils and sins, and the

many others which are in me. Having known
the truth through Thy clemency, I have found
Thy charity, and the love of my neighbour.
What has constrained me? Not my virtues, but
only Thy charity. May that same charity constrain Thee to illuminate the eye of my intellect
with the light of faith, so that I may know and
understand the truth which Thou hast manifested
to me. Grant that my memory may be capable
of retaining Thy benefits, that my will may burn
in the fire of Thy charity, and may that fire so
work in me that I give my body to blood, and
that by that blood given for love of the Blood,
together with the key of obedience, I may unlock
the door of Heaven. I ask this of Thee with all
my heart, for every rational creature, both in
general and in particular, in the mystical body
of the holy Church. I confess and do not deny
that Thou didst love me before I existed, and
that Thy love for me is ineffable, as if Thou wast
mad with love for Thy creature. Oh, eternal
Trinity! oh Godhead! which Godhead gave
value to the Blood of Thy Son, Thou, oh eternal
Trinity, art a deep Sea, into which the deeper I
enter the more I find, and the more I find the
more I seek; the soul cannot be satiated in Thy
abyss, for she continually hungers after Thee,
the eternal Trinity, desiring to see Thee with
light in Thy light. As the hart desires the
spring of living water, so my soul desires to
leave the prison of this dark body and see Thee
in truth. How long, oh! Eternal Trinity, fire

and abyss of love, will Thy face be hidden from my eyes? Melt at once the cloud of my body. The knowledge which Thou hast given me of Thyself in Thy truth, constrains me to long to abandon the heaviness of my body, and to give my life for the glory and praise of Thy Name, for I have tasted and seen with the light of the intellect in Thy light, the abyss of Thee—the eternal Trinity, and the beauty of Thy creature, for, looking at myself in Thee, I saw myself to be Thy image, my life being given me by Thy power, oh! eternal Father, and Thy wisdom, which belongs to Thy only-begotten Son, shining in my intellect and my will, being one with Thy Holy Spirit, who proceeds from Thee and Thy Son, by whom I am able to love Thee. Thou, Eternal Trinity, art my Creator, and I am the work of Thy hands, and I know through the new creation which Thou hast given me in the blood of Thy Son, that Thou art enamoured of the beauty of Thy workmanship. Oh! Abyss, oh! Eternal Godhead, oh! Sea Profound! what more couldst Thou give me than Thyself, Thou art the fire which ever burns without being consumed; Thou consumest in Thy heat all the soul's self-love; Thou art the fire which takes away all cold; with Thy light Thou dost illuminate me so that I may know all Thy truth; Thou art that light above all light, which illuminates supernaturally the eye of my intellect, clarifying the light of faith so abundantly and so perfectly, that I see that my soul is alive, and in

this light receives Thee—the true light. By the
Light of faith I have acquired wisdom in the
wisdom of the Word—Thy only-begotten Son.
In the light of faith I am strong, constant,
and persevering. In the light of faith I hope,
suffer me not to faint by the way. This light,
without which I should still walk in darkness,
teaches me the road, and for this I said, Oh!
Eternal Father, that Thou hast illuminated me
with the light of holy faith. Of a truth this
light is a sea, for the soul revels in Thee, Eternal
Trinity, the Sea Pacific. The water of the sea
is not turbid, and causes no fear to the soul, for
she knows the truth; it is a deep which manifests
sweet secrets, so that where the light of Thy
faith abounds, the soul is certain of what she
believes. This water is a magic mirror into
which Thou, the Eternal Trinity, biddest me
gaze, holding it with the hand of love, that I
may see myself, who am Thy creature, there
represented in Thee, and Thyself in me through
the union which Thou didst make of Thy godhead with our humanity. For this light I know
to represent to myself Thee—the Supreme and
Infinite Good, Good Blessed and Incompre-
hensible, Good Inestimable. Beauty above all
beauty; Wisdom above all wisdom—for Thou
art wisdom itself. Thou, the food of the angels,
hast given Thyself in a fire of love to men;
Thou, the garment which covers all our naked-
ness, feedest the hungry with Thy sweetness.
Oh! Sweet, without any bitter, oh! Eternal

Trinity, I have known in Thy light, which Thou hast given me with the light of holy faith, the many and wonderful things Thou hast declared to me, explaining to me the path of supreme perfection, so that I may no longer serve Thee in darkness, but with light, and that I may be the mirror of a good and holy life, and arise from my miserable sins, for through them I have hitherto served Thee in darkness. I have not known Thy truth and have not loved it. Why did I not know Thee? Because I did not see Thee with the glorious light of the holy faith; because the cloud of self-love darkened the eye of my intellect, and Thou, the Eternal Trinity, hast dissipated the darkness with Thy light. Who can attain to Thy Greatness, and give Thee thanks for such immeasurable gifts and benefits as Thou hast given me in this doctrine of truth, which has been a special grace over and above the ordinary graces which Thou givest also to Thy other creatures? Thou hast been willing to condescend to my need and to that of Thy creatures—the need of introspection. Having first given the grace to ask the question, Thou repliest to it, and satisfiest Thy servant, penetrating me with a ray of grace, so that in that light I may give Thee thanks. Clothe me, clothe me with Thee, oh! Eternal Truth, that I may run my mortal course with true obedience and the light of holy faith, with which light I feel that my soul is about to become inebriated afresh."

A Letter of Ser Barduccio di Piero Canigiani, containing the Transit of the Seraphic Virgin, Saint Catherine of Siena, to Sister Catherine Petriboni in the Monastery of San Piero a Monticelli near Florence.   In the Name of Jesus Christ.

Dearest Mother in Christ Jesus, and Sister in the holy memory of our blessed mother Catherine, I, Barduccio, a wretched and guilty sinner, recommend myself to your holy prayers as a feeble infant, orphaned by the death of so great a mother.   I received your letter and read it with much pleasure, and communicated it to my afflicted mothers here, who, supremely grateful for your great charity and tender love towards them, recommend themselves greatly, for their part, to your prayers, and beg you to recommend them to the Prioress and all the sisters that they may be ready to do all that may be pleasing to God concerning themselves and you.   But since you, as a beloved and faithful daughter, desire to know the end of our common mother, I am constrained to satisfy your desire; and although I know myself to be but little fitted to give such a narration, I will write in any case what my feeble eyes have seen, and what the dull senses of my soul have been able to comprehend.

This blessed virgin and mother of thousands of souls, about the feast of the Circumcision, began to feel so great a change both in soul and body, that she was obliged to alter her mode of

life, the action of taking food for her sustenance
becoming so loathsome to her, that it was only
with the greatest difficulty that she could force
herself to take any, and, when she did so, she
swallowed nothing of the substance of the
food, but had the habit of rejecting it. Moreover, not one drop of water could she swallow
for refreshment, whence came to her a most
violent and tedious thirst, and so great an in-
flammation of her throat that her breath seemed
to be fire, with all which, however, she remained
in very good health, robust and fresh as usual.
In these conditions we reached Sexagesima Sunday,
when, about the hour of vespers, at the time of
her prayer, she had so violent a stroke that from
that day onwards she was no longer in health.
Towards the night of the following Monday,
just after I had written a letter, she had another
stroke so terrific, that we all mourned her as
dead, remaining under it for a long time without giving any sign of life. Then, rising, she
stood for an equal space of time, and did not
seem the same person as she who had fallen.

From that hour began new travail and bitter
pains in her body, and, Lent having arrived, she
began, in spite of her infirmity, to give herself
with such application of mind to prayer that the
frequency of the humble sighs and sorrowful
plaints which she exhaled from the depth of her
heart appeared to us a miracle. I think, too, that
you know that her prayers were so fervent that
one hour spent in prayer by her reduced that

dear tender frame to greater weakness than would be suffered by one who should persist for two whole days in prayer. Meanwhile, every morning, after communion, she arose from the earth in such a state that any one who had seen her would have thought her dead, and was thus carried back to bed. Thence, after an hour or two, she would arise afresh, and we would go to St. Peter's, although a good mile distant, where she would place herself in prayer, so remaining until vespers, finally returning to the house so worn out that she seemed a corpse.

These were her exercises up till the third Sunday in Lent, when she finally succumbed, conquered by the innumerable sufferings, which daily increased, and consumed her body, and the infinite afflictions of the soul which she derived from the consideration of the sins which she saw being committed against God, and from the dangers ever more grave to which she knew the Holy Church to be exposed, on account of which she remained greatly overcome, and both internally and externally tormented. She lay in this state for eight weeks, unable to lift her head, and full of intolerable pains, from the soles of her feet to the crown of her head, to such an extent that she would often say: " These pains are truly physical, but not natural; for it seems that God has given permission to the devils to torment this body at their pleasure." And, in truth, it evidently was so; for, if I were to attempt to explain the patience which she practised, under

Y

this terrible and unheard-of agony, I should fear to injure, by my explanations, facts which cannot be explained. This only will I say, that, every time that a new torment came upon her, she would joyously raise her eyes and her heart to God and say: "Thanks to Thee, oh eternal Spouse, for granting such graces afresh every day to me, Thy miserable and most unworthy handmaid!"

In this way her body continued to consume itself until the Sunday before the Ascension; but by that time it was reduced to such a state that it seemed like a corpse in a picture, though I speak not of the face, which remained ever angelical and breathed forth devotion, but of the bosom and limbs, in which nothing could be seen but the bones, covered by the thinnest skin, and so feeble was she from the waist downwards that she could not move herself, even a little, from one side to another. In the night preceding the aforesaid Sunday, about two hours or more before dawn, a great change was produced in her, and we thought that she was approaching the end. The whole family was then called around her, and she, with singular humility and devotion, made signs to those who were standing near that she desired to receive Holy Absolution for her faults and the pains due to them, and so it was done. After which she became gradually reduced to such a state that we could observe no other movement than her breathing, continuous, sad, and feeble. On account of this it seemed right to give her extreme unction, which our abbot of Sant' Antimo did, while she lay as it were deprived of feeling.

After this unction she began altogether to change, and to make various signs with her head and her arms as if to show that she was suffering from grave assaults of demons, and remained in this calamitous state for an hour and a half, half of which time having been passed in silence, she began to say: "I have sinned! Oh Lord, have mercy on me!" And this, as I believe, she repeated more than sixty times, raising each time her right arm, and then letting it fall and strike the bed. Then, changing her words, she said as many times again, but without moving her arms, "Holy God, have mercy on me!" Finally she employed the remainder of the above-mentioned time with many other formulas of prayer both humble and devout, expressing various acts of virtue, after which her face suddenly changed from gloom to angelic light, and her tearful and clouded eyes became serene and joyous, in such a manner that I could not doubt that, like one saved from a deep sea, she was restored to herself, which circumstance greatly mitigated the grief of her sons and daughters who were standing around in the affliction you can imagine.

Catherine had been lying on the bosom of Mother Alessia and now succeeded in rising, and with a little help began to sit up, leaning against the same mother. In the meantime we had put before her eyes a pious picture, containing

many relics and various pictures of the saints.
She, however, fixed her eyes on the image of the
cross set in it, and began to adore it, explaining,
in words, certain of her most profound feelings
of the goodness of God, and while she prayed,
she accused herself in general of all her sins in
the sight of God, and, in particular, said: "It is
my fault, oh eternal Trinity, that I have offended
Thee so miserably with my negligence, ignorance,
ingratitude, and disobedience, and many other
defects. Wretch that I am! for I have not
observed Thy commandments, either those which
are given in general to all, or those which Thy
goodness laid upon me in particular! Oh mean
creature that I am!" Saying which, she struck
her breast, repeating her confession, and continued: "I have not observed Thy precept, with
which Thou didst command me to seek always
to give Thee honour, and to spend myself in
labours for my neighbour, while I, on the contrary, have fled from labours, especially where
they were necessary. Didst Thou not command
me, oh, my God! to abandon all thought of myself and to consider solely the praise and glory of
Thy Name in the salvation of souls, and with
this food alone, taken from the table of the most
holy Cross, to comfort myself? But I have sought
my own consolation. Thou didst ever invite
me to bind myself to Thee alone by sweet, loving,
and fervent desires, by tears and humble and
continuous prayers for the salvation of the whole
world and for the reformation of the holy

Church, promising me that, on account of them, Thou wouldst use mercy with the world, and give new beauty to Thy Spouse; but I, wretched one, have not corresponded with Thy desire, but have remained asleep in the bed of negligence.

"Oh, unhappy that I am! Thou hast placed me in charge of souls, assigning to me so many beloved sons, that I should love them with singular love and direct them to Thee by the way of Life, but I have been to them nothing but a mirror of human weakness; I have had no care of them; I have not helped them with continuous and humble prayer in Thy presence, nor have I given them sufficient examples of the good life or the warnings of salutary doctrine. Oh, mean creature that I am! with how little reverence have I received Thy innumerable gifts, the graces of such sweet torments and labours which it pleased Thee to accumulate on this fragile body, nor have I endured them with that burning desire and ardent love with which Thou didst send them to me. Alas! oh, my Love, through Thy excessive goodness Thou didst choose me for Thy spouse, from the beginning of my childhood, but I was not faithful enough; in fact, I was unfaithful to Thee, because I did not keep my memory faithful to Thee alone and to Thy most high benefits; nor have I fixed my intelligence on the thought of them only or disposed my will to love Thee immediately with all its strength."

Of these and many other similar things did that pure dove accuse herself, rather, as I think, for our example than for her own need, and then, turning to the priest, said : "For the love of Christ crucified, absolve me of all these sins which I have confessed in the presence of God, and of all the others which I cannot remember." That done, she asked again for the plenary indulgence, saying that it had been granted her by Pope Gregory and Pope Urban, saying this as one an hungered for the Blood of Christ. So I did what she asked, and she, keeping her eyes ever fixed on the crucifix, began afresh to adore it with the greatest devotion, and to say certain very profound things which I, for my sins, was not worthy to understand, and also on account of the grief with which I was labouring and the anguish with which her throat was oppressed, which was so great that she could hardly utter her words, while we, placing our ears to her mouth, were able to catch one or two now or again, passing them on from one to the other. After this she turned to certain of her sons, who had not been present at a memorable discourse, which, many days previously, she had made to the whole family, showing us the way of salvation and perfection, and laying upon each of us the particular task which he was to perform after her death. She now did the same to these others, begging most humbly pardon of all for the slight care which she seemed to have had of our salvation. Then she said certain things to Lucio and to another, and finally to me, and then turned herself straightway to prayer.

Oh! had you seen with what humility and reverence she begged and received many times the blessing of her most sorrowful mother, all that I can say is that it was a bitter sweet to her. How full of tender affection was the spectacle of the mother, recommending herself to her blessed child, and begging her to obtain a particular grace from God—namely, that in these melancholy circumstances she might not offend Him.   But all these things did not distract the holy virgin from the fervour of her prayer; and, approaching her end, she began to pray especially for the Catholic Church, for which she declared she was giving her life.   She prayed again for Pope Urban VI., whom she resolutely confessed to be the true Pontiff, and strengthened her sons never to hesitate to give their life for that truth.   Then, with the greatest fervour, she besought all her beloved children whom the Lord had given her, to love Him alone, repeating many of the words which our Saviour used, when He recommended the disciples to the Father, praying with such affection, that, at hearing her, not only our hearts, but the very stones might have been broken.   Finally, making the sign of the cross, she blessed us all, and thus continued in prayer to the end of her life for which she had so longed, saying: "Thou, oh Lord, callest me, and I come to Thee, not through my merits, but through Thy mercy alone, which I ask of Thee, in virtue of Thy Blood!" and many times she called out: "Blood, Blood!"   Finally, after the example of the Saviour, she said: "Father, into Thy Hands I commend my soul and my spirit," and thus sweetly, with a face all shining and angelical, she bent her head, and gave up the ghost.

Her transit occurred on the Sunday at the hour of Sext, but we kept her unburied until the hour of Compline on Tuesday, without any odour being perceptible, her body remaining so pure, intact, and fragrant, that her arms, her neck and her legs remained as flexible as if she were still alive.   During those three days the body was visited by crowds of people, and lucky he thought himself who was able to touch it.   Almighty God also worked many miracles in that time, which in my hurry I omit.   Her tomb is visited devoutly by the faithful, like those of the other holy bodies which are in Rome, and Almighty God is granting many graces in the name of His blessed spouse, and I doubt not that there will be many more, and we are made great by hearing of them.   I say no more.   Recommend me to the Prioress and all the sisters, for I have, at present, the greatest need of the help of prayer. May Almighty God preserve you and help you to grow in His grace.

If you have enjoyed this book, consider making your next selection from among the following . . .

Prices guaranteed through December 31, 1992.

NOTES

NOTES

NOTES

NOTES

NOTES

NOTES

NOTES